Husbands Should Not Break

Husbands Should Not Break

A Memoir about the Pursuit of Happiness
after Spinal Cord Injury

Shane Clifton
with
Elly Clifton

RESOURCE *Publications* · Eugene, Oregon

HUSBANDS SHOULD NOT BREAK
A Memoir about the Pursuit of Happiness after Spinal Cord Injury

Resource Publications
An Imprint of Wipf and Stock Publishers
199 W. 8th Ave., Suite 3
Eugene, OR 97401

www.wipfandstock.com

ISBN 13: 978-1-4982-2579-3

Manufactured in the U.S.A.   07/29/2015

To my family, for showing me the meanings of faith, hope, and love. With a family like mine, a person can make it through anything.

Contents

Preface

I experienced some trepidation standing at the top of the jump, although no inkling of a catastrophe, merely an embarrassing hesitation. I wasn't afraid. What was there to fear? A jump, then a landing into a soft foam pit? I'd seen athletes practicing jumps into pits of this type, whose very purpose was to make falling safe. But I was nervous and a voice in my head reminded me, "You're getting older. You're turning forty." So an activity like the mega-ramp, which previously would have given me no pause for thought, now had me feeling my age. I figured that was as good a reason as any to take the jump. And so I did.

On the way down, I remember the feeling of my stomach making its way to my throat, and of having time to look ahead at the jump and wonder, "am I mad?" But the foam looked soft, and I was committed; so down, up, and down again . . . headfirst.

I knew straightaway that I'd broken my neck.

There it is—the turning point of my life. I will come back to it later, but for now it is enough to say that on October 7, 2010, I had an accident that left me a quadriplegic. Since this book tells the story of that accident and my rehabilitation, it is what is sometimes called an "illness memoir"— more recently I heard it labeled "sick lit." *Husbands Should Not Break* (a title taken from a painting my wife did for me in the hospital) had its origins in the need to work through my experience and, in particular, the struggle to transcend the sometimes crippling unhappiness that came with the losses inherent to spinal cord injury. Books of this sort are normally either tragedies, inspirational, or some combination of the two. In this case, the narrative deals with sadness, but I hope that it is not a sad book to read. Indeed, for all of the frustrations that go with disability, paralyzed bodies are often stupidly funny; and while this book is a long way from being a comedy, I hope it is a relatively compelling read, and one that draws out at least the occasional smile. But if it is not a tragedy, then neither have I intended to inspire you. I have come to the view that there is not much that is heroic in dealing with an acquired injury. Heroes choose to run into burning buildings, but the rest of us just do the best that we can with the circumstances life throws at us. Instead, this book is an invitation into my head; an opportunity to imagine what it might be like to experience the loss that comes with spinal cord injury and, thereafter, to think about life, loss, disability, happiness, faith and doubt, and through it all, hope.

If there is an overall meaning to the narrative, it's summed up in a quote from *The Princess Bride* (the book, not the film). Apart from the fact that my wife has always fantasized about Wesley—with his derring-do adventures all for the passionate love of Buttercup—*The Princess Bride* has nothing to do with what follows. But the quote, which is borrowed from the final paragraph of the book, makes a lot of sense to me:

> I'm not trying to make this a downer. . . . I mean, I really do think that love is the best thing in the world, except for cough drops. But I also have to say, for the umpty-umpth time, that life isn't fair. It's just fairer than death; that's all.
>
> —William Goldman, S. Morgenstern, *The Princess Bride*

Prelude

September 15, 2010 (Wednesday)

Shane Clifton Journal

"What do you do for a living?"

"I teach theology."

"Oh, right. What's that exactly?"

"It's the study of God."

Awkward silence.

"I write and teach about faith . . . about religion."

"Well that sounds interesting," forehead wrinkled in a "tell me more" look of curiosity—or, same words, but a blank and subtly hostile flattening of the mouth that says clearly, "Quick, get me out of here. I've run into a religious nutcase."

So I teach theology for a living, but if you are expecting spiritual insight, you'll be sorely disappointed. I've spent (far too many) years studying, just to learn that I don't know very much. I am a mess of faith and doubt, and more irreverent than religious. I guess I would say I'm a liberal, even if my friends hate that term with its wishy-washy connotations. To me, being a "liberal" suggests a certain "open-mindedness" and "generosity" . . . and I'd like to think I've learned at least that much. In any event, this is not a theology textbook or a spiritual guidebook. It's a journal . . . of sorts. Let me explain.

As part of a class I teach on social justice, my students are spending the night "sleeping rough" on the streets of Sydney with Hope Street Urban Compassion, trying to get a feel for what it would be like to be homeless.

I've asked them to write a journal. Not merely to record what happens, but to explore their own reactions and express something of the horror and hopelessness of homelessness.

Setting the assignment has inspired me—not the horror and hopelessness—but the process of writing a journal. I guess I should start by saying something about myself. I'm a middle-aged guy, husband to Elly, father of three boys: Jeremy (Jem, 15), Jacob (13), and Lachlan (Lochie, 10), with a mortgage and house in suburbia. You know the type; Hollywood might imagine me as Lester Burnham (Kevin Spacey) in *American Beauty*—"I feel like I've been in a coma for the past twenty years. And I'm just now waking up." In reality, middle class suburbia isn't so bad, but as I said, I feel inspired to write—to try to make sense of my day-to-day existence—to see whether it has any meaning. No, hang on, that sounds too much like I've been listening to some self-help guru. How's this? I've been inspired to write just for the sake of it; because I want to express myself, perhaps even reveal myself. Although it's never likely to see the light of day, I'm going to pretend I have an audience—you, my imaginary reader.

I do need to warn you though. This isn't the first time I've tried to journal. I hope I can do a little better than I did at age thirteen, during my first year of high school:

- *December 25, 1982*: Dear Diary, Christmas morning. I have been up all night thinking about what I would get for Christmas. I received exactly what I wanted (a water proof watch, a Camera, and this diary). This has been the best Christmas ever.

- *February 15, 1983*: Dear Diary, Today I got my head smashed in by a year-eight student, Adam Shed—a dickhead and a Catholic mind you!

- *February 28, 1983*: Dear Diary, Today I started going with Leanne Stone (a spunk in my class—7L1, the top class).

- *April 17, 1983*: Dear Diary, Today we had a history excursion. We had a great bus trip and I got to *pash* Leanne for the first time. Me and Leanne also broke the kissing record with a time of three minutes, four seconds.

- *April 30, 1983*: Dear Diary, Today and the past few weeks I have been getting on unreal with Leanne (doing things even at school). I made a debate team to play against year eight. I have been writing to Helen (a girl across the road from Oma's place) as a kind of a pen friend (don't tell Leanne).

- *May 8, 1983*: Had a fight with Leanne. Dropped the silly slut.

September 19, 2010 (Sunday)

Shane Clifton Journal

I'm completely knackered . . . tripping over my own feet, stumbling into walls, and slurring my words knackered. I've spent the entire weekend implementing one of Elly's grand landscaping ideas, increasing the size of the backyard pond to accommodate her growing bale of turtles. She now has four: Sushi, Kamikaze, Squirtle, and Shelby, as well as a school of koi. I don't understand it myself, this fascination with turtles; and she keeps lizards too, not to mention our cat and dog. When you take three teenage boys into account, we live in a zoo. Anyway, Elly has a few passions and maybe they are all-of-a-piece. She loves weird and wonderful miniature creatures (crabs, lizards, dragonflies); gardens, preferably of the higgledy-piggledy cottage variety, awash with color; and art, of every variety. She's an experimenter. I suppose these passions all came together in the creation of this pond.

I shouldn't be so exhausted from a little pond-expansion project, though. I thought I'd set myself up for an easy ride. The otherwise impossible task of digging through clay was achieved by hiring a one-tonne bobcat fitted with rubber tank tracks, an excavator, and backfill blades. Ha! Just writing that makes me feel manly! Honestly, this is the way to do yard-work . . . or so it seemed at first. I picked up the bobcat early Saturday morning from Kennard's hire and enjoyed the jealous stares of the blokes at the petrol station while I filled it with diesel. Back at home, I managed to back the beast off the trailer down a forty-five-degree slope—like a nervous L-plate driver trying his first reverse park. The controls took some getting used to, but after a few hours I'd managed a pond that Ian Thorpe could feel at home in. Resisting the temptation to dig up the entire backyard for a giant hot tub, Elly and I set to the task of tidying up, lining the pond with rubber and fixing up the mess created by the excavator. Two hours of digging was followed by two days of backbreaking work, and I'm sorely in need of a beer and a massage, although the latter seems unlikely. I guess I'll be content to collapse, semiconscious, in front of the TV. Did I tell you I'm knackered?

Maybe Hollywood's hatred of suburbia has some merit? But then I see Elly, looking like a mud wrestler at the end of a winning bout, and the effort seems worthwhile.

September 25, 2010 (Saturday)

Shane Clifton Journal

It'll be the big four-O on October sixteenth. I know I'm supposed to be crying in my whiskey, changing my job, getting fit and then bingeing out, having an affair, and all that midlife crisis jazz. But, I'm a little embarrassed to admit, I'm happy enough with life. Sure, I could be richer, but I have about enough. Of course, it would be great to live in a beachside mansion, but being a *bogan* in Sydney's southwest has its own warped satisfaction. I've also have a great girl. I mean, I could try to hook up with some hot twenty-year-old, but who'd choose a porcelain doll over the skills and experience, the lumps, bumps, and stretch marks that have established character? Besides, as far as mid-life crisis milestones go, I've already changed professions, leaving a potentially "successful" career with Price Waterhouse to become a student and then teacher of theology (madness), and I already own a raincoat-yellow convertible MX-5—an alternative to the Harley-Davidson my wife won't let me have—so I'd say my crisis has come and gone.

Turning forty does provide a good excuse to party though! Elly and I are teaming up—joining forces for a combined fortieth celebration. Everyone's going to have to dress up as their favorite movie character. We spent the morning at a hire shop, opting to go with Jem's favorite film, *Pirates of the Caribbean*. Elly looked drop-dead gorgeous as a pirate's wench. Seeing her strut through the shop, skirt billowing, brought back memories of her parading about in her wedding dress with its 80s-style puffy frills and her *trendy* perm.

While I flirted with Elly, my boys were also prancing around as pirates. They looked impressive, although I'm a bit worried about them handling swords! We seem to be accident and emergency junkies. If it's not broken bones from skateboarding, it's a school sports injury or any number of things. Just last month, Jacob whacked Lochie on the nose with a stick, drawing blood, while re-enacting fight-scenes from *The Matrix*. Only seconds before impact, I heard Jacob quoting Morpheus, "What are you waiting for? You're faster than this. Don't think you are; know you are. Come on. Stop trying to hit me and hit me." As I said, what will happen when they carry metal swords?

September 26, 2010 (Sunday)

Shane Clifton Journal

While the kids slept in, dead to the world, I took the opportunity to wake Elly with breakfast in bed. It's about as romantic as I get, so it's the sort of gesture that sometimes pays dividends, as it did this morning. We made love, enjoying the thrill and the intimacy, and we finished with a cuddle in the sunlight that was streaming through the window. Is there anything better than Sunday morning sex?

We were still in bed when I noticed the time—10:15 a.m.

"Crap, we've got to be gone in fifteen minutes. Crap, I shouldn't be swearing on my way to Church . . . Crap!"

What followed was a hubbub of noise:

Me: Bolting half dressed down the hallway, bellowing at the kids, "get out of bed, we've got to go, now!"

Kids: Incoherent teenage grumbling interspersed with a whining, "Do we *have* to go to church?"

More yelling, reluctant movement, followed by the chaos of showers, breakfast, and questions about missing shoes. We managed to scramble into the car only a few minutes later than planned and made it to the service halfway through the first song.

I spent the afternoon pirating scenes from movies to run on a continuous loop at our party. Here are a couple of my favorite quotes:

- *Fight Club*: "How much can you know about yourself if you've never been in a fight? . . . It's only after you've lost everything, that you're free to do anything."

- *Amélie (Elly's favorite film)*: "Amélie still seeks solitude. She amuses herself with silly questions about the world below, such as, "How many people are having an orgasm right now?"

- *Zoolander*: "Have you ever wondered if there was more to life, other than being really, really, ridiculously good looking?"

- *Shawshank Redemption*: "Hope is a good thing, maybe the best of things, and no good thing ever dies."

September 28, 2010 (Tuesday)

Shane Clifton Journal

The previous owner of my little yellow convertible upgraded the muffler system, so it accelerates with a deep rumbling roar. People stare as I go past, probably because a middle-aged giant (194 cm/6' 5") looks absurd in such a car. But there is something spectacular about driving to work on a sunny, spring morning with the top down, hair getting mussed in the breeze.

The romance was diminished somewhat by my arrival in Chester Hill. They say Sydney is a beautiful city, but the tour guide rarely ventures to the glorious western suburbs. As I drove up Waldron Road, past Chester Square with its kebab takeaways, moneylenders and pawn brokers, a chocolate brown paddle pop—lobbed from a group of loitering teenagers—landed in my passenger seat. I forced myself to keep driving.

October 2, 2010 (Saturday)

Shane Clifton Journal

School holidays started today, so we made our way down to my parents' place in Callala Bay for a two-week break. Mum and Dad (Olga and Ken) are in their early sixties, working but semi-retired, and keen to play some golf and to give their citified grandchildren the chance to enjoy the benefits of coastal life. My brothers Troy and Kurt and their families also live nearby (Daniel further afield in Hervey Bay). I plan to spend my time surfing, golfing, reading, eating, and drinking—although I'll try to constrain the latter.

Elly has more relaxing goals; she plans on painting, reading a romantic novel, going craft shopping at Berry with her Mum, and—more importantly—doing as little as possible. She has university assignments to finish (it's the last semester of her study to finish a Bachelor of Arts), but I suspect she'll keep study to a minimum.

The boys have but three ambitions: first, to learn to surf; second, to go jumping off Big Red (a ten-meter cliff that descends into the Shoalhaven River near North Nowra); and third, to have a go at the mega-jump that Nowra City Church recently installed for the youth group. The mega-jump involves a skate ramp leading to a pit of foam, which is intended to soften your fall. The pit is similar to one you'd find at a gymnasium or an indoor skate park. The church recently posted photos of the youth group kids launching themselves into the pit, along with a few church elders taking their turn. It left the boys salivating, so I telephoned ahead and the pastor arranged to meet us at the church on Thursday afternoon.

As I'm writing, we're unwinding and reading (in my case journaling) with a glass of champagne. It's a bubbly end to a day of packing and driving with the frustrating whine and recalcitrance of three boys who seem to feel no obligation to help out. Two and a half hours locked in a tin can as the two youngest punched, yelled, giggled, and cried. Jem managed to ignore it all with the help of an iPod, but Elly and I were frazzled. We tried the strategy of old Mr Fredricksen in the movie *Up*—you know, "Let's play a game. It's called 'see who can be quiet the longest.'" Unfortunately, this was to no avail. At one point, I got hit in the head with a tennis ball—a disconcerting experience when driving down the freeway at 110 km an hour.

October 3, 2010 (Sunday)

Shane Clifton Journal

Spiritual giant that I am, I skipped church today for a game of golf, playing with Mum and Dad at Nowra Golf Club. It's a relatively short but magnificent course, lying under an escarpment on one side and next to the Shoalhaven River on the other. The course features a number of tee shots set into the cliff face. It is a spectacular feeling to drive a ball from a tee mound, already situated twenty meters high, and to watch it soar down the fairway—provided you hit it straight. In theory, I go round with a handicap of eighteen, but I haven't been playing enough and scored twenty-five over. Hopefully some extra rounds in the holidays might restore some form.

October 5, 2010 (Tuesday)

Shane Clifton Journal

Callala Bay is a small town located on the northern shores of Jervis Bay, on the south coast of New South Wales. It's staggeringly beautiful! Elly and I took a walk this morning. From Mum's place, we followed the creek some one hundred meters down to the shores of the bay. The path drew us immediately to a harborage for about thirty yachts and cruisers. There was no breeze, so the water was crystal clear except for the almost stationary clouds mirrored on its surface. We dawdled to the boat ramp and past the stinky fishermen, who were filleting two good-sized kingfishes, along with a pile of ink-blackened squid (later on, Dad took the boys fishing and they brought home a healthy catch, enough for a calamari dinner). Further on we climbed a coastal cliff face to continue our walk around the headland. Gazing south across the bay, we could see the small and trendy town of Huskisson—a scattering of sailboats and a whale/dolphin-watcher making their ways out toward the open ocean. It would be an idyllic place to live, except that the waves don't find their way into the bay. For me, perfection is the roar of the surf crashing into the sand!

We walked on around the headland, past the multimillion-dollar, cliff-top houses (we can dream can't we?), and then followed a shortcut back through town to return home. Along the way we passed the Callala skate ramp, seeing Jem being admired by a gaggle of try-hard primary school skaters, including Lachlan, and Troy's boys, Aiden and Taylor. They gaped at his perfectly executed kick flips and rail slides, and winced at his crashes. I hate watching them skate on concrete. It was only six months ago that I broke my wrist skateboarding with the boys at Leumeah. I sometimes forget that I'm nearing forty, and skateboarding moves have changed since I was a teenager. I tell Jeremy that we used to skate a little like we surfed; we had a smooth style, but there were no ramps, half pipes, or jumps, so we would scrape our skin off but rarely break bones. For whatever reason, perhaps in an effort to be the "cool" father, I had deluded myself into thinking I could join them. I'd spent $200 on a skateboard, and on my first session, discovered that my body no longer bounced on concrete. I swore off the skate park and Jeremy succeeded in winning himself a new board. It's taken me six months to heal and I've only recently been able to bare weight back on my wrist. Thank God I can now push up on my surfboard. Thank God that water is softer than concrete!

October 6, 2010 (Wednesday)

Shane Clifton Journal

The swell is slowly picking up, so Troy and I went out for an early morning wave. Surfing is our brotherly glue—it marks our togetherness. Troy had to go to work afterwards, so we got up at 5:30 a.m. and traveled to Culburra, up the north end of the beach at Crookhaven Heads. The waves break just off the point and have a nice hollow left and right peak. We had the beach to ourselves for an hour or so before the school-holiday crowds joined in and, after about twenty minutes, a pod of dolphins appeared and started surfing the waves. It gave us one heck of a fright, but swimming with dolphins in the wild is an encounter with the divine—both fearful (they're scary-big creatures when they bob up next to your surfboard) and sublime. Incredible! They didn't hang around long, and after a couple of hours we were spent. We arrived back at Callala Bay at nine o'clock, and the family was only just getting out of bed—lazy sods.

I've spent some time today reading Alasdair MacIntyre's *Dependent Rational Animals*. He notes that the ill and the disabled are almost never considered in the pages of moral philosophy books, and when they are, it is inevitably as subjects of charity, so:

> We are invited, when we do think of disability, to think of the 'disabled' as 'them,' as other than 'us,' as a separate class, not as ourselves as we have been, sometimes are now and may well be in the future. (p. 2)

His purpose is to contemplate the virtues necessary to *be with* and *be* the disabled. I'm only part way through the book, but in the light of my early morning surf, it's at least interesting that he includes three chapters focusing on dolphins. To be honest, I'm finding his argument a little hard to follow (perhaps my brain is going soft on holiday, but what have dolphins got to do with dependency?). He's not beaten me yet, though, so I'll keep reading.

[Editorial comment: In the light of my surf with dolphins and the events that are about to unfold, this journal entry seems either providential or fabricated. In terms of the latter, I can only say the record is true, and you can believe it or not as you will. Is this evidence of providence; of God's work in my life prior to my accident, preparing me for what was to come? It may be, but if so, providence has a diabolical sense of humor.]

October 7, 2010 (Thursday)

Shane Clifton Journal

Up for an early surf again today. Troy had to work, so I dragged Jeremy out of bed and he reluctantly accompanied me to Culburra. It was a cold and damp morning, so the boy decided to stay in the car and sleep. Wimp! The good news was that I had the beach to myself. There was a slight offshore breeze, a few drops of rain bouncing off the surface of the water, glassy left and right barrels, and an empty line-up. I surfed for one and a half hours, mostly on my own. It was a sublime and spiritual encounter—the ocean a temple, the wind of the spirit making ripples on the surface, the waves a revelation of transcendence. Elly only sees the wet and cold, but surfing can be prayerful. "Hughie" is supposed to be the God of the surf. As teenagers, my friends and I would sacrifice food to Hughie—baked beans or whatever was on hand—in the hope of an increased swell. And, while my faith today is a little more orthodox, the ocean is still a reminder of the beauty, wonder, and the untameable nature of God.

As I write, I'm relaxing over a late breakfast with a full day in front of me. This afternoon I'm taking the boys to the mega-ramp at Shoalhaven City Church. Afterwards, we're going to jump off Big Red. I want to give my western suburbs kids a taste of my coastal childhood!

PART 1

Hospital

CHAPTER 1

Broken

[The following journal entries recount my accident, as well as the time spent in the intensive care unit (ICU) of Prince of Wales Hospital. For obvious reasons, the journal entries were written more than a week after the events described, but for the sake of clarity, they have been placed here in chronological order, as though written on the day being described. Since I was unable to handwrite or type, my entries were dictated to Elly. She also kept an occasional journal and, even though there is a little repetition, I have included her account alongside my own.]

October 7, 2010 (Thursday)

Elly Clifton Journal

Thursday, October 7, 2010, was the worst day of my life. I've never been through anything as terrible. What should have been a fun and unique opportunity turned into a tragic nightmare. Shane has long been an athletic go-getter, so I've always seen his body as an indestructible machine . . . and I think he's always used it that way too. He grew up loving adventure and speed: skiing, surfing, skating, etc. He's not an adrenaline junkie, but a sports lover. One of the things I've always loved about him is his stature and strength. Besides that, he is the best-looking man I know!

Shane was hesitant to try the mega-jump on the skateboard. He had kept his vow never to skateboard again after fracturing his wrist earlier in the year, so he decided to use a bike instead, practicing on the flat before tackling the ramp. He'd watched his boys take turn after turn, enjoying the thrill and landing softly. After a while, he decided to give it a shot. After all, what could go wrong when you're landing in a foam pit? As he launched the bike off the end of the ramp, he went up and over and rotated forward as he fell into the pit. It looked like nothing at all, totally harmless, funny—I even laughed. We had no idea he'd injured himself until he called out, "I've broken my neck."

At first I thought he was joking, but he repeated himself, "I've broken my neck," his voice oddly matter-of-fact, but with a hint of rising panic. As I scurried into the pit, I was torn between desperation and disbelief, hoping that he was wrong, that before I reached him he would sit up and tell me that he was okay. But, in my gut, I knew he wouldn't.

He was hard to get to, with the foam moving about like lumpy jelly, but Jem helped out and we reached him—and seeing him there, his body crumpled, twisted, and squashed into the foam, broke my heart. He was struggling to breathe, and he wanted me to lift his head, but as hard as it was not to pick him up and hug him close I knew better than to move him. Instead, I supported his shoulder and tried to make enough space for him to inhale. He had intense pain in his neck but couldn't feel anything else.

"I'm sorry, I'm sorry," he kept saying (God knows why), and as he cried, I held my own sobs in check, dying inside but trying to be strong for him. "It's okay, my love, we'll be okay," I whispered in reply. It was all I could say, even if I was not sure whether I could believe it myself.

Before I knew it, the ambulance had arrived. I didn't even hear the sirens. I'd been absorbed into a world where there was only the two of us, and looked up to find us surrounded by paramedics. Jeremy was asked to move out of the pit, and to do so in triple-slow-motion so that nothing moved. I was allowed to stay with Shane, supporting his shoulder, but was relieved to cede control to someone who knew what they were doing. I felt so utterly helpless, but I at least needed him to know I was there—that he wasn't alone.

The paramedics found working in the foam a challenge—they knew that every movement they made risked further damage to the spinal cord. But after cutting the hood off his jumper, they were able to apply a brace and carefully remove the pieces of foam from under his head. Then they "log" rolled him onto a stiff plastic tray. When he was finally held securely on his back I let out a sigh of relief—and realized that I'd been holding my breath, my fist and shoulder muscles clenched tight, sweat running down my face. As the tension eased, Shane looked at me and asked, "Have you got me over yet? Because it feels like I'm still in the foam, face down."

Shane was still crying and in a lot of pain. It felt like an eternity before the paramedics (a troop of at least eight) decided he was stable enough to be carried out. Olga (who had come with us for the adventure) said that during the interminable administrations of the paramedics, it seemed to her the world had changed—that as she stood there helplessly and watched, she was assaulted by memories of Shane's swimming, surfing, and jumping off cliffs, set against a black future that she just could not envisage. Try as she might, she had no categories to imagine Shane paralyzed, and her mind flitted from the past to the present to the future in an uncontrollable whirr. She was crying when I came out of the pit and we hugged, and the boys came over and buried me in a three-way embrace. Jem, towering over me like his Dad, kissed me on the forehead (like his Dad), Jake put his cheek against my wet face, Lochie burrowed his head into my neck, and they held me tight; and somehow in our shared hopelessness we found a little bit of strength. About this time, Ken turned up from work and stood with us as we watched his son; my husband; their Dad, lying motionless. Of course, the bloody dog played hole-digging games next to the pole he was tied to, completely oblivious to his master's demise.

Then I heard the sound of a helicopter and watched one of the paramedics waving a flare to show it where to land. It was an enormous beast, like an army chopper, but painted red. Though it landed a fair distance away, it blew up a ferocious dust storm that almost knocked us off our feet. It was so strong that it flipped one of the ambulance trolleys on its head. The dog would have flown through the air if the Jacob hadn't held him down.

While the paramedics continued attending to Shane, there was nothing left for me to do. I felt utterly helpless and desperately tried to call Mum and Dad, but they were on a caravan holiday somewhere on the Nullarbor Plain and weren't answering, so I called my best friend instead. Rowena was fabulous. She listened to what had happened (God knows how she understood anything I said, with me sobbing into the phone)—just letting me speak. And she didn't say much, but I (almost) believed her when she told me that Shane would be okay and that I had the strength to get through this. We only talked briefly, but it helped me to find the courage to take a breath and face the next minute.

They told us Shane was being taken to Prince of Wales (POW) Hospital in Randwick, but said they couldn't let me ride in the helicopter with him. I couldn't understand why and I pleaded with them, but they insisted, telling me there were no spare seats. I know it's irrational, but it felt like he was being kidnapped, and I was devastated. When we were saying "goodbye" Shane seemed much calmer and was joking with the paramedics—God knows how or what about. But as his Mum and I kissed him and prayed for him, he started crying again and looked so frightened. It was heartbreaking! Jake was also sobbing, while Jeremy and Lachlan looked stunned with disbelief. Watching them fly away with the love of my life was the most horrid thing I've ever faced.

So of course, we needed to chase that helicopter! What was going to take them twenty-three minutes would take us three hours. We decided that Ken and I would drive straight to the hospital, while Olga would take the boys back to her house to collect our things before following behind. It was going on dusk when we left, and I remember watching a pink and blue sunset, wondering why God had the gall to paint the sky so beautifully at a time like this. The trip dragged on for an age, like one of those dreams when you're sprinting away from danger but don't seem to be getting anywhere. To make matters worse, my bladder decided to dance a jig and we had to stop four times on the way so I could to go to the bathroom. I'm sure Ken was thinking, "Again? You have to go again??!!"

When we arrived at the hospital and made our way to accident and emergency, Rowena was there waiting with some of Shane's work mates; Steve, Jacqui, Greg, Kate, and Andrew. We said our hellos, more hugging and kissing. They were in the dark about what had happened and what *was* happening, so Ken filled them in while I went hunting for Shane. The triage nurse informed me that Shane's condition was critical, but that he was undergoing tests and I would have to wait to see him. "He needs me," I said, and didn't really believe her when she responded with a glib "he's in good care." It was maddening, and I felt like pushing open the doors and doing a room-to-room search, but instead went back to the others and sat and waited. And waited.

Sometime later, Mum arrived with my boys, along with Shane's brothers Troy and Kurt in tow. Kurt was carrying a bottle of Scotch, even though I knew he hated the stuff. Apparently, on a whim, they had stopped on the way and brought a bottle as a gift for Shane. They knew he couldn't drink it tonight, and while it was, perhaps, a stupid waste of money, it was also a statement of faith—a tangible symbol that there would come a time when they could share a dram. To that end, Kurt was even prepared to learn to like whiskey.

It was somehow comforting to have everyone around, even though there was nothing anyone could do or say. It was just better to be with friends than to be alone. So we sat together and waited some more. I heard whispered conversations, but I just sat there and brooded. Rowena bought me a cup of tea and I wrapped my hands about it, noticing the heat but not caring. I didn't drink, but just sat there staring at the cup. Sometime later she took it back—I'm not sure whether empty or full—and then she came and put her arms around me. Resting on her shoulder, I closed my eyes, and I could see Shane going down the ramp and jumping. It was just so innocuous, just a little jump into a soft bed of foam. How can something as innocent as that jump have led to this? Why, God?

It was 10 p.m. before I was finally allowed in. Six and a half hours since the bloody accident. They'd given Shane some painkillers and he was doing better, calm and pain-free, and pleased to see us. But when Jem was confronted with his Dad, lying in a hospital bed, he burst into tears. I was too relieved to see him to cry, but I understood. Shane looked small and frail, like he'd aged two decades in an afternoon. This wasn't the same man who had taken Jeremy surfing that morning.

Yet it was the same man, my man. I reached down, smiling, and held his hand. It came as a shock to realize that he hadn't noticed—that he hadn't responded. Holding hands is one of the glories of marriage. It's a reminder that someone else is with you, sharing the good times and bad, "in sickness and in health" as the old vow goes. I have always loved his hands. They are huge, but not fat—long and thin—so that when we place our hands palm to palm, his fingers bend at the knuckle over the top of mine. When we hold hands, mine are engulfed, and nothing in the world can make me feel so secure, so loved. But now, no response. Just when I most needed his strength—and him mine—his hands deserted me. I kept smiling, hoping he wouldn't notice as I placed his arm back on the bed and went to stroke his hair.

All this time the doctors and nurses had been hovering in the background, and now they came over to give us an update. We were hoping there would just be bruising to his spinal cord, but an MRI showed he'd fractured both C4 and C5. The damage to the spinal cord was inconclusive, but they felt it had been pinched in some way. They couldn't give a prognosis, they said, but there were more tests to do and the picture should be clear tomorrow. One of the doctors asked if I wanted to have any more children. I couldn't believe the question. What an idiot! Pregnancy and childbirth were the last things on my mind, although I was wondering whether or not we'd ever have sex again, which brought to mind all kinds of questions; "had I known the last time we *did it* might be the last time we would *do it*, would I have *done it* differently?"

Later, when I raised the topic with Rowena, she tried to comfort me by reminding me "you've had twenty good years of sex," but it wasn't helpful. I want more—I'm supposed to be coming into my prime!! The unknown nature of his injury leaves the brain fried. We can't plan anything. We don't know what level of movement he'll have or what equipment he might need. We're in limbo! If he needs a wheelchair, we'll have to buy a new house. But where would we go? Will I need to be near relatives who can help me lift him? The thoughts and questions keep whirling around my head. Enough.

Before long (we had been waiting for hours and this visit seemed over in an instant) the doctors told us it was time to go. Shane needed his rest, and so did we. He was lying on his back, staring at the ceiling, unable to scratch his bloody nose. Out of nowhere he told me to finish my degree and sell his car. These things seemed so absurdly trivial but, so that he could rest easy, I reassured him—"sure, will do." I glanced over at Olga, who rolled her eyes and shook her head, laughing.

On the way out, Steve Fogarty said that the college would continue to pay Shane's salary indefinitely, which was a huge relief. We can eat! Hope School gave us $500. Blake and Coral Edwards said they'd take care of our lawns. Someone organized a roster for meals. It is all a blur, but we were enveloped in kindness, generosity, encouragement, and prayer.

Shane Clifton Journal (October 7)

I experienced some trepidation standing at the top of the jump, although no inkling of a catastrophe, merely an embarrassing hesitation. I wasn't afraid. What was there to fear? A jump, then a landing into a soft foam pit? I'd seen athletes practicing jumps into pits of this type, whose very purpose was to make falling safe. But I was nervous and a voice in my head reminded me, "You're getting older. You're turning forty." So an activity like the mega-ramp, which previously would have given me no pause for thought, now had me feeling my age. I figured that was as good a reason as any to take the jump. And so I did.

On the way down, I remember the feeling of my stomach making its way to my throat, and of having time to look ahead at the jump and wonder, "am I mad?" But the foam looked soft, and I was committed; so down, up, and down again . . . headfirst.

I knew straightaway that I'd broken my neck. There was no temporary unconsciousness, no moment of wondering why my arms and legs wouldn't respond, just a flash of nightmarish insight. I knew my life was irrevocably changed. The rising panic was palpable. I could taste it—a tangy bile on the back of my tongue. I called to Elly for help and tried to get my fear under control, forcing myself to take a breath and slow down. But the foam was in my face and I felt as though some alien force was pinning me down, denying me movement, smothering me. I gasped for air, still trying not to lose it.

I couldn't see a thing, but I could hear Elly stumbling over the fence and into the pit, fighting through foam, calling to me, wanting to know whether I was okay. I could think of no answer, so as she carefully made her way over, I clenched my jaw and prayed with the "wordless groans," the "incoherent grumblings" that Paul describes Romans 8:26. When eventually she got to me, I begged to be lifted up and given room to breathe away from the stifling foam, but she refused and I felt momentarily betrayed. "You have to be still, my love," she said, "I cannot move you, but I will clear the foam so you can take in some air." She spoke deliberately, calmly, and her voice, along with her hand touching my face, eased my fear. I felt a surge of pride at her strength, and then my mind raced and I began to think of what this injury might mean for her, for us.

"I'm sorry," I said, my voice cracking. "I'm so sorry. What have I done? Darling, I'm sorry."

"Don't be silly," she replied. "I love you, and we'll get through this together."

But I couldn't help myself, and we cried together as I went on apologizing, like a drunk trapped in regret, unable to change the past and equally sure that tomorrow would bring more of the same.

The only good news, "thank God it wasn't one of our boys," I whispered to Elly.

When the paramedics arrived, (whether quickly or slowly I had no idea—time after the accident had no meaning) Elly moved aside and a man with a husky but reassuring voice took over, introducing himself as Chris. He stood behind me, his forearms clenched firmly along my head and neck, reaching down to my shoulders and keeping my spine rock-steady as the remainder of the team (and Elly) gingerly raised me to the surface of the foam and rolled my body onto the tray of the gurney. Other than an intense pain in my neck and Chris' strong grip, I couldn't see or feel what they were doing and it was some time before I realized that I'd escaped the foam.

While all this was going on, Chris distracted me with small talk, asking mundane details about my life, my family, my holiday—you know, the sort of conversation you might have with a friendly stranger at the beach. Inevitably, we got onto my job, and I gave the usual explanation:

"A theologian?"

"Yeah. I teach people about faith."

"Oh, right."

"We discuss issues like the problem of pain—why bad things happen to good people."

The topic was a little too close to home, so we returned to more prosaic matters. My T-shirt read, "Trust me, I'm a doctor," (a PhD in theology, not really useful in these circumstances) and we laughed at the irony.

I'd never flown in a helicopter before, but this wasn't the view I'd been hoping for—my bed at right angles to the nose of the aircraft, surrounded by six paramedics looking down on me like pallbearers staring at an open coffin. I lay there as the living dead, an immobilized body capable of nothing but speech. Headphones were placed on my ears and the giro began winding up. Even with the ear protection the sound assaulted me, and the craft shook violently as we took off. Although I could see faces looking down on me, it was far too noisy to talk. I was completely alone. It felt like even God had abandoned me.

The trip was torture. It seemed interminable and the panic soon returned, but there was nothing to be done about it. I couldn't sit up, run away, punch a wall, bury my head in a pillow, go back in time, plan a way forward. So my brain ran in circles and turned to mush as I cried and cried.

I had no idea where the helicopter landed. Accident and emergency I guess. I was strapped down, looking at the ceiling (or up the noses of my attendants), with no perspective on my surroundings, no sense of where I was. For the first time in my life I had no say about my next *step*. Chris and the paramedics said goodbye as I was handed over to the doctors and nurses who asked the basics: name, birth-date, what happened? [*Little did I know, I'd have to repeat these details a thousand times over in the months to come. I never did come up with a creative answer, although I sometimes joked about my age . . . my favorite, "At forty, it takes longer to rest than it did to get tired."]*

Soon after, a nurse bustled over with a pair of scissors and unceremoniously cut away my clothing (so much for my "Trust me . . ." T-shirt). I guess I was naked, but I don't remember caring or even thinking about it. I was given the pin test—poked from top to toe, hoping for a squeal. From my head down to my upper chest I had normal feeling, almost everywhere else I felt nothing (oddly, I could sense a toe being pricked and a spot on my bum). It's hard to describe what this feels like (or doesn't feel like, as the case may be). It's normally disability that's the metaphor: she was *blind* drunk; he was *paralytic*! But this experience was brutally literal. It felt like I was paralyzed from the neck down.

By and by, the doctors and nurses had done with their prodding and left me in peace. Well, not peace exactly. They let me be, but the emergency room was a train carriage bustling at peak hour . . . all stations to the city, medical personnel boarding and departing, and me with no way to get off. I was asked a few questions, but most of the time they talked *about* me; a cacophony of voices, sometimes speaking gibberish, other times speaking English, but at all times frightening. The word "tetraplegia" bounced off the walls and into my skull with an ominous cadence, like a ball bearing in a maze.

Next, I was prepped for scanning: x-ray, CAT scan, and MRI. I was transferred from bed to gurney to machine and back, tasks performed like I was glass. Over the days to come, these tests were to become routine, but on this first night in hospital, closed off in machines that would forecast my destiny, the experience was religious—not an encounter with friend Jesus, but lying on an altar in the presence of a fearful God. I spent some of the time praying, but found that I couldn't finish my sentences, that I had no words to express my fears and hopes. The MRI was the worst of the tests, one hour enclosed in a tube, being attacked with noise and light. Too scary for prayer—all I could do was grit my teeth till my jaw ached.

Eventually, the last test was completed, and a porter returned me to accident and emergency where another physician greeted me. Dr. Lucy introduced herself as the registrar of POW's spinal unit and the person who would oversee my care when I got out of ICU. She was blonde and attractive, a model wearing a stethoscope.

"Call me Lucy," she said, but any infatuation on my part was quickly smothered by what she had to tell me. "We have the results of the scans, which show that you have broken your fourth and fifth cervical vertebrae (C4/5)."

It was an explanation with little meaning. "I heard the doctors use the word 'tetraplegia.' Is that what I have? What does it mean?"

"It's another word for quadriplegia. You'll be a quadriplegic."

I knew this already, but on hearing it out-loud a lump swelled in my throat. I couldn't deal with the gravity of the news, so I turned to something mundane—"Why the two terms?"

"*Tetra* is derived from the Greek, and *quadri* from the Latin, for four. Since your injury affects four limbs, you have quadriplegia . . . or tetraplegia."

[Editorial note: For those of you grammar nerds, plegia is derived from the Greek word plēgē; paralysis/wound/blow/affliction. Thus, tetraplegia is a compound of two Greek words while quadriplegia is a compound of a Latin and a Greek word. This, perhaps, explains the tendency for medical staff to prefer tetraplegia. Americans tend to say quadriplegia, Europeans tetraplegia]

I knew nothing about spinal injury, but it wasn't the time for long-winded explanations. Lucy gave me the basics.

"While we know you have damaged your spine, we don't yet know the impact on the spinal cord. It's sometimes the case that people with injuries like yours have some recovery. The difficulty is that we don't yet know the extent of the damage. It's just too early to make any guesses about the future. Tomorrow, surgeons will examine your scans and decide what to do next, whether we need to operate. For now, what you need is a good night's rest."

As she finished up, Elly, the boys, and Mum and Dad came over to my bed. It was so good to see them. They lined up one by one and kissed me. Elly gave a long and gentle cuddle, leaving wet tears on my cheeks that I couldn't wipe off—she pulled out a tissue and did it for me. I could tell it was hard for them, seeing me like this. None of us knew what to say, but "I love you" was enough. It was late, and the nurses wanted me to get some rest, so I said goodbye to my tribe and was transported in and out of elevators and down a maze of higgledy-piggledy corridors to ICU. I was attached to a Christmas tree of monitors, and encouraged to sleep with the in-out rhythmic swish of the oxygen mask that covered my nose and mouth. It was then I realized that I was no longer in pain and that I couldn't hold my eyes open. I fell asleep and didn't wake until morning.

October 8, 2010 (Friday)

Elly Clifton Facebook

By now I guess that most of you have heard about Shane's awful accident. For those of you who have sent your prayers and support—you are invaluable. He has fractured two vertebrae—C4/5. They are going to operate tomorrow to stabilize the neck and spine, using some of his hip bone to repair the vertebrae. He can't move his arms or legs but, oddly, does have some feeling in his feet. He is fluctuating between panic and resignation. I am feeling devastated and shocked, while at the same time strengthened by the support of my dearest friends and Shane's Mum and Dad. Shane turns forty next Saturday, October sixteenth. Please pray that his breathing will remain stable.

Shane Clifton Medical Records

CT brain and cervical spine upper/mid thoracic spine performed, CT Abdomen and Pelvis with Contrast performed. MRI Brain and Spine. No sensation below C7. Landed on head, axial load. Clinical details: Trauma with paralysis and loss of sensation below C4 following a fall onto head from a bicycle accident. No brain injury or sinus damage. There is a 3–4 mm anterior displacement of C4 on C5 and a fracture involving left osteo-inferior corner of the C4 vertebral body with a 10 mm linear bony fragment displaced posteriorly. C4–5 disk injury. Spinal cord contusion from C3–4 to C6 level. No rib fractures. All internal organs are normal as are small and large bowel.

CT Angiogram Head and Neck performed. Result—Incomplete C4 quadriplegia.

Shane Clifton Journal

I woke on Friday morning to a team of doctors surrounding my bed, reviewing my charts, and checking the monitors. Seeing me wake, they removed my facemask, pointlessly introduced themselves (I'd no chance of remembering their names), and then repeated the pin test. "Can you feel this?" Prick into my ear, "yes." "And this?" Neck, "yes," shoulder, "yes," elbow, "no!" Fingers, one at a time, "no," chest, "yes," belly button, "maybe" (some surprise), stomach, "no," bum, "yes," pause again, "yes, not a sharp prick but a dull sensation." And so it goes on, thigh, knee, shin, "no," "no," "no," toe, "yes." "Which one?" "Big toe." "And now?" "Middle toe, I think."

"Close enough" (but no cigar), and on it goes, down one side, back the up other, prick, prick, prick, prick, prick; "yes, no, no, no, yes," . . . the occasional surprise.

So it turns out I have some scattered sensation in areas below the level of injury. This seemed like good news—great news even—but the doctor's response was muted. "It doesn't mean much," he tells me. Apparently sensation is common, but it doesn't indicate whether further sensory improvement is likely or whether there's a chance of regaining movement. "For now," he says to me, "the question is whether we need to operate. I think we will, but the final decision rests with the surgeons. I will tell you when we know more." And with that, the doctor and his acolytes moved on to the next bed, doing the morning rounds.

They left me with a nurse, who gave a friendly "howdy" with an American twang, and declared that I had her undivided attention—apparently ICU nurses care for a single patient over a twelve-hour shift. She was young and pretty, and after telling me her name was Cindy, I plied her with twenty questions. Where are you from? Why Australia? How long? Do you have a boyfriend? She laughed at this last question and told me she was all mine. For the first time that morning I smiled, the light-hearted fun of flirtatious banter providing some relief against the stark reality of my situation.

With my neck encased in a brace, my head was rigid. I could see straight ahead and then only as far north, south, east, and west as my eyes could circle in their sockets. I noticed the flashes and beeps and buzzes of the machines that form a halo around my bed. I asked Cindy what it all does. Lifting my right arm she showed me an attached board with a tangle of wires stretching from key points on my body to the machines, intended to monitor my vital signs. I looked like a *cyborg*, but she told me not to worry about any of it, except for a single machine that sits over my left shoulder. Among other things, this shows my heart rate.

"When that line goes flat and an alarm screams, then you can worry!"

This ludicrous statement was surprisingly funny, and I found myself already attached to this nurse.

Soon after, Elly and Mum came into the ward, having spent the night at Aunty Ineke's place nearby. It didn't look like they'd slept very much, but they weren't interested in talking about their own difficulties. I brought them up to date and we set about the hard task of waiting and worrying, wondering when the surgeons were going to advise us of their plans. When they eventually stopped by, it was only to confirm that I'd be heading off to surgery the next day. They intended to take a slice of bone from my hip and attach it to my fourth and fifth cervical vertebrae to fuse the joint and stabilize the bone that surrounds the fragile and damaged spinal cord. They told me there was a small risk that the operation could further damage the area (or worse), but I had no option other than to take their advice and proceed with the surgery.

The news, while expected, was surprisingly scary—a reminder of the fragile state of my health, and of the fact that death was near. Cindy noticed a spike in my heart rate and some shortness in my breathing, and placed the oxygen mask back over my face. My tears eventually gave way to tiredness, and I fell back to sleep.

The rest of the day proceeded apace. Visits from family. Sleep. Medical rounds. The generous solicitations of Cindy. In the blink of an eye it was evening. At 7:00 p.m. there was a changeover of nursing staff, and not long after, my family headed home. This is the worst of times, in a crowded ward, utterly alone. There's nothing to do, no place to go, no book to read (and no hands to hold it), no computer to write on, no television to dull the mind. There are only thoughts circling my head, repeating themselves, utterly useless "what-if's?" and "what-will-I-do's?" that force their way to the front of my consciousness and can't be set aside by my usual dreams of surf and golf and friendship and sex. Every imagination draws me inexorably down the same path, "my God, my God, why hast thou forsaken me?"

October 9, 2010 (Saturday)

Olga Clifton Facebook

Just want to let all of Shane's friends know that he is being operated on at 11:00 a.m. to fuse and stabilize his vertebrae, so as to avoid any further injury to the spinal cord. Elly and the boys are holding up amazingly well and are very grateful for all the prayer and support they are receiving.

Shane Clifton Journal

I woke with the changeover of nurses (it must have been 7 a.m.). I hoped that Cindy was on again, but was told that the nurses rotate beds; that ward policy dictates they're not to be given the same patient twice. I felt irrationally cheated, like a teenager that has been dumped by his girlfriend, the flirtations of yesterday proving to be meaningless. I knew the feeling was absurd, that my anger at today's interloping nurse (I cannot remember her name) was unjustified, but I found it really hard to get past the connection formed on the first day of my dependency, the day that Cindy became my hands and feet and took care of my broken body.

Fortunately, Elly arrived early, wanting to see me before I was taken off to surgery. We chatted for a while, about nothing in particular. I kept my nursing infatuation to myself as Elly read me get well cards and encouragement from Facebook. It was all too overwhelming and again I found myself crying. Of course, it didn't help that I couldn't blow my own nose, but Elly—who always has tissues handy—reached over and let me have a good snort. A wet face and dripping booger brought us both to laughter, another transition on this rollercoaster emotional journey.

We waited. "They'll be here soon," the nurse informed us. We waited some more. "Soon." Waiting was a pretty nerve-racking business, an operation on the spine being no small matter. Then suddenly it was time. Hasty goodbye kisses, a quick prayer, and I was wheeled off along another dizzying trail of ceilings to surgery. Handed over to a surgical nurse, I was asked the standard questions: name and date of birth (I certainly don't want someone else's surgery). A doctor arrived and explained the nature of the forthcoming surgery. Then an anaesthetist placed a mask over my face: ten, nine, eight, seven . . .

Elly Clifton Facebook

6:00 p.m.: He went into surgery at 1:00 p.m. (bloomin' hospital times!). They told me it went really well. Doctors said it would take four to eight hours, but he was out in less than four. I haven't yet had a chance to speak with the surgeon. Shane has a tube down his throat and is to be ventilated tonight, more as a precaution and to give his lungs some help. A doctor had suggested that he might need tracheal intubation (a tube through the throat). Thank God that wasn't necessary. The ventilation tube should be removed tomorrow. For now, he needs to rest and begin his recovery. I'm exhausted, and finding it hard to come to terms with tubes, blood, and everything really. I don't have much idea what is going on, but will let you know more when I do.

9:00 p.m.: Thank you all so much for your prayers and kind wishes. I feel like I'm connected to a beautiful worldwide family, and it staggers me how thoughtful you are. I am holding onto God so tightly. He is my comfort and strength when I feel it's all too hard, and you are all God's beautiful gift to us at this time. The doctors said he might regress in the days after the surgery due to swelling—but I'm praying and hoping for good things as his body begins its healing journey.

October 10, 2010 (Sunday)
Elly Clifton Facebook

I finally spoke to a neurosurgeon that was part of the team that operated on Shane. He was pleased with the way it all went. The surgeons spliced bone from his hip and inserted it between his C4 and C5 vertebrae, which are now fused, pinned, and bolted (I imagine he'll set off alarms going through airport security). They also removed a shard of bone. It hadn't pierced the spinal cord, but if left there it'd be a potential threat. I have been shown an x-ray, and it's utterly surreal to see his neck held together by screws.

They don't know the full extent of the spinal cord damage as the membrane wasn't broken, and they don't like to break it just to see. They said that his injury is severe and that it will have far-reaching consequences, but cannot give us any idea of what to expect. We just need to learn patience.

He has been on a ventilator all day, and heavily sedated. He would open his eyes when woken by the nurse, but wasn't able to respond much. I'm glad he can rest. The nurse asked him to lift his arms and he bent both elbows, the left better than the right, which was encumbered by UV lines and the like. The most encouraging thing was that he could feel them touch his belly button.

I know so many people are doing things for us behind scenes, and I'm sorry that I can't thank you all personally. Your prayers and kind thoughts are giving us the strength we need each day to walk through this, and I cannot put in words what that means. Bless you all.

October 11, 2010 (Monday)
Facebook

Josh Dowton: Hi Elly, I just thought I'd share a beautiful, simple prayer for Shane from our three-year-old tonight. In the middle of dinner, she stopped, got us all to hold hands, and then said, "Grace to Jesus for Daddy's friend with the sore neck. Make him be better soon."

October 12, 2010 (Tuesday)

Elly Clifton Facebook

I finally heard my husband speak today. For a few short moments I saw a glimmer of my darling man. He's so tired. He will need to remain in Intensive Care until he can breathe without assistance for more than an hour at a time. At that point, they will give him another MRI and determine the success (please God) of the surgery. After that, he should be moved into the Acute Spinal Ward. Could be days, could be a week.

October 10–12, 2010 (Sunday to Tuesday)

Shane Clifton Journal

The days following surgery were a dizzying blur. I was often woken by the activity of nurses attending to the various needs of my body. They'd talk to me briefly, but my attention waxed and waned. I couldn't reply in any case. I had double-barreled tubing on my face, one tube feeding oxygen down my throat and the other pumping vomit-colored food through my nose and into my stomach. It was uncomfortable, but I was distracted by tiredness and morphine kept me in a near comatose state. Sometimes I'd awaken to the kisses and encouraging whispers of my family, but I couldn't keep my eyes open and would soon fall back to sleep.

I am led to believe that on the fourth day (two days after surgery) the oxygen pump was removed. It was a relief to have it out, but my throat was sore and raspy and speech seemed beyond me. The tubing was replaced with an oxygen mask and all I felt like doing was sleeping.

On the fifth day, I woke up with a start. I had been dreaming about my accident and the horror of falling upside-down. I woke with a scream as my head hit the foam. A nurse rushed over (another fresh face) but there was nothing she could do. Later that day I was dozing, and I found myself rushing down a water slide, to and fro at break-neck pace (a phrase that has never carried more meaning). The slide went on interminably, and the feeling of falling became more and more frightening. Once again, I awoke with a start. It felt like I was covered in sweat, but Mum was right there and assured me my vital signs were normal.

What was not normal was my breathing, which moved in and out of my chest with a gurgling rumble. It felt like I was breathing through water and the struggle to find oxygen was making me panic. The nurse (Susan, a

Pom, who speaks with the sophistication of the Queen) put her hand on my chest and encouraged me to slow my breathing, to concentrate on taking deep breaths; in and out, in and out. The gurgle remained but I was calmer. Susan suggested we call the physiotherapist to help remove the phlegm from my lungs. This seemed a bit weird. All I knew of physios was that they massaged your muscles, but I was open to any suggestions.

Peter—sporting the red polo shirt that I'd soon come to identify with POW physios—was medium-height, muscular, and strong. He had fiery red hair and bounded into the room with a burst of energy. He put me at ease at once, which was good because his strategy sounded quite alarming. He was going to give me an assisted cough, which involves a vigorous push immediately below my rib cage, timed with my outward breath and attempted cough. While Peter and I worked, the nurse was instructed to hold a suction machine over my mouth to suck up the mucus (essentially a phlegm vacuum cleaner). A "vigorous push" turned out to be a bone-rattling wallop, although he told me my rib cage would hold up. It took a couple of tries before I timed my cough correctly, but when I did, we achieved a thoroughly satisfying expectorate (such a cool word). Twice more and my lungs were clear and breathing was smooth. It is difficult to describe the euphoria of cleared lungs after a fight to breathe. I imagine the terror of emphysema, and am thankful that I've never smoked.

Later that night, the problem returned, and Peter came back to give me another wallop. I experienced relief, but began to worry about the night shift when the physios would go home, and I'd be left to breathe on my own. I asked why the nurses weren't trained in this skill, but Peter assured me that he was on-call, available if I needed him—my new best friend!

I fell asleep easily enough, enjoying the free drugs and the opportunity to legally "chase the dragon." Before long I started to dream again, a repetitive cycle of falling—the dragon biting back. I was only vaguely conscious of the details of the fall; it may have been the accident running through my mind or some other imaginary flight. Whatever the case, my panic increased and I eventually scared myself awake again. Immediately, the fear of falling was replaced by the struggle to breathe. With a croaky and teary voice, I called to the nurse, who removed my oxygen mask and tried to calm me down. He went to the sink and wet a hand-towel to wipe my forehead with, encouraging me to slow down and take deep breaths. I knew the routine by now but after an episode like this, it takes time to believe that I'm neither falling nor choking. I asked the time and I begged for Peter, but it turned out to be only 11 p.m. It was not long enough since my last assisted cough, and it'd be too long before morning if Peter came now.

The nurse stood next to the bed and left his palm on the towel over my forehead. His presence and the gentle weight of his hand calmed me enough that I could close my eyes.

October 13, 2010 (Wednesday)

Shane Clifton Journal

I fell back to sleep, but the nightmarish cycle repeated twice more—dream, fall, wake, panic. I was developing a clock obsession, but the damned thing was not in my line of sight. "Time please, nurse, and get Peter, please!" My gurgling, labored breath resulted in the physio being called. The nurse remained by my side as I struggled to breathe until Peter arrived and worked his magic. I've fallen in love with him and his red curly hair, but he refused my offer of marriage. "Only because it is illegal in Australia," he said.

I slept through to the change of shift (7:00 a.m.). My breathing was phlegmy, but the morning brought me some courage. Another new nurse told me it'd be a couple of hours before a physio would be free to help me cough, but I was confident enough to gurgle in and out till he came.

It was Nick who helped me expectorate this morning, and soon after, the senior ICU doctor and his entourage arrived at the foot of my bed. I explained the troubles of my evening and he added Endep, a mild antidepressant, to my long list of drugs (apparently at low levels this also provides pain relief). He also said it was time remove the nasogastric tube and start feeding me by mouth. This seemed like a step forward, so I tolerated the sickening sensation of the tube being pulled out of my gullet, through my throat, and out of my nose.

When the crowd moved on, one of the nurses (after a while they all start to blend into one) fed me yogurt, a teaspoon at a time. I wasn't hungry, but I hadn't eaten in six days (vomit brown goo down the nose doesn't count), so I savored the feel of the velvety liquid sliding down my throat.

Exhausted from last night, I nodded off and was asleep when Elly and Mum arrived mid-morning. Again I'd dream, fall, awaken, and panic, but a wifey kiss and cuddle worked wonders. With my tubes removed I was able to talk more freely, and I took the opportunity to find out how everyone had been holding up. My family shares my ordeal, but for the first time in my life I could do nothing to help them out. We were all tired and spent the day dozing, although I began to dread falling asleep.

The physios and I agreed to a routine; they're to come before breakfast, lunch, and dinner, and are on-call if needed at night. Following the evening clear out of my lungs, the nurse invited my Mum to feed me. She was a little reluctant, but went ahead and placed a dollop of apple mash on the spoon, pretending to fly an airplane into my cave of a mouth. A little comedy—however silly—helps. I took a couple of spoonfuls, but the third got stuck in my throat and I started to choke. It felt like the food had gone down my airway, but my cough was too weak to shake it loose. As I spluttered and coughed, Mum frantically called the nurse who pushed on my chest in a move that would make a physio proud. The food dislodged, but I was too fearful to try again.

Facebook

Elly Clifton: Shane is very weary, but being very brave. I cannot imagine how frightening it must be to have your body suddenly stop responding. His condition is still serious, as he is constantly at risk of blood clots, pneumonia, and bedsores. These threats will dramatically decrease once he can sit in a wheelchair. So please pray for his breathing to become stronger and more regular. I am feeling stunned that tomorrow will be a week since the accident. I feel like I've lost seven days somewhere. If only I could go backward in time, to last Wednesday to make different plans for Thursday . . .

David Parker: Had a great time with Shane tonight, lots of talking and banter. It was so good to see the difference from when I last went in; he's so much more like the Shane I know. Breathing by himself was a bit exhausting and so I had to leave after thirty minutes, but it did me good, and I hope it did him good too, Dave.

October 14, 2010 (Thursday)

Shane Clifton Journal

I'm starting to develop something of a macabre routine, one that I am increasingly cognisant of as my mind recovers from its morphine haze. Night and day I am "turned"; rolled onto my left side (held up by pillows), two hours later onto my back, two hours onto the right side, all with the goal of preventing bedsores. This explains part of my difficulty sleeping. Last night

I made it through to 3 a.m., when, once again, I needed to ask the nurse to get the physio out of bed. I felt guilty, but he consoled me by letting me know that night-time call-outs pay handsomely.

Anyway, back to that routine. Following a change of nursing shift in the morning, the first order of duty is the toilet (although no toilet is involved). I'm rolled onto my left side (apparently, pressure on the colon helps the process) and an enema is inserted into my anus. With time, I shit in bed (sometimes, only a swear word will do), normally with the help of what is politely called a PR (per rectum) but which is, in fact, a finger up the bum; the massage stimulates the rectum creating a reflex in the muscles that are no longer under my control. The process can take up to an hour, and even without substantive sensation, it has to be endured. It is not merely the stink, but the thought that I'm shitting in bed and lying in poo.

Next, I am cleaned. Not just my bottom, but my whole body from head to toe is sponged down with soapy water. It is an intimate task, and the strangeness of the newly met female nurse seeing you nude and cleaning your body is topped only by the shock of the same task being performed by a man. Once I'm empty and clean, I'm ready for the doctors and their morning rounds.

Today it was decided that the nasogastric tube needed to be reinserted, and one of the trainee doctors was left to perform the task. Last time this was done I was unconscious, but today I was asked to resist gagging as the tube was inserted through my nose and down my throat. I tried my best, but the doctor miscued and hit my airway, causing me to gag like a drunken teenager. Out came the tubing and then back in for a second try—with the same result. He urged me to relax, but as the third and fourth attempts got caught in my throat, I struggled to control the rising anger, barely managing to keep myself in check. He convinced me to try for one last attempt, but when my frustration bubbled over in teeth clenched obscenity, he was at last smart enough to leave me alone.

Later that morning, when Elly and my Dad arrived to visit, my fury had given way to fear. At times like this I feel like a coward, afraid to sleep, afraid to eat, afraid of the nasogastric tube. The doctors soon returned which only added to my distress, but the tube had to be reinserted ("no, you can't go for a few days without eating"). The senior doctor promised he could get it done without too much bother. Before I could mount a defense he had the tubing in my nose, down my throat, and into my gullet. I stared daggers at the trainee who at least had the decency to look embarrassed.

Sometime later I was sent off for another MRI to check the success of the operation. I have bad memories of this machine, but this time it proved bearable. I just tried to think of it as an 80s disco hall; lights, sounds, and cramped spaces. It was certainly a test worth enduring. If my pinned and screwed neck looks stable, occupational therapists will be tasked with sitting me up in bed, and then transferring me to a wheelchair. I've had a horrible week, and I'm tired of staring at the ceiling, so this is a pretty exciting thought.

The rest of the day was straightforward. I enjoyed the company of a few visitors and spent the rest of the time napping. Fortunately, my nightmares seem to be subsiding, and I mostly avoid panic. I still find it difficult to breathe, though, and the physios remain my close friends. I have received an early birthday present. Elly brought me a clock that projects the time onto the ceiling. At least my time fetish can be satiated.

Elly Clifton Facebook

Our lives have been thrown into an unrecognizable state of rush and exhaustion, and today I felt like punching someone. I know things will settle into more of a routine in the next couple of weeks. God, give me patience.

October 15, 2010 (Friday)

Elly Clifton Facebook

The MRI showed more swelling, but that is not surprising following surgery. Shane was distressed and over-tired this morning, so I snuggled up to him as much as I could, and at least for a while, he calmed and fell into a deep sleep. The doctors decided not to try to sit him up till Monday, which was so annoying. The hospital shuts down on the weekend, so Shane feels like he is making no progress, just lying around and waiting.

This is the hardest thing I have ever had to face or walk through. I feel like someone has cut off my legs (yes, I see the irony), and yet I'm expected to walk stronger than ever. I am a zombie, unthinkingly going through the motions. I crawl out of bed, head into the hospital, and spend my day in and out of ICU (only two people allowed at Shane's bedside at any one time, so I have to go outside when people come to visit). I am all the time waiting, always powerless, feeling more hopeless as the days wear on. I am sleeping badly, and spend too much time in the bewitching hours watching the fluorescent clock turn over the minutes. In the lonely darkness, I have to stop myself reaching for the barren side of the bed; the person I've turned to for the last twenty years is miles away, and I can't even cuddle up to him and cry.

Then, during the day I find myself nodding off, snoozing at awkward angles on the chair in the waiting room and waking with dribble running down my chin. When I'm up and about I bump into things. Today I almost knocked over Shane's drip. At least I haven't crashed the car.

Shane Clifton Journal

I woke at 12:15 a.m., again at 2:15 a.m., and by 3:30 a.m. I was really struggling to breathe. I asked the nurse to call the physio, but she didn't see the need to wake him up. Half an hour later I tried again, but she insisted that I was breathing properly and my vital signs were fine. Later, I again pleaded for help, but she told me the problem was in my head; "if you just calm down and breathe slowly, you'll be fine." I felt like I was drowning, but I forced myself to suck in air—inhale, exhale; in, out; focusing on each breath for a minute, a half-hour, an hour.

Watching the time tick over, I mouthed curses to damn the nurse (evidence of my deep spirituality) and stayed awake until the 7:00 a.m. change of shift, then jumped at the new nurse, pleading for a physio. It was Nick who arrived to help me out—shove, cough, suck. I felt relieved and intensely grateful, like you might feel toward a fire fighter who had just rescued you from a burning building. I made it clear to whoever was listening that the over-night nurse had tried to kill me! But the fact that I was still alive (if not kicking) weakened my case. At least the system of rotating nurses means I shouldn't have to put up with her again.

I slept for much of the morning but woke in a cold sweat, dreaming again of falling. This is starting to get me frazzled. I'm so tired, but I dread going to sleep.

Later in the day, I enjoyed the company of friends. Kate and Andrew Tennikoff gave me an early birthday present: a pair of headphones and an iPod full of music, as well as audio books. When they left, I asked the nurse to jack me up and pump up the sound. I wanted something mellow, and the album I selected was Norah Jones, *Come Away with Me*, but I soon realized my mistake. Her music has a haunting quality and is intensely emotive. I was already tired and fragile and within a minute I found myself sobbing, but I'd been left with the oxygen mask over my face and I couldn't attract the attention of the nurse. Norah Jones was singing "Don't Know Why":

I waited 'til I saw the sun
I don't know why I didn't come
I left you by the house of fun
I don't know why I didn't come
I don't know why I didn't come
When I saw the break of day
I wished that I could fly away
Instead of kneeling in the sand
Catching teardrops in my hand
My heart is drenched in wine
But you'll be on my mind
Forever
Out across the endless sea
I would die in ecstasy
But I'll be a bag of bones
Driving down the road alone
My heart is drenched in wine
But you'll be on my mind
Forever
Something has to make you run
I don't know why I didn't come
I feel as empty as a drum
I don't know why I didn't come
I don't know why I didn't come

I experienced Norah Jones as torture until someone finally saw me crying and turned off the music.

CHAPTER 2

Staring at the Ceiling

October 16, 2010 (Saturday)

Facebook

Elly Clifton: Fortieth birthday in ICU. Patients are usually only allowed three visitors at one time, but today the nurses let in more people. Shane couldn't eat his lovely big cake made by Karina Smith (Cake Smith), so we're saving some for when he can. The nurses were more than happy to take some off our hands.

We read our cards to him. It had been difficult to find ones that were appropriate, e.g.,

- "It's your 40th, do what you want."

- Or another, "It's your 40th birthday, it's all downhill from here."

- Or another, with a fisherman on the cover, and inside the punch line, "We all know you're a master baiter." I said to Lochie, "we can't get Dad that card since he might be sad if he can never do that again." Lochie was horrified, saying, "Dad would never do that!" I responded quickly, "No, you're right."

I tried to bring some levity to the day, buying the family funny hats. Jem wore his all day—a tall, purple, cat-in-the-hat-styled piece, and Olga dazzled the ward with a multi-colored Mohawk wig. Shane had the traditional Clifton birthday hat with pastel candles, which he kept on his headboard. Jacob refused to wear anything, saying, "I have hair." I had thought that was true of all of us but, apparently, in comparison to his stylish spike, we may as well have been bald—the wonders of male teenage vanity.

Shane and I have now been married for half of our lives. He slept well last night; at least as well as you can in the hubbub of an ICU ward when you're being turned over every two hours. Even so, he struggled today to keep his eyes open, and it looked to me like he was faking being upbeat. This is not how anyone would want to celebrate a birthday. At the end of the day he became quite philosophical, and asked me to post Shane's thoughts on his Facebook page; so I will be hacking into his account to do so!

The first of "Shane's Insights"

How to wake on the morning of your birthday: Kurt, Emma, and their troupe singing happy birthday over the phone, followed by my own melodic sons and parents . . . Being loved by family and friends, what more could a birthday boy want?

Shane Clifton Journal

I had a better night, perhaps because I was allowed my 3:00 p.m. tryst with the physio (a girl this time, a trainee working with Nick). This morning, while lying in poo, I received some early-morning birthday calls, launched in song. It is a good thing the phone transmits sound and not smell!

It was a busy day with friends and family filing in and out of my cubicle, all of us trying to pretend that there was something worth celebrating. And there was. I'm alive (the most important thing) and blessed to be on the receiving end of a massive outpouring of love: cards, calls, prayers, and encouragement.

My cubicle was festooned with color, although the attempts to hide the drab square-ness of an entirely functional hospital ward (which looks exactly the same as any other ward in any other hospital) was like applying makeup to a six-foot five transvestite—we could pretend she is female but what is underneath the skirt is obvious. I wasn't allowed flowers (although Elly has enjoyed taking home those that were meant for me), but I was surrounded by balloons and streamers, a happy birthday banner, and the family wearing crazy hats.

To capture the celebrations, Elly had on hand the video recorder. Sometime during the morning a nurse asked her how I had my accident, and she realized that she was holding a record of the event. She was far too nervous to look at it herself so she gave the video to Rowena, who watched it and said, "It looks like nothing, totally harmless." That may be, but I was nowhere near ready for that video.

At 4 p.m., I was informed that I was to be moved from ICU to HDU (high dependency unit). It's in the same ward, and I have to stare at the same damn ceiling (for the sake of those of us who get no other view, surely the hospital could add a lick of paint. I don't need Michelangelo, but a splash of color would do wonders for the mood). In any event, the only difference between ICU and HDU is that one nurse looks after two patients. It's a sign that things are improving, or at least stabilizing, but it makes me feel a little vulnerable. What will I do if a nurse is occupied with another patient and I'm struggling to breathe? I was assured that they will always be close at hand and that machines will scream if anything goes wrong. This makes perfect sense, but logic doesn't help. I can't seem to shake off this relentless dread.

October 17, 2010 (Sunday)

Elly Clifton Facebook

Throughout the week, Shane has been struggling to breathe at night. This, added to his nightmares, has become a vicious circle. Waking throughout the night makes him tired and eats away at his emotional resources. This exacerbates his fear, and causes him to panic about sleeping (and dreaming) and, paradoxically, about not getting enough sleep! And his inability to rein in this restless panic him leaves him feeling pathetic. More than once he's said to me, "I feel like a sook." The male nurse told him that he was amazed at how well he was coping and that he thought he was marvelous. I've been telling him not to be hard on himself. If it were me, I would've been crippled by one continuous panic attack from the moment of the accident.

I've spent much of the day helping Shane journal. There is something therapeutic in the process, although it feels like we must be describing someone else's life.

Shane Clifton Journal

Aside from ever present nurses, on weekends doctors are "on-call" only, and there are no OT's or physios on-site, so we are mostly left to our own devices. Today I enjoyed a visit from Troy, Kristine, and their kids. Three-year-old blonde bombshell, Ameliese, is normally too shy even to talk to me, but today she came into my cubicle with a sunflower smile, a hug, and a wet kiss on my cheek. Spinal cord injury (SCI) does have its upside; kids seem to be captivated by me! The rest of the day I relaxed with Elly, reflecting on what has been one hell of a week, and dictating this journal.

I have been thinking about dependency. While at Callala Bay, I was reading a book by Alasdair MacIntyre, *Dependent Rational Animals*, which explores the virtues associated with dependency. To have been reading that book at that time is just a weird, although I have not finished it and I don't fully grasp its argument. But I do know something about the tradition of virtue ethics.

Virtues are the habits of character that enable a person to succeed, and a family and community to flourish. In terms of the virtues needed to help those in need, I have seen them displayed magnificently this week. On the whole, I have been treated with uncommon care by all the hospital staff (excepting the nurse who tried to kill me). I honestly don't know how they do it. What sort of character does it take stick your finger up someone's bum and clean up crap, and to do so with kindness, gentleness, and good humor? How do you remain patient with a patient who has you woken up and dragged into the hospital at 3 a.m. every night for a week, especially when it's likely that he's driven more by fear and panic than real physical need (perhaps the murderous nurse has a point)?

Then there are the virtues that I need to make a go of things. To be honest, the transition from independence to dependency is something I haven't yet got my head around. I have gone from being able to do most things for myself, and now I rely on others for almost everything. What are the habits of character that I will need as a dependent person striving for some level of independence? I don't know the answer right now. At the moment, I'm simply trying to learn to be grateful, to express my appreciation to the staff and to my family and friends. Gratefulness is a reciprocating virtue; it creates an atmosphere that encourages the best in others. Yet it does not come easily when life is hard. How do I say thank you to a nurse for cleaning my bum when I hate what is happening to me? How do I keep saying thank you, time and again throughout the day, when I'm forced to ask for help at every turn?

How do I say thanks when I feel like shouting *piss off*?

October 18, 2010 (Monday)

Second Facebook Hack by Elly—"Shane's Insight No. 2"

"Dignity is not what happens to you. Someone can play with your bum, wipe your balls, and strip you naked—but if it's done with respect, then it's dignified."

Shane was crying as he said this and I wrote it down word for word.

Elly Clifton Facebook

Well, he no longer needs the breathing machine, which is a relief. Its Darth Vader-like wheezing was adding to his night-time restlessness. The drips on his arms and hands and the electrodes on his chest have also been removed, so he's looking much less like a cyborg. But before he had time to enjoy the freedom, the OT arrived with a new neck brace. It extends from his neck down through his chest and back, and now he looks like a storm trooper; a little less evil than Vader, but still wicked enough! It is for a good cause, though—to hold him rigid so he can sit up.

I am getting tired of ICU. You have to wait outside the ward and buzz the nurses and hope it's not too long before they let you in. Not only do I need to ask permission to see my husband, but because only two visitors are allowed in at a time, I need to leave every time someone comes; I seem to spend half a day waiting in the hall outside the wall. It's uncomfortable, frustrating, and boring.

When Rowena was at the ICU door waiting to visit him this morning, the nurse asked Shane how he knew her, and he said, "she's my girlfriend"—meaning a friend that's a girl. I'm sure it raised a few eyebrows since I'm in there regularly and known to be his wife!

Shane Clifton Journal

Greg Cortese dropped in today with a late birthday present from the college, an iPhone 4. He has included a hands-free Bluetooth receiver, although I will still need someone to put it on my ear. It also has a built-in recorder, which will give me the independence to be able to dictate my journal. So at forty, I have joined the ranks of the Apple cool.

The ward has again returned to life. During the morning rounds we discussed my on-going nightmares and decided that taking me off morphine might reduce my hallucinations. It seemed obvious enough that I wondered why the suggestion wasn't made earlier. I will take four hourly Endone, an opioid that apparently blocks nerve receptors in the brain.

The big news of the day; Peta (OT), has been helping me to sit up in bed, getting me ready for a wheelchair—hopefully later in the week. If I had to guess, I'd say she was in her thirties. Her blonde hair was pinned back in a no-nonsense ponytail that matched her gym-toned physique and straightforward attitude. She was gentle enough with me, but I could also tell that she wouldn't hesitate to give me some needed tough love. Indeed, I'm shocked at how stupidly hard it was to sit up. I was just looking forward to a nicer view of the world (bye-bye ceilings), but the elevation caused my blood pressure (BP) to crash (75/50). And while I didn't faint, I spent most of the time with my eyes closed, spinning through a galaxy of speckled stars and black holes. I managed about a half hour, until the dizziness, as well as pain in my shoulders and neck, overcame my determination—Endone has only so much power.

Through the rest of the day, I repeated the exercise twice more. Now as I dictate this journal, I feel the satisfied joy of an aching body. Two weeks ago sitting up was unremarkable, but now I consider it an achievement.

October 19, 2010 (Tuesday)

Shane Clifton Journal

Keith was today's nurse, a lanky (six and a half foot) pommy with blonde hair and the beginnings of a creepy looking mo (his defense is that he's readying himself for Movember). He had me rolled on my side with his finger up my bum when he decided the time was right to tell some jokes:

> A nurse walks into a bank to deposit his paycheck. Asked to sign the payslip, he reaches into his top pocket and pulls out a pen. In its place he discovers a rectal thermometer. "Damn," he says in annoyance, "some asshole has my pen!"

> A middle-aged patient has been giving the nurses a hard time. When a trainee nurse comes out of his room crying, the matron decides she has had enough. Marching over to his bed she informs him that she needs to take his temperature. The man opens his mouth, but the matron says she needs to take a rectal reading. Asking him to roll onto his knees and bend over, she tells him that the thermometer needs a little time to come to the correct reading and, since she has forgotten his notes, she will be back in a minute.

Some time later the man hears laughter and realizes that his door has been left ajar. Hearing the commotion, a doctor enters the room and asks him what is going on. He replies grumpily, "haven't you ever seen anyone having their temperature taken before?" The doctor responds, "No, not with a carnation."

During the morning (when Elly and her parents were visiting), Peta came into my cubicle to tell me that today was to be the day for the wheelchair. She would be back in a half-hour to get me up. It was sooner than I had thought, and while I was excited, I also had a sudden attack of nervousness; like a virgin on honeymoon. While brides and grooms are calmed with champagne, I was given a tablet of Endone. Nicely mellowed, I was fitted to my storm trooper brace and sat up in bed (to stabilize my BP), awaiting my date.

Peta returned with FB in tow (not real name, acronym explained below)—a surgical dresser; "it's a clever title for a man who spends his day helping you lot to shit, shower, and dress," he says.

He arrived pushing a hoist and carrying a green sling over his shoulder. With Peta on one side of the bed and FB on the other, I was rolled onto my side and the sling was shoved under my back. I was wearing a hospital gown and, laughing at my exposed bum, FB growled, "your arse is so hairy I'm going to have to use a comb to take you to the bathroom." My wife looked shocked, and Peta rolled her eyes (apparently used to this sort of thing). I couldn't help but laugh as I realized who it was he reminded me of—a beardless Fat Bastard (of Austin Powers fame); rolls of flab but strong as Satan, and just as crude. I pictured him in my kids' favorite scene:

> *Fat Bastard*: "First things first: *Where's your shitter*? I've got a turtle-head poking out."
>
> *Dr. Evil*: "Charming."
>
> *Fat Bastard*: I'm not kiddin'. I've got a crap on deck that could choke a donkey. Aww, it's *squidgy*. I'm gettin' all emotional from it, ya know?

With the sling fitted under my back, around my thighs, between my legs, and hooked onto the hoist, I was raised slowly into the air and, like a sack of potatoes, transferred to my first wheelchair. In keeping with my rabid feminism, it had a bright pink frame (although as I write, I can hear my more perceptive students complaining that the presumption that a pink chair is necessarily suited for a male feminist is itself sexist—ah, the circumlocutions of political correctness). The high-backed seat was on a forty-degree tilt and as I was lowered into it, my head spun, the black holes eviscerated the stars, and I passed out. I awoke what seemed to me like an instant later to the worried looks of my family, but Peta was calm, telling us that it's normal to pass out after having spent so long lying down.

With my head still spinning, she invited Elly to push me slowly to the nearby door and out onto the ward balcony. I hadn't been outside for what felt like a lifetime (in fact, it had only been twelve days—did I really exist before this accident, or was my previous life a phantasm?), and although the glare was intense, the salty northeasterly breeze reminded me of the surf and I felt a surge of hopefulness.

Only a few minutes later, my neck and shoulders started to ache, and together with the glare and my light-headedness, I dry-wretched. My mood turned 180 degrees, and I felt like screaming at God. "It is so bloody unfair. If I can't last ten minutes, how on earth am I going make a go of a lifetime in a chair?" Assurances from Peta that "this is normal," that "I'm doing well," rang hollow.

And so I was returned to bed crying (again). Lying on a flat bed, having escaped from the storm trooper brace, was enough to put me to sleep. There is nothing like the healing power of unconsciousness.

Chapter 3

Acute Spinal Unit

I don't think I could stand being quadriplegic.

October 20, 2010 (Wednesday)

Elly Clifton Facebook

I stayed in a lodge with my folks last night and turned up at the hospital at 9 a.m. feeling fresh and sprightly. Much better than the smog-ridden, traffic-jammed nightmare I endure most mornings (that trip is really wearing me out). I arrived to discover that sometime during the evening, Shane had been moved from HDU to the acute spinal ward. He has been given a bed directly opposite the nurses' station, to ease his fear about another reduction in the nurse/patient ratio. While the nasogastric tube remains in place, I have been given the opportunity to feed him "thickened liquids." He says it is delightful to taste food again (yogurts and custard), but thickened water is "blech."

Elly Clifton Facebook (later in the day)

Shane started to feel sick during the day and his temperature has been rising; now 38.8 degrees (C). I am concerned for him, as fevers make him feel pretty icky. They tested his urine and he has a bladder infection, so they have put him on antibiotics. Thank you everyone for your support and prayer. You are all such an amazing extended family, and we're so blessed to be connected with you all!

October 21, 2010 (Thursday)
Elly Clifton Facebook

Shane has had a bad morning, with temperatures nearing 40 °C. He started shivering and ended up with uncontrollable shakes. They sent him off for tests and have found that he has clots in his lungs. Apparently there is a high risk of pneumonia. Please pray.

October 21, 2010
Shane Clifton Medical Records

CT Neck and Chest, Pulmonary Angiogram tests due to fevers of unknown source. Result: Multiple pulmonary embolus in right lower lobe [blood clots in lungs] . . . patient commenced on therapeutic clexane [needles] after consultation with haematology team. Blood test every second day.

October 24, 2010 (Sunday)
Shane Clifton Journal

I've had a rugged few days. When novels describe a "teeth-rattling fever," they are not being metaphorical. What started as a shiver became an uncontrollable shake, at times so bad that I couldn't stop my teeth from crunching. While nurses tracked my rising temperature, I felt cold and no amount of blankets helped. I was hot ice on a snare drum being beaten to death by Animal from *The Muppets*. After a midnight visit from the doctor in charge of "infectious diseases" (what a title), I was placed on an antibiotic drip and drugged up. And so I slept . . . and slept for days.

I have felt much better today. My temperature has dropped, and while I'm still fragile, I'm starting to feel normal again (whatever that is in this paralyzed body).

Now that I'm up to it, I should say something about my new digs. My cubicle is directly in front of the nurses' station. It's an open ward and my space is nondescript—a bed and curtains in an area that houses six other patients (it reminds me strangely of Forest Gump, lying face down on his bed with his shot-up butt in the air, next to a crippled Lieutenant Dan and a ward of injured soldiers). In addition to our six, there are others in the ward; anonymous patients imprisoned in their private rooms. The ceiling is as boring as it was in ICU; dirty white tiles, hole punched, ten holes wide and thirty long (and me with nothing better to do than count).

It is a chaotic environment, with nurses coming and going and talking endlessly, no attempt at library-like quiet. I hear things about other patients that I probably shouldn't, but this suits my nosiness (X has returned to the ward because her drug habit caused her to ignore the early warning signs of pressure marks; Y is a new patient who disgorged three condoms full of narcotics during his bowel treatment; Z is on suicide watch, a 200 kg paraplegic who repeatedly smashes his head against the wall). Of my direct neighbors, the cubicle to my right is occupied by an older lady (sixty or seventy) who likes to keep the television on all night. I sleep nevertheless, thanks to earplugs, plentiful drugs, and the rhythmic, soothing whispers of a C-PAP breathing machine. I recall mentioning that I hated the Darth Vader breathing machine in ICU, and was pleased to be rid of it. When I arrived at this ward, the Doctor insisted that I sleep with this new machine (a gentler, less invasive version that covers just my nose rather than my whole face), and my spirited complaints lost out to my doctor's insistence. I'm now a little embarrassed to admit that I am starting to like it. Perhaps this is a type of Stockholm syndrome.

I was lazing in bed this morning, waiting for the day to get started, when the curtains were pulled around the bed of my neighbor on the left— Dennis. Almost immediately he started to complain, and a few minutes later I heard a moan and then an ear-bending scream. Then, in a strong American accent, "get that f**king thing away from my dick and get someone who knows what the hell they're doing."

The cursing continued as the nurse scurried from the cubicle, returning a few seconds later with her boss. More abuse, and then screams that went on and on. Eventually things quieted down, although the curtains remained closed; presumably, the poor bugger needed some peace.

Not fifteen minutes later and a (thankfully) different nurse drew my curtains and introduced herself as Louise. "Time for your catheter change," she said, and I hoped this was her dark sense of humor.

It wasn't. Apparently, catheters need to be changed once a month, or immediately after a bladder infection has been treated by antibiotics. I fall into the latter category, and although I already have a catheter, I cannot remember it being inserted. Presumably, this was done soon after the accident, either in the helicopter or accident and emergency. It is oddly disconcerting that I cannot say which . . . it just seems like the sort of thing you should know about.

But I wasn't given time to panic, and I didn't have the courage to ask Louise what went wrong next door. On went the latex gloves (you know the scene in the movies where the nurse, with a wicked gleam in her eye, pulls on her gloves with a flick). The blanket was pulled down and my gown up. Out came the old catheter. That was easy enough, but the memory of my neighbor's torture pressed itself on my mind.

"Is this going to hurt like it did next door?" I asked, directing my gaze at my neighbor's curtain.

"Do you have feeling down here?" Louise responded.

"I'm not sure. I sometimes think I can tell when I'm being touched."

"No problems," She said. "I will use some lignocaine gel, which has an anaesthetic effect."

"Did he get the gel?"

"Yes."

What could either of us say to that?

So Louise filled a plastic syringe with the lignocaine, grabbed hold of my penis and squirted in the gel. Apparently it takes a few minutes to be effective, so we waited and chatted. It was a surreal experience. There I was, lying in bed with a pretty, young nurse fiddling with my manhood (is that the right word for a non-functioning penis?). I wondered whether she thought I was attractive, even though I knew it was a stupid thought. It is difficult to accept the fact that I'm not sexy (if I ever was), and that to the nurse my naked body is uninteresting, except as the subject of a medical procedure. I still feel sexual, and this exposure was getting my imagination going, even if the inane conversation and my lack of an erection said otherwise.

She gave the gel five minutes and then inserted a catheter, but the exercise caused a mini-erection, so she held my penis while it subsided. Again, this is so bloody strange. I cannot "think" and become erect, but I have what is called a reflex erection—the thing expands and shrinks as a reflex response to touch or movement. I hope this might prove useful later (although it is a half-hearted and temporary expansion), but it was damnably embarrassing this morning. There I was with Louise holding my (semi-erect) penis; what the hell was I supposed to talk about (and think) while that was going on?

It subsided and Louise inserted the catheter. I didn't feel a thing, and in the light of my neighbor's screams I was immensely relieved. Then I got to thinking; this temporary relief at my lack of feeling has to be set against the darker reality that I really do want to be able to feel this part of my body. It was a thought I couldn't face up to then, and I still can't now.

Louise asked me to cough. She needed to inflate a small balloon that sits on the end of the catheter to prevent it from pulling out, and could only do this once the urine was flowing—evidence that the tubing had made it out of the urethra and into the bladder.

[I was later to have the one of the junior nurses inflate the balloon early. I bled like a stuck pig and spent three days with an infection and high temperatures].

With everything in place, a 750 ml bag was fixed to the catheter line, and my first (conscious) catheter change was complete.

Elly Clifton Facebook

Shane has been amazing me with how well he is mentally coping with this injury. He doesn't want to use the TV because he doesn't want to miss what God wants him to learn from this awful experience. He said that TV is just an escape, and he'd rather sit with his thoughts.

[This did not last long. In fact, one month on and my friends worked out how to override the television payment control box, providing permanent access to the TV for free. I justified this theft on the basis that a charge of $21 a week for access to free to air television was immoral, especially for people forced to spend months in hospital.]

October 25, 2010 (Monday)

Shane Clifton Journal

Elly transcribed my journal of yesterday and then teased me about an entire day's entry being taken up describing a few minutes of changing the catheter. She thinks men are wimps; "women have faced up to this sort of invasive procedure for years without complaint," she quipped (I saw her Facebook post of yesterday, so I know she is teasing). She seemed more amused than jealous of my nurse fantasies.

After the transcription, Elly read me some of the dialogue from Facebook. I'm a little embarrassed by Elly's publication of my capacity to cope, and my so-called deep spirituality. I wonder whether this is a facade I put on for others. Is it that I want to appear heroic or that I'm trying to make things easier for my friends and family—since the extent to which I'm coping will influence their ability to muddle their way through this nightmare? Even this observation is an attempt to be bloody heroic—enough of this circular nonsense! The truth is I am coping okay in the morning and during the day. It's night-time that's hardest, trapped in bed, hours away from my family, with nothing to do but think about loss and a restricted future. It isn't getting easier. In fact sometimes I think it's getting harder as it becomes more obvious that this journey is not a dream. I am starting to get mad at God, but for now I'm trying to push theology to one side so I can focus on more practical matters.

It turns out that my screaming neighbor is a gem of a bloke, a sixty-year-old American who broke his fourth vertebrae while representing his country playing "old fellas" rugby (who knew Americans and old men played rugby?). Dennis' injury is an incomplete one, and he has been regaining movement and feeling each day (explains yesterday's reaction). This, along with his cheerfulness, makes him an encouraging companion.

On most days, my medical care is supervised by the spinal unit registrar, Jasmine (who has replaced Lucy), but today she was accompanied by her boss. Dr. Bonnie Lee is short—tiny in fact—and he never stops moving; he rocks backwards and forwards on the balls of his feet, picks up a medical chart then puts it back down, and turns his gaze from one person to another; a doctor charged up with Eveready batteries. He was engaged in rapid-fire strategy, in planning the next steps of my rehabilitation with Jasmine. They talked about medicines and procedures and goals for physiotherapists. I'm sure all this is important, but in the weeks I have been in hospital I have yet to receive a straight answer to a question that was becoming increasingly urgent.

When a gap opened in the conversation, I asked, "What is my prognosis? Will I recover or is this all there is?"

Bonnie stopped moving, gave me his full attention (and even slowed down the pace of his speech).

"This may be all there is. You may get no further neurological recovery, or you may regain almost everything. There is just no way of knowing."

He continued (speeding up again), laying before me the basics of spinal cord injury. The spinal cord is approximately the diameter of a finger, consisting of millions of nerve fibers that transmit information from the brain down to every part of the body (instructing the muscles of the body to move), and in the reverse direction, providing feedback (sensation, both pleasant and painful). In their traverse to and from the brain, the nerves of the spinal cord are protected by the vertebrae that make up the spine. Nerves that exit the cervical vertebrae (C1 to C8—the upper section of the spine) control breathing and supply movement and sensation to the neck, upper-trunk, arms, and hands; those that exit the thoracic vertebrae (T1 to T12) supply movement and sensation to the trunk and abdomen; those that exit the lumbar and sacral vertebrae supply movement and sensation the legs, bowel, bladder, and sex organs.

(He gave a thoroughgoing description, which I have paraphrased. He was treating me as an intelligent adult, and I appreciated it)

"Your break," he went on to say, "is the fourth and fifth vertebrae, but you seem to have most of your C5 function; shoulders and bicep. Everything below C5 level is impacted; wrist (C6), triceps (C7), fingers (C8). Obviously, everything else below the trunk is damaged."

I have asked other doctors the same question, but I asked again. "Is it a good sign that I have some feeling below the level of my injury, however muddy?" (I can sense touch, but not hot or cold. I cannot feel needles, which is some compensation.)

Bonnie's response confirms what I have already been told. "Motor neurons and sensor neurons traverse distinct parts of the spinal cord. It is possible for a person to have feeling and no movement and, conversely, to be able to move without feeling"; he went on to describe the surprising difficulty of walking without sensation in your feet and legs.

In terms of prognosis, the problem is that science has not yet reached the point that it can scan to the level of the neuron (which is more than 1000 times thinner than a human hair), so we have no way to determine the extent of the damage in the case of an incomplete injury. At the time of an accident, the area of injury swells and goes into shock—a little like a swollen ankle. Over time, the swelling subsides, and undamaged neurons are able to resume their function. Most recovery occurs in the first few months—and there is something of the J-curve effect thereafter. By six months to a year, the injury has largely stabilized, but recovery may continue through the following year, sometimes later. There is simply no way of knowing, and so no real way of planning for the future.

His conclusion is worth quoting in full (I can pretty much remember it verbatim). "An incomplete injury is a blessing; it means that recovery is possible, we just don't know how much or how little, or how long it might take. It can also bring challenges; it not only makes it difficult to make plans, but it can give rise to additional hardships—not least of which can be pain below the level of injury. Increased sensation is not always positive, but is better than having no feeling at all."

It was a lot to take in, but Bonnie's thorough and brutally honest explanation was precisely what I needed. He finished with a challenge:

"Whatever your neurons do and don't do is largely out of your control. But if you work hard, if you use the muscles you have and exercise those areas that are experiencing improvement, you can make the most of whatever level of return you get. Even if that return is minimal you can learn to function and flourish, with wheelchairs and mechanical aids and computers. You still have some say in the shape of your future."

I like that. It is incentive enough, at least, to help me cope with what is coming next.

Medical records: Nuclear Medicine Bone Scan. Whole body bone scan. No evidence of calcification in the hip region. (More tests, the routine of SCI)

October 26, 2010 (Tuesday)

Elly Clifton Facebook

Shane didn't get to sit up too long today, as his blood pressure suddenly dropped and he looked white in the face. The nurse was worried he might pass out. Apparently, there's a pressure strap they can wrap around his tummy (a theraband) that the helps control BP, so hopefully he won't have that dizzying experience again! He wanted to stay up longer, but he looked awful and I was glad he went back to bed. I saw Peter Garrett (from Midnight Oil) in the car park at the hospital, so I dashed out of the car and chased him into the lift to tell him that Shane has always had a "boy-crush" on him. He said he would try to visit him in the next week or two. Shane was chuffed!

[He never did visit. No more "boy-crush"!]

Shane Clifton Journal

I wake up pretty well the same way every day, to the incessant babble of nurses rambling during the change of shift (they pretend to be doing business, but I hear them going on about nothing at all). It is an eternity before they pay me any attention (seriously, time is interminable when you have to wait for a nurse to pay you some attention before you can do something as simple as sitting up), and I almost always spend some of the interim trying to get myself out of bed. Bonnie Lee has encouraged the habit, but it is something of a black comedy. I move my legs, or rather, try to do so. It is not as simple as being unable to feel my toes wriggle and my knees bend. Rather, in my mind, they are present and functional, but simply too heavy to move or lift. I close my eyes and bend my fingers, one at a time, I clench my bum cheeks, and I move my legs, ankles, and toes. It is all imaginary, a mind-over-matter exercise, but though matter always wins I cannot help but go through the ritual . . . just in case.

Louise served breakfast this morning, for the third time this week. This is so much better than the ICU rotation of a new face every day. I bombarded her with questions:

"Age?" . . . "Twenty-six."

"Nursing for?" . . . "My second year as a registered nurse, and I'm completing an honors degree at Sydney University."

"Cool. A nurse. Good looking. Smart. Boyfriend?" "Aw, shucks! No, but I went on a date this weekend."

"He good-looking?"

She shows me a photo, and I go on asking questions. She obviously thinks I'm nosy (well, I am), but I'm excited for her, and I want her to live a brilliant life.

When Louise moved on to other patients, I wondered about my response to her—my need to know her. In thinking about it again now, I realize that dependency is not only a physical reality, but also a psychosocial one. For three days Louise has woken me, bathed and dressed me, brushed my teeth, dressed me like a storm trooper and helped me sit up, and all this with gentle and solicitous care. Three days is nothing in the scheme of things, and yet the intensity of this journey elevates the importance of her care. As this hospital becomes my "home," Louise becomes a member of my family. That, at least, is how things feel to me, even though as I record this journal I'm aware that this attachment cannot be reciprocated. Primary school students feel the same way about teachers, whose oversight of pupils is (properly) only professional. Even so, in a sterile and challenging environment, Louise does her best to make me feel at home, and even to feel loved.

Toward the end of the day (around 5 p.m.) I was surprised by a visit from my parents and the boys. My Mum and Dad (their Oma and Opa— my Dutch heritage) brought them to the hospital after school. My parents are amazing. Even though much of their care happens beyond my view, they have moved from their home in Callala Bay to stay with Elly, help run our house and manage our teenage boys. No doubt this is a challenge for them all; Mum and Dad are part of a more "diligent" era of parenting, and my children are used to slacker parents. While this journal entry has not been full of lovey-dovey soppiness, it has to be said that I love my family—that if I manage to get through this experience, it will only be because I have been well loved.

But I am getting side-tracked. The kids came to the hospital feeling optimistic and motivated. In the two-hour drive to POW (damn that Sydney traffic) they listened to the audiobook *It's Not about the Bike*, the autobiography of Lance Armstrong. Apparently they sniggered every time the story mentioned testicles, but they have also been reflecting on Armstrong's courage and his success after the horrible experience of testicular cancer. It got them thinking about their Dad, and the courage we would all need to flourish through this accident.

For the first time, Jacob took on the job of feeding me. He was tentative, and he whispered (I had to ask him to repeat himself) about how odd it was to be feeding his Dad. He got all teary (my loving boy) but made us both laugh by the standard choo-choo train spoon technique, and a joke he heard at school—"Practice safe eating—always use condiments." My plateful of food was mashed, and while the vegetables were edible, the pureed meat—soaking in what the menu promised was gravy—was inedible. Earlier in the day a speech pathologist (for some reason responsible for judging my capacity to swallow) removed the nasogastric tube (yippee) and urged me to finish my meals, but I didn't think I had what it takes to deal with beef that looks and tastes like cat vomit (or what I imagine cat vomit must taste like). I asked how much was left and Jem grabbed the bowl to make a guess, but lost control and dumped the plate upside down on my chest. He was apologetic, but I was relieved.

October 27, 2010 (Wednesday)
Shane Clifton Facebook

Ten Worst Hospital Experiences (in random order):

1. Enema—best and worst (glad for the clean out, but preferred the old way of doing it!).

2. Nasogastric tube insertion (6 times before successful).

3. Choking on my own phlegm—being unable to breathe.

4. Dead weight of my own body.

5. Life as a pin cushion.

6. Night terrors (thank God, now over).

7. Tablets that don't go down.

8. Constant neck brace discomfort.

9. Being rolled every three hours during the night.

10. Thickened water.

Olga Clifton replied: Nasal Gastric Tube, gone; Night terrors, gone; Thickened water, gone. Three down and seven to go!

The Ten Best Hospital Experiences:

1. Elly—her arrival, and along with visits from all my family and friends.

2. Amazing care of nursing staff and doctors.

3. Overwhelming care, prayer, and generous support of friends from our community and around the world.

4. Life saving physios—getting rid of phlegm.

5. Painkillers!!

6. Slow but steady progress.

7. Friendly fellow spinal patients.

8. Getting up in a wheelchair—new view of the world.

9. Brief glimpses of the outside world.

10. Thinking time and a slower pace of life.

Elly Clifton replied: slower pace—you've got to be joking!!

October 28, 2010 (Thursday)
Medical Report

Nuclear Medicine Gallium Study. Gallium injection on Oct. 26. Whole-body gallium scan on Oct. 27. Repeat Gallium scan on Oct. 28. Investigating fevers. Sternum fracture discovered.

Olga Clifton Facebook

Shane scared me by fainting today after they put him in his chair "I think I just fell asleep," he said.

Elly Clifton Facebook

Shane had a hard day today; he was tired and ended up in a lot of pain when sitting in his chair. It was really difficult to watch him suffering; hurting in the one part of his body he can still feel! I have decided that I don't want to play anymore. I want my life and my husband back please.

October 29, 2010 (Friday)
Shane Clifton Journal

It seems that each day I'm learning something new, making progress. It may be two steps forward and one back, but I am moving. Today, I was fitted with a battery-powered wheelchair. I was giddy with excitement, like a teenage boy getting the keys to his first beat-up car. The chair is nondescript black, second-hand, battered and bruised, and held together by duct tape. It has obviously been smashed and crashed by amateurs such as myself, and I wondered how, without the use of my hands and arms, I was going to be able to steer. Peta assured me that the function I have would be enough. So once again, I was hoisted out of bed and this time plonked into the chair, which was tilted back twenty-five-degrees to prevent me from falling forward. It has gears and a tilt function that are accessed by tapping a chunky red button on the side of the chair arm. Steering is with a simple joystick, topped with a half tennis ball (literally), which rests under my clawed hand. As promised, I can steer with movement controlled through shoulders and biceps.

Hospital corridors are wide, and given my control of the machine, that was a good thing. From her bag of goodies, Peta made a show of withdrawing an L-plate and tagging it to the back of the chair; "ha-ha," I said, without much humor, but everyone else was amused. I snaked my way up the corridor and back, with nurses laughing and giving me an exaggeratedly wide berth. My progress was slow and uncertain, but I wasn't being pushed and having control of my next "step" was exhilarating. With my family following in a ragtag conga line, I made my way out of the spinal unit toward the common room, showing off my new-found mobility. I've heard it said that paralyzed people are trapped in their chair, but this felt like freedom to me. Even the pain in my shoulders, which eventually sent me back to bed, was nothing more than a trifling inconvenience.

November 1, 2010 (Monday)
Shane Clifton Journal

"Bom dia! Sair da cama!" (Portuguese—Good Morning! Get out of bed!) trumpets FB as he barreled to my bedside. "Off to the bathroom," he continued, pulling back my covers and screwing up his nose before declaring, "you stink."

Before I had time for embarrassment he burst into laughter and my nurse (Lauren) rolled her eyes and shook her head. It dawned on me, more importantly, that this rude pronouncement heralded a new first . . . I wouldn't be crapping and washing in bed. Instead, I was transferred to a high backed commode and pushed to the loo. While the procedure was the same (enema, finger, crap), it was weirdly liberating to hear the splash of poo in the water; to put behind me the dehumanizing experience of laying in "it" in bed.

And I was properly showered for the first time in weeks, the soggy-toweled top-to-tail wash in bed replaced by a delicious stream of warm water that was allowed to run over my head and shoulders and stream (unfelt) over the rest of my body. Holding the nozzle in one hand, FB shampooed my starchy unkempt hair, scrubbed my body with a soapy sponge, and then proceeded to rub my pink body dry with a scratchy white hospital towel. Stupendous. I felt born again . . . as clean as Mary Magdalene.

Later that morning, I was taken to the gym to start my formal exercise program, supervised by physiotherapist, Keira. She is in her mid-to-late twenties, average height, mousy-brown hair (again) tied back in a single pony, deliberately functional but still pretty. She looks fit—like a physio should—not a skerrick of fat, but not skinny—athletic. I noticed the young boys stealing glances, paraplegic males in their twenties preening, like all young men at the gym, hoping she would look their way. If she was aware of this, she was unaffected, and as she walked about the room, she treated every person with generous friendliness. When she introduced herself to me, a surprising sense of hopefulness warmed my heart. Not love-at-first-sight, but something like that; an instinctive confidence that I was in the hands of someone who cared. In this first meeting, we discussed my history and goals, and Keira set out a plan of attack that is intended to strengthen the muscles I have that function and to set alight any that show the merest spark of potential.

I started with a simple cardio workout: an arm crank (an exercise bike tied to my hands and driven by shoulders and biceps). Next, I was strapped to a set of pulleys that were attached to a rack above my head, allowing my arms to move up and down within the limits of their range. I tired quickly. It was a small start, and I am no Kurt Fearnley (wheelchair para-Olympian and marathoner), but both Keira and I were satisfied.

I returned to the ward and remained in my chair till I could no longer stand it—four and a half hours in total. A record.

November 2, 2010 (Tuesday)

Shane Clifton Journal

When I awoke this morning, I was subject to odd looks, with nurses glancing my way and laughing. Lauren (the nurse most fancied by the young boys on the ward) came over and said,

"Hey, old man, it's a glorious pink morning."

It wasn't an expression I heard before—pink morning—but I assumed it had something to do with the sunrise that I couldn't see in the windowless ward. She continued,

"I feel like some music and I'm in a pink mood. What do you reckon? Do you like Pink, 'Funhouse'?"

"I guess so. Probably not my first choice," I replied. It was an odd conversation, made weirder by Lauren dancing away laughing. I'd heard of black moods, but pink?

Later that morning, Elly arrived and laughed at me, but also betrayed a little annoyance. It turned out Lauren had painted my toenails pink. Spinal patients at POW wear ugg boots with their toes cut out (I have yet to be given an adequate reason for this, although someone suggested it is because one size fits all—my friends think I should ask for a refund), which had given Lauren the opportunity for some mischief, made easier by the fact that I couldn't feel her at work. Elly's annoyance was because she had planned a similar stunt. In fact, before my accident, Elly would paint my toes when I slept on the lounge. I think she feels like Lauren has stolen her thunder!

I am writing this journal entry using *Dragon Nuance* voice recognition software that Bill, a volunteer I.T. geek whose deteriorating muscular dystrophy now has him confined to a chair, downloaded onto my laptop. It takes a bit of getting used to, but it is remarkably accurate, although it too easily picks up the background noise of hospital life. Much more difficult is the mouth-mouse. It looks something like a snake microphone, clamped to the side of the desk and attached to the computer by USB; it extends to my mouth and is easy enough to move with my teeth in an up-and-down, side-to-side shake of the head. Yet it causes me pain in the neck, and I simply cannot work out right and left click, which are meant to follow a blow and a suck, but are too easily confused with my breathing; to say nothing of the fact that I end up with spit dripping from the mouthpiece. The whole exercise makes me dizzy and frustrated.

I have been told that there is an enlarged trackball desk mouse that I should be able to use, even without hands. Fingers crossed! (Don't you love the English language?)

November 4, 2010 (Thursday)
Elly Clifton Facebook

I made Shane some homemade risotto, and he ate and ate and ate, which was awesome and very heart-warming (loves his wifey's cooking!). My brilliant husband has been sitting up in his motorized wheelchair for over five hours, and he's still going and quite comfortable!

November 5, 2010 (Friday)
Elly Clifton Facebook

Shane tried to turn 360-degrees in the lift today, and it was a tad tight. He dragged his feet around the edges, then he drove out saying, "I've probably broken all my toes." A wheelchair can be dangerous, especially with Shane driving. FB told us that, only a few months ago, a patient purposely ran into a surgical dresser, leaving them on compo for a month (not sure whether he can be believed, but it's a good story).

November 6, 2010 (Saturday)
Shane Clifton Journal

I have gone back to the use of a dictation machine; voice recognition software in a noisy ward and the annoyance of the mouth-mouse having defeated me. It's getting difficult to keep up the pace of writing, in part because the days are getting busier, but also because the routine of hospital life blends one day into another, so there is nothing worth saying. Wake, breakfast, bathroom, physio, visits, occupational therapy, food, more visits—sleep.

Weekends bring some relief, and today my brother Kurt arrived with my nieces and nephews. They are fascinated by everything. They rode the hoist up and down, trialed my voice recognition software (I draw the line at allowing them to access to the mouth-mouse), and then on my lap for the thrill of a go-kart chair as we terrorized the nurses (at breakneck speeds of 5 km an hour). Seven-year-old ball of energy, Joel, hit me up for an arm wrestle and grinned ear to ear when he won.

As I mentioned earlier, on the day of my accident, Kurt and Troy were driving up to the hospital and decided to buy me a bottle of scotch—an odd decision, perhaps, but it was all they could think to do at the time. It was not single malt, but a blend—Black Label Johnnie Walker, so not too bad (gifts of scotch always welcome—lightly peated single malt ideal). Kurt decided that today was as good as any to have a dram, so he poured the two shots directly in front of the nurses' station, helping me to a quaff. Given hospital policy, I felt like a schoolboy defying the headmaster. The act of rebellion was exhilarating, added to the pleasure of scotch warming the back of my throat, and watching my brother choke and cough; "disgusting swill," he concluded. The boy has no class.

Before they left, Kurt handed over a homemade envelope the size of a quarter of my bed, which he opened to reveal fifty or so drawings and homemade cards from Joel and Bryce's schoolmates in Nowra. It was overwhelming, the primary school artwork along with heartfelt good wishes and prayers. I had a flash of insight into Jesus' meaning when he called the little children to himself and declared, "The kingdom of God belonged to such as these." I didn't know any of these children, but they were thinking of me. Symbolic of the lot was a card from a girl named Lucy. She had drawn a picture of herself holding the hand of a man in a wheelchair and wrote:

"Dear Mr. Clifton, I love you, because I pray for you every day."

I think Lucy might have captured the meaning of prayer.

Elly Clifton Facebook

Shane keeps fainting (or nearly so) whenever he gets up in his chair. His blood pressure dropped to 80/50 today when he sat up. He fainted, and I had to slap his face and call him for almost a minute as the nurses held up his legs. It was freaky, and the male nurse, Alberto, said he was so close to calling for resuscitation . . . Shane claims he was faking it just to get me going.

When he returned to bed, Jacob and Lachlan stole his wheelchair. We told them not to go far, but later discovered they had taken the lift up to the tenth floor—Shane is on the first.

November 12, 2010 (Friday)

Shane Clifton Journal

I spent the day today with Mum, while Elly had a well-earned rest. We decided to go for a coffee, which is not worth reporting except that it was my first time outside of the hospital in thirty-six days, and my first ever in a chair. What stood out initially was the uneven surface. I'd failed to appreciate how flat and smooth hospital floors are until I rolled outside and felt the instability of every slope and bump. We traveled at a snail's pace up the driveway and headed toward the pedestrian crossing that leads to the busy and trendy shop-fronts of the eastern suburbs. Randwick is an old town and its footpaths are cobbled and uneven, but more than just the bumpy ride, I was overwhelmed at being outside. In the spinal ward, I lived in a bubble where disability and wheelchairs are the norm, but outside I felt the weight of my difference. I was obviously handicapped (a designation I had not used before), struggling even to make my way along a footpath. I imagined that I was being looked at, pitied—a newly inducted member of the circus freak show. And at that moment I was pitiable, feeling thoroughly sorry for myself.

My tears convinced Mum that it was best to return to the hospital, so we made our way to the in-house cafe. I felt foolish, forty years old and afraid to be outside.

After lunch I had an appointment with Keira, who was taking me for a swim. Another first. Getting ready was something of an effort, since getting changed is a production. I was hoisted into bed, undressed, re-dressed in my board shorts and neck and chest braces, and lifted back into my chair; looking like a half-naked storm trooper. The pool itself is indoors and heated to 34 °C, so the air was a misty, pungent, chlorinated fog. Once again, I was hoisted from my chair into a swinging gurney, which was swiveled over the pool and lowered. Fitted with a floatie under my neck and a noodle under my knees, I was able to relax into the water while Keira towed me around the pool, like a tugboat maneuvering a bent and broken-down ship. I'm not sure whether there are any real physical benefits to the exercise, but with my normally heavy and unwieldy body weightless, Keira did take the opportunity to stretch my shoulder muscles and rotate my arms.

There is an intimacy between a physio and a patient that comes from the elimination of personal space and the need for manhandling. As I am recording this journal entry, I have attempted to analyze my emotional response, wondering whether the sublime joy I felt while being held by Keira was sexual. I am as liable as anyone to self-deception, but I don't think it was. But as I was cuddled, floating around the pool, I did feel loved; mothered might be a better term.

While swimming, and again now as I record this journal, I have been flooded with memories. I have spent my life in water—swimming and surfing. From the age of eight I trained and competed, in my early teens winning medals and making my way to State and Australian Championships, eventually to the Pan Pacific games. My best event had been backstroke, and here I was again, staring at the ceiling of the pool. It seemed like a homecoming, but I was also reminded of my handicap, of my complete uselessness. At one point, I looked over and saw my Mum at the side of the pool. Over the years, she has spent countless hours watching me swim, and today, seeing me like a dead whale in the water, I suspect she shared my mixed emotions. I didn't know whether to enjoy myself or to scream in frustration at the reminder of loss.

November 15, 2010 (Monday)

Shane Clifton Journal

Before the accident, Elly and I had purchased U2 tickets for their December thirteenth concert, so this afternoon she called Ticketek, trying to get them to change our tickets for accessible seating. I was nearby, listening nervously and staring blindly at the thumb on my right hand, which was twitching like a leaf in the breeze. After a brief discussion, she was put on hold, and I suddenly became aware that I was doing more than simply watching the thumb quiver. I told it to be still, and it was.

Shock. Unbelief. Hope.

I told it to move, and it resumed its twitching. I focused on the rest of my hand, and I could get my pointer finger to move as well.

I looked over to Elly, "watch my hand," I said.

Her face lit up, but the ticket office came back online, so she forced herself to talk about our tickets while watching my finger move, stop moving, and move again. When she got off the phone, she launched herself out of her chair and grabbed my hand. "Do it again," she whispered passionately, and I repeated my party trick.

The movement is tiny and adds no real function, but it represents possibility—hope. It tells us that some recovery is likely. Elly was effervescent and let her mind run, imagining this small movement as the first step toward walking, the beginning of God's answer to our prayers. I am more circumspect—I can't seem to help my innate realism/pessimism. I simply cannot allow myself to hope for what may never come. Right now I'm struggling with prayer. Is this the work of God? A natural process? How do I locate God in the movement of fingers when my body remains broken?

But Elly's enthusiasm turns out to be contagious. I can move my finger, and we have been allocated new seats for U2! This is a good day.

November 16, 2010 (Tuesday)

Elly Clifton Facebook

Shane moved his thumb!! I hardly slept last night I was so excited! His pointer finger and his middle finger moved ever so slightly too. It's his right hand, which is awesome. I am so thrilled—he's really chuffed too. When we told the boys they were all thrilled, and Jake jumped around the house yelling out with excitement. Thank you, Jesus! He can only bend his elbows, his wrists just flop, no leg movement at all—but he can now move his thumb and pointer fingers. It is a small movement, but rich in promise.

The boys came to the hospital today. Lochie got ill and ended up sleeping in Dad's hospital bed. The other two went down to Coogee Beach and came back raving about all the topless girls Lochie had missed. There is no way he'll let the boys go down to the beach without him again.

November 19, 2010 (Friday)

Medical report

CT IV Pyelogram—CT Upper Abdomen and Pelvis. Five weeks post surgery. Septic. Raised white cell count. On Warfarin.

Elly Clifton Facebook

Shane ended up with the shivers last night and couldn't get rid of them. Then his temperature rapidly escalated to 39.7 degrees (C). He was very unwell, burning up and feeling awful. It was distressing how quickly he went downhill; he'd been so well and happy with visitors earlier in the afternoon. They put him back onto an antibiotic drip and replaced his catheter (which makes him nervous, but he felt nothing). He was exhausted this morning, although his temperature was much better. They did multiple tests and think that he must have a bladder infection. I did tell them about Lochie and our virus, but they think the fact that the antibiotics are keeping the temperature down is a sign it's bacterial. The rollercoaster nature of this journey is exhausting and frightening. It seems that I move from elation to depression, up and down and round in circles, and I never get the chance to find my equilibrium.

November 20, 2010 (Saturday)

Elly Clifton Facebook

After a fever-free day yesterday, he hit the highs again last night so they were planning to change his antibiotic today. As a result, he was again exhausted as his body fights with bugs. I am renting an exorbitantly priced unit across the road from the hospital for three months over the X-mas holidays so that the boys and I can be closer to the hospital. I get the keys on Monday. The western Sydney bogans are becoming inner city hipsters.

November 21, 2010 (Sunday)

Shane Clifton Facebook

Free at last, I am free at last. (Neck brace finally came off).

Progress notes: fever gone, able to spend day in chair, using trackball mouse, learning to drink water from cup—not spilling too much!

November 23, 2010 (Tuesday)

Shane Clifton Journal

I have spent Sunday through to today with my brother Daniel, down from Hervey Bay in Queensland. He is here with Bianca and their two beautiful children, Kailani and Iluka. I have had such a wonderful time with them all—indeed, as horrible as this accident has been, it has reminded us all of the importance of family. I am not sure what else to say about their visit. The girls have enjoyed riding on my lap through the corridors. Daniel has pushed me to keep up my exercise—no weekend rest. Bianca has used her talent for massage on my shoulders, arms, and hands; using her pungent, homemade massage oils and leaving my cubicle smelling like a temple. She's been thinking about my diet and has come prepared with healthy breakfasts and natural supplements.

It is J. R. R. Tolkien who notes that good times make boring tales, and perils the best stories (if memory serves, this is in the Hobbit, while Bilbo and the dwarves rest in Rivendell). Tolkien knows a thing or two about storytelling. We have had such a nice time these few days that I don't have anything to write about!

November 25, 2010 (Thursday)

Alice McCullum Letter

Dear Shane,

After having my world rocked by you—in particular, after a semester of ethics—rather than asking, "what would Jesus do?" I often wonder, "what would Shane do?" So as I sit in the library during study week contemplating what topic to revise, I ask myself, "WWSD?" And instantly I know that he would abandon all academic priorities and write a letter to himself. So, as a true disciple of Shane, here I am doing just that.

I've wanted to write this letter for a little while, but kept thinking to myself, who am I to encourage Shane? But really, who am I not to? After all, I am one of your admirers, one of the loyal fans, one of the many people praying, desperately praying, for your recovery.

After three years of intense theological discourse, I occasionally struggle with the concept of prayer. Torn between the extremes of Calvinism and Arminianism, Piper and Pinnock, I struggle for faith to lift my eyes heavenward and trust solely in the creator of the universe to, A) care enough to listen, and B) listen enough to do something; however, when hearing of your accident, all of a sudden those questions didn't seem to matter, as all I could do was rely on Her anyway [reference to class discussion of divine transcending gender]. Whether God is the most moved mover, the unmoved mover, or perhaps the most moved un-mover, prayer became a necessity. After all, prayer is potentially about the pray-ers, and I think those of us praying were in need of some peace. So I have been praying, in fact begging God for her goodness to move in this situation, her peace to reign in your family, her strength to overcome your weakness, and the healing power to move from the "not yet" into the "now."

Most often, I take the advice of Jesus and pray for God's will to be done, but occasionally, and now is such an occasion, I pray my will and the will of your family, friends, and followers (not followers in a Jesus sort of way, more a collective understanding that "Shane's 'the shit'" sort of way). I pray that everything will go smoothly, that recovery will come and it will come rapidly, and that it will be as though none of this has ever happened. And why? Because clearly that is the ideal, convenient, and happy ending—but most of all, I pray this because the world needs you. Not only do those who are closest to you need you (and like heck, they *do*), but also those a little bit further away, as well as those a long way away. Even those who don't know you need you. They need you to keep going; keep believing. They need you to keep asking, to keep questioning and seeking—to challenge the status quo. They need you to keep living so selflessly, living so dedicated, living devoted to a cause beyond yourself; to keep dreaming and imagining a church that is more like the bride of Christ than what we are at the moment. We need you to keep challenging us, destroying our mind-sets, fighting for better concepts and greater ideologies. We need you keep speaking out about what redemption really is. Women need you. Relationships need you. Families need you. Leaders need you. Goodness, *people* need you.

Now, it may seem that I am speaking very highly of you, and that I am. I do hold you in the highest regard, but the message I'm trying to convey in all of this is that the man that you are is too great an asset to the world, too great a gift to humanity, for it to be just stripped from us here and now. This you may deny, but with all sincerity—and I am 100 percent convinced— your openness to God, your willingness to serve, you receptiveness to the grace of God, and your absolute humility have allowed you to become a hero to many. A bloody legend to the Aussies, awesome to the Americans, as good as gold to us Kiwis, and a champion to all those at Hillsong. So thank you. Thank you for your openness, willingness, receptivity, and humanity. I for one appreciate it greatly.

Suffice it to say, you are greatly loved and appreciated. And you are greatly needed. So with all that is within me, I beseech thee to continue on with such things. To keep fighting, keep living the dream in your heart, and loving. Because, as I have mentioned, we need you.

I look forward to hearing great reports of you being able to engage in your favorite activities again—food, drinks, and of course, Elly (referring to the opening line in your lecture on sexual ethics). I look forward to the day when you are back at home, sitting on the couch with a glass of red in one hand, Elly's hand in the other, your eyes closed, head back, and the soundtrack to *The Mission* playing in the background.

Best of luck, all my prayers, and a touch of love,
Alice McCallum, Wellington, New Zealand

November 28, 2010 (Sunday)
Shane Clifton Journal

Sex does not seem to be a topic that features in the POW rehabilitation program, although we have been able to spend time with the in-house psychologist, Annalisa. She is the sort of person who makes you feel immediately at ease. It probably helps that she is somewhere near our age; she has mousy-brown hair, cut between a pixie and a bob (which are the only two hairstyles I can name, so this may not be saying much), and wears colorful earrings and necklaces—a hippie with class. Last week, Annalisa spent a couple of hours with Elly and I, and at her recommendation, Elly purchased three books:

- Robert W. Baer, *Is Fred Dead? A Manual on Sexuality for Men with Spinal Cord Injuries.*

- Ken Kroll and Erica Levy Klein, *Enabling Romance: A Guide to Love, Sex and Relationships for People with Disabilities (And the People who Care About Them).*

- Miriam Kaufman, Cory Silverberg, and Fran Odette, *The Ultimate Guide to Sex and Disability: For All of Us Who Live with Disabilities, Chronic Pain, and Illness.*

After nearly twenty-one years of marriage, two months is a long time to be celibate, so we have started to read our way through these books. Given its title, we began with *Is Fred Dead?* It turned out to be pedestrian reading, assuming a kindergarten level of anatomy and zero sexual experience. It is supplemented by a series of hilariously explicit drawings, cartoons of the penis and vagina, of different sexual positions, of oral sex and the like. Our favorite is of a nude woman sitting on the face of a supine quadriplegic; his eyes open wide and startled. The picture had us laughing out loud. Elly proceeded to show the book to the nurses on the ward and soon these bizarrely pornographic, but un-erotic cartoons had everyone in stitches.

We did manage to find some useful material. Despite what people generally assume, SCI is not the death of sex (although it sure feels like it). Some people with incomplete injuries fully recover their sexual function. For others, while psychogenic erection (a brain powered stiffie) is not possible, reflex erections are enough to enable coitus (a horrible word), often with the help of Viagra and other related drugs, or startling pieces of equipment such as a vacuum pump. Orgasm is unlikely, so fertility will be affected—not a concern for us at all! There is talk of learning to orgasm through stimulation of another part of the body—shoulders or ears. It sounds absurd to me, but what would I know.

There is a big focus on oral sex, since it enables a quadriplegic male to give pleasure . . . and enjoy the giving! *Is Fred Dead?* contains helpful advice: "do not bite your partner's genitals with your teeth. The genitals are very sensitive part of the body. The genitals will bleed profusely if the skin is broken. So no biting!" Wow, who would have thought it? Thank you, Robert Baer, for this profound insight.

Notwithstanding the comedy, I could see Elly's mood darken. Despite a robust and enjoyable sex life, oral sex is not something she has ever liked. This has nothing to do with prudishness (as anyone who knows her would be aware). Like many women, Elly has experienced sexual abuse, and this has its on-going impact.

As we put the books to one side, we were not sure whether all of this information was encouraging or depressing. It is certainly the case that reading SCI porn in an open ward was not romantic.

November 29, 2010 (Monday)

Shane Clifton Journal

There is talk of moving me from the acute to the rehab ward, located adjacent. It is another sign that I am moving forward, but I am a little alarmed about the proposed accommodations. There are two alternatives; private single bedrooms or four bed, shared accommodation.

This morning, my attending nurse, Francis, showed me the planned transfer to bed fourteen. It is a four-bed room, occupied by three old men, including Jim [not real name], who is the ward whinger. I make my view crystal clear:

"I will not be sharing a room, let alone with Jim. Get me a private room, or leave me where I am."

I think I was calm enough, but I could tell that Francis was a little taken aback. He promised me he would see what could be done.

Half an hour later, the shift manager, Kristy, approached me. "Unfortunately, Shane, there is a shortage of beds in rehab. No private rooms are available, and we don't have any choice but to move you to bed fourteen."

"I am not moving to that bed," I said icily. "I've been in open wards for almost two months and I need some privacy. I want to be able to use my computer with voice recognition software, and it's about time I'm able to kiss my wife without the whole world watching."

Kristy stood firm. "If we could, everyone would have a private room. But this is a hospital and not a motel, and we just have to make do as best we can."

Weeks of forced gratitude came undone and I lost it, shouting "You say 'we,' but you go home every night while I live here. This is not just a hospital; it has become my hellhole of a home. I don't give a shit what you say; I am not moving to bed fourteen."

This war of words was going on next to my bed in an open ward. I managed to get everyone's attention, and Kristy was wise enough to know when to withdraw.

The fact that my outburst was surprising at least got it some attention.

It was just before dinnertime, and I was in bed when the Nursing Unit Manager (NUM) stopped by for a chat. We were both calm, but our positions were entrenched. I demanded a private room, insisting that I would not allow myself to be moved. We both knew that this was an idle threat. Quadriplegia means that the hospital can do with me what it wants.

And so here I am, again, trapped in bed recording this journal and feeling like a prisoner, subject to the whims of hospital administration. To be honest, my beef is not really with the hospital, but goes deeper. I feel like I'm being steered by a capricious providence that's taking me on a journey into hell, or at least to its outer reaches—perhaps Dante's second level, where the lustful are tossed around by endless storms?

November 30, 2010 (Tuesday)

Shane Clifton Journal

A few days ago a new patient, let's call him Max, was placed two beds down from my own. He is the worst sort of Aussie bogan—loud, demanding, crass—so much so, that in an effort to minimize his harassment, a nurse removed his buzzer from his bedside. The dramas continued this morning when he started to demand medication that the nurses seemed reluctant to give. Every five minutes for what felt like hours, he shouted and swore at the nurses to give him his drugs.

Now, the staff of the spinal ward are used to abusive patients. There is a transvestite on the ward who is always telling them to f**k off. Another female patient regularly screams at the attendants—recently leaving one of the newer nurses in tears. In these few months in hospital, I have learned that there is nothing especially laudable about disabled people. People who were bastards before the chair remain so when in it. Indeed, the fact that people are being served by nurses seems to exacerbate the problem, and nurses have no meaningful recourse. They mostly just cop it.

This morning, Max was targeting my favorite nurse, Louise. It was making my blood boil, and at a certain point I couldn't stand it anymore. "Shut the f**k up." I yelled.

I was tense and shaking, and not a little surprised at my outburst and my language. Louise came over and thanked me for the support, but went on to say that Max has suffered a brain injury and his behavior is one of the consequences.

So it turns out that I've told a mentally disabled patient to F-off. Perhaps Dante's cause is just.

I went to Max and apologized, and he didn't hold a grudge (truth be told, I'm not sure he even understood what had happened). He went on to tell me about his injuries and his pain, as well as his need for medication, and I put up with his lengthy conversation as penance.

December 1, 2010 (Wednesday)
Shane Clifton Journal

The NUM and I seem to have arrived at a standoff since I have not been moved, and nothing has been said about Monday's "discussions." I have been booked in for an MRI, and when I asked for an explanation, Jasmine (registrar) was evasive, but eventually conceded that my "abnormal" behavior this week was discussed in a team meeting, and Bonnie Lee was concerned about the possibility of brain injury!

My family had a good laugh about the test. Mum commented, "That's just Shane. If he feels strongly about something, he'll fight for it." More to the point, surely an acquired disability and life in POW (a truly apt acronym) is enough to explain a little anger, without needing any reference to brain damage.

Medical records: cranial MRI, no abnormality identified.

December 3, 2010 (Friday)
Elly Clifton Facebook

Shane has been moved to the rehab ward today. A private room, bed nineteen.

CHAPTER 4

Rehab

December 3, 2010 (Friday)

Shane Clifton Journal

The rehab ward has a reception and nurses' station that faces the main corridor, with open-plan, four-bedder rooms adjacent, and private accommodations in a U-shape surrounding. The rooms each have a window to the outside, but the view is limited to the ramshackle red brick and concrete buildings that make up the rest of the hospital, which seems to have been built like a kid's Lego set, with no obvious design or coordination.

Room nineteen is tucked away in the corner of the ward, and as I entered for the first time, despite my behavior during the week, I confess to feeling surprisingly isolated. It is only two corridors and a hop, skip, and a jump away (the ironic joy of metaphor), but I no longer have nurses who can keep their eye on me. There is a buzzer, but I've seen how long it sometimes takes for those to be answered. For the briefest of moments I contemplated asking to be moved, but pride stayed my hand. Anyway, if the window doesn't have any view to speak of, it at least lets in some natural light, and this engenders a hopefulness that has been absent from the windowless bomb shelters I have lived in until now. The room is a compact box, with its own sink and bathroom—luxury. The walls, painted in the typical hospital off-white, are pockmarked with the dings of wheelchair miscalculations and the blue-tack remaining from posters that have been stuck up and pulled down with each new patient. The ceiling is a dirty white, exactly the same as everywhere else.

Elly has been waiting for the opportunity to decorate and got into it straightaway, pinning up two of her own art works. The first is a macabre painting of an x-rayed skull, embossed with the bloodied words "husbands should not break." She tells me she painted this in a moment of inspired anger. Most people don't seem to know how to take it, but I revel in its darkness. The second is its opposite; a colorful series of interlocking painted hands that I take to represent the love and support of our extended family (for Elly, the focus on hands expresses the sadness she feels at mine no longer functioning). With her artwork in place, Elly added color to the remaining wall-space with a selection of cards. She gave pride of place to little Lucy's drawing and her encouragement, "Dear Mr. Clifton, I love you, because I pray for you every day." She added some Christmas tinsel, and the previously drab, boxy room became gloriously gaudy.

While Elly was embellishing my "home," my parents installed a bar fridge and kettle, and filled the cupboards with clothes, food, and some precious bottles of single malt. It was almost dinner by the time they finished, and after kisses and hugs goodbye I made my way to the dining room. Until then my meals had been served at my bedside, and this was my first communal meal. The food was presented on a portable buffet, and while the finishing touches were being prepared, a convoy of wheelchairs waited to be served. Choices were limited and appear to be the same bland fare that was served in acute. I made my choice and my tray of food was carried to the common table, and while I waited for a nurse to come and feed me, I made my introductions and enjoyed the company.

K, paraplegic, Motocross accident; P, paraplegic, pushbike hit by a car; G, paraplegic, car crash; I, paraplegic, shot five times; Jo, quadriplegic, fell down stairs carrying a case of beer; Ja, paraplegic, surfing fall. We are an eclectic bunch, and while we probably have little in common in terms of typical measures (age, profession, education, hobbies, and the like), the shared challenge of SCI brings some camaraderie.

Sitting next to me was Sid—who looks tall and gangly, although it's a little hard to tell in a wheelchair—and his gorgeous wife Mary. They are a little older than Elly and I, perhaps in their fifties, and hail from Cooma; they are sheep farmers (truly iconic Australians). Sid told me about his journey. He had been a long-time snow skier—he and Mary were supposed to be on the slopes in Japan as we spoke—and was doing his usual run down the slopes of Mt. Perisher, when he crashed through an unmarked hole in the snow and was sent catapulting. He was transferred by helicopter to Canberra, and he vividly remembers his discussion with the doctor:

"When she told me that I was paralyzed from the neck down, it sent shivers down my spine. I think."

The accident left him an incomplete quadriplegic with the seemingly back-to-front difficulties of central core syndrome, which has him regaining movement in his legs while remaining constricted in his trunk, arms, and hands. He complains of pain in his shoulders, and while he talks he fidgets with the small amount of movement he has won back in his fingers, stretching them open and closed, and pushing them backwards and forwards. It turns out he is my neighbor in room twenty, and I can tell almost immediately that I am going to enjoy his company.

December 5, 2010 (Sunday)

Facebook

Zella: Still standing with you all for a miracle.

Shane Clifton Journal

Elly was in stitches after reading Zella's unintentionally priceless Facebook post. She has her father's sense of humor—sick, that is.

Speaking of sick, I am spending the weekend in bed (again). This time the problem is not my health, but a broken down wheelchair. As Murphy's Law dictates, the electronics that drive the chair blinked out on Friday night, not long after the occupational therapists departed for the weekend. No amount of tinkering by nurses, surgical dressers or tech-savvy visitors could solve the problem. So here I remain, two days later. Grrr.

There is not much to journal about, except it is worth describing one incident. Just after lunch, five Korean colleagues came for a visit. They were immaculately dressed; the three men in suit and tie, accompanied by two glamorous women, obviously having come straight from church. They arrived bearing gifts, including five liters of Aloe Vera juice, which they assure me has cleansing and healing properties. David and Hannah are the senior pastors in the group and, as always, they greeted me warmly, treating me like a privileged son. I have previously traveled to Seoul with them both and witnessed first-hand the intensity and passion of Korean spirituality. They came today to pray, and before long they had crowded around my bed to pray—whether in Korean or tongues, I am not sure. I was little surprised when a hand was placed on my head, and I was rocked back and forward as they prayed loudly and vigorously, and I wondered whether they had forgotten my broken neck and recent release from a spinal brace? The neck seemed to hold together, however, and I appreciated their concern and passion. They prayed for my "total healing," that I might walk again, and they encouraged me to exercise faith.

P.S. I am writing this journal using voice recognition software. It is a relatively slow process, because instead of just making spelling mistakes, it gets words and phrases confused and I am not yet efficient at fixing errors. Even so, I feel liberated: no longer dependent on a scribe. Thank God for a private room, and *Dragon NaturallySpeaking*.

December 6, 2010 (Monday)

Shane Clifton Journal

Sid and I were sitting at the table in the dining room waiting for the nurses to feed us breakfast, when Mary approached, accompanied by Ally (occupational therapist). After some small talk Ally asked:

"Tell me, Sid. What's your current rehab goal?"

"To pick my nose," he responded immediately, prompting laughter from everyone at the table.

When she had regained her composure, Ally asked:

"Why not try to learn to feed yourself?"

"I've got Mary for that," he replied dryly.

He earned a slap for this, and both Mary and Ally insisted that he feed himself breakfast—Mary certainly had no intention to help. All this interaction captured the attention of the room, along with their encouragements ("go on, you lanky wimp"), which forced his hand.

With some difficulty, he picked up his spoon, tentatively loaded it with muesli and milk, and then raised his hand almost to his mouth, at which point his grip loosened and the spoon, with all its contents, fell to the table.

A second time and the same result.

A third effort, and that time the spoon touched his mouth before he dropped it.

Sid was red-faced and frustrated, but the rest of us were laughing. As he made his fourth and fifth attempts, the laughter reached a fever pitch and the whole ward, nurses and doctors included, came over to watch the show. Max was chortling and almost choked himself, spraying his own cereal across the table. All of this was too much for Sid, who joined in the merriment. A sixth effort saw him raise the spoon and get the cereal in his mouth. We all cheered, and Mary rewarded Sid by feeding him the remainder of his breakfast.

For twenty minutes, we laughed at a handicapped man spilling his breakfast. Surely this captures the absurdity of SCI.

December 7, 2010 (Tuesday)
Shane Clifton Journal

Throughout my stay in hospital, I have been flooded in prayer. There have been so many varieties: prayer for healing, for comfort, for God's will, for faith. I've been prayed for by pastors, laity, friends, relatives, strangers, Christians, and Muslims (a very encouraging visit from an Imam). My brother Daniel is an atheist, but I suspect even he has prayed—I know he joined his wife Bianca in lighting candles in my honor. All of this has been an expression of love and hope (and maybe of pity), and appreciated in all its variety.

Today I received a prayer hanky that has apparently been blessed by Marilyn Hickey, supposedly based on the scriptures ("God did extraordinary miracles through Paul, so that even handkerchiefs and aprons that had touched him were taken to the sick, and their illnesses were cured and the evil spirits left them." Acts 19:11–12). Again I was encouraged to exercise faith, to believe that God will heal, and as an expression of that faith, to place the hanky underneath my pillow. My Dad said that I had nothing to lose by giving it a go, but as much as I am trying to be generous to the varieties of spirituality of my pray-ers, I am getting a bit tired of this sort of absurdity. If God were to heal me, why would he use a hanky blessed by a TV evangelist from another country over the heartfelt prayers of my friends and family? So I asked Elly to blow my nose and throw the hanky in the bin. She laughed, before carefully folding the hanky and putting it away.

On a related note, Elly has spent a fair chunk of the last couple of days designing a Christmas sign for the spinal ward, "Have a wheelie great Christmas." The nurse, Lauren, has gone crazy bedecking the ward with tinsel and lights, trying to win the POW hospital Christmas decoration competition *[her mother's ward ultimately beat her, and I heard her mumble, "the bitch!"]*. As a result of all this activity, Elly has had a thumping headache all day. I have no idea what to do with prayer at the moment, but it feels right to ask God to heal her!

December 8, 2010 (Wednesday)
Elly Clifton Facebook

Shane was all ready for his monthly excursion with the spinal-wardians: his first excursion out of the hospital. This time it was to Bondi Junction to go X-mas shopping. Shane's never liked shopping much, and mysteriously developed nausea upon arriving. Coffee didn't put it right, so he got back on the bus and returned to POW to bed. I don't think the problem was his dislike of shopping.

December 9, 2010 (Thursday)
Shane Clifton Facebook

Twenty-one years married yesterday. Elly is the delight of my heart. Whatever the challenges of life, I remain the most fortunate of men.

Elly's comment: God has blessed us. My heart is yours, darling. Xx

Shane Clifton Journal

I was at breakfast when Elly came into the dining room with a present: a very cool Salvador Dali *Persistence of Memory* melting clock that bends and flops over the edge of the shelf, "because," she says, "time has gone wonky for us." I was horrified to discover it is our anniversary. I have not been watching the calendar and nor has this anniversary been on my horizon. I burst into tears, which turned out to be the only reaction capable of garnering some sympathy for such an unforgivable oversight (also, a little embarrassing in front of everyone in the dining room). I am truly sorry. Elly has been extraordinary over these last couple of months, but much more so over the course of twenty-one years of marriage.

We have now been married more than half of our lives, and it is hard to remember what it was like to be single (will I think the same way about before and after this accident?). We were school sweethearts, dating in year eleven and twelve, and getting married at the end of my first year of university. We were both (just) nineteen, and my Dad used to respond to people's surprise at our engagement by saying, "it's okay; Shane is marrying an older woman." (Three months.)

I'm not sure how you summarize a lifetime together in a journal entry. In an era characterized by high rates of divorce, we have been extraordinarily fortunate. We have never had a shouting (or physical) argument—perhaps because, when we were courting, Elly used to cry if I yelled at her. If there has been tension, it has been the shared difficulty of raising three boys, but we have managed to fight those battles together. Over the course of decades I have not been as romantic as I should've been, and Elly has suffered from a fairly long-term postnatal depression (which has been managed by counseling and drugs). But we have been mostly happy, survived financially, and raised a family. In this light, our marriage might be judged a success—except for today's forgetfulness. I think we have what it takes to survive SCI, although, no doubt, this is also a topic that warrants prayer. It is still too early for us to have faced up to the impact of this injury upon our relationship.

Which reminds me, my exercise regime has been progressing, and I am learning to make some use of the fingers on my right hand for small tasks; eating (messily), brushing my teeth, picking my nose, and scratching—these latter might sound like insignificant activities, but spend an hour with your hands tied behind your back and see how annoying it is to be unable to dislodge a booger or a scratch an itch. Today, Keira noted some slight return in my right triceps. Elly thinks this is the best possible anniversary present.

December 10, 2010 (Friday)

Shane Clifton Facebook

Immediately after breakfast this morning, Ally and Peta (OTs) loaded me on the hospital bus and took me on my first trip to my home since my accident. Our goal was to work out what modifications might be necessary to allow me to function upon my hospital discharge.

We had purchased this house six years prior, located in Narellan Vale, so close to the outskirts of southwest Sydney that we have sometimes been able to kid ourselves into believing that we live in the country. It's a middle-class suburb, made up of quarter-acre blocks and project-built, brick homes. Residents tend to be house-proud, and lawns and gardens are neatly manicured. I've heard it said that the overriding effect is a bland sterility, but it's a good environment to raise children, and Elly enjoys the opportunity to garden.

It's hard to describe my feelings as we approach the house. The first thing I saw was the mulberry tree that we planted in the middle of our lawn (a previous anniversary present), surrounded by the gloriously messy remnants of the spring harvest. Elly's cottage garden flowerbeds—she would be able to name the varieties, but it is all a blur to me—were looking a little rundown, but were still a tangle of color. The house is single-story, four bedroom, and brick; in and of itself quite plain, but made homely by Elly's creativity—her garden makeovers and painted murals. I was a potpourri of emotions as I was loaded off the bus, delighted, nervous, sad; a mess of feelings that I couldn't begin to understand or explain.

There were hugs, kisses, and tears when I arrived, but I couldn't access the house through the front door, so I needed to go through the garage and enter via the sliding door out back. I could make it into the lounge room, but only barely managed to negotiate the narrow corridor to my bedroom. It was immediately apparent that it would be too small for Elly and myself to share. Because I am susceptible to pressure sores, I need to sleep on a hospital bed with an alternating air pressure mattress (its air cells inflate and deflate to alternate pressure on the skin). We will need space for two beds, and sufficient room to accommodate a wheelchair and maneuver a hoist. But the bedroom is not nearly roomy enough, and the en suite is too small for a commode.

Bustling around the house with a tape measure and pad, Ally and Peta concluded that it would be possible to convert Jeremy's bedroom into a space that could accommodate my paraphernalia. It would require renovations, and a complete dismantling and rebuilding of the main bathroom, and mean that Elly and I would sleep in separate rooms while Jeremy would join Jacob and Lachlan, three teenage boys bunking together. Jeremy declared, "no way am I moving in with those two," and notwithstanding his bluntness, he spoke for us all.

There is the added problem that Narellan Vale has poor access to public transport—no railway station. Given that I will be unable to drive, this is a real drawback. We looked up Google maps on the iPad, and it suggested that it would take one hour and fifty-seven minutes for me to get to my workplace in Parramatta using a bus and train.

For the occupational therapists, this was not a social visit, and before I had time to digest the implications of their measurements, we were on the bus, making our way back to the prison.

The trip home has turned out to be gut wrenching. Indeed, the word "home" seems inappropriate; I felt like a stranger in someone else's house—worse, like I was an interloper in someone else's life. It has dawned on me that I have probably seen the last of Narellan Vale. I knew from the beginning that this accident has changed my life, but the magnitude of that change is only slowly coming into focus.

December 11, 2010 (Saturday)
Shane Clifton Facebook

We spinal patients have problems with our bowels. Here are some lessons that I've learned:

1. Shit happens.
2. Shit happens anywhere, anytime.
3. Don't worry, be cool, it's only shit.

Relax. If you ask politely and wait long enough, someone will clean it up.

December 15, 2010 (Wednesday)
Shane Clifton Journal

U2! I'm normally forced out of bed, but after a late night I've been allowed to sleep in. Yesterday was a great day.

It was 4 p.m. when the taxi (actually, it is more like a minibus) met us at the High Street entrance of the hospital. I rode a lift into the back where my chair was anchored to the floor. It was my first disabled taxi (more like a courier van), and I soon discovered that it's a sickening experience. The problem was not only that I was in the back of the vehicle, but also that the windows were below my eye level. Since all I could see was the road flashing by, I was unable to anticipate the driver's speedway, dodgem-car movement through Sydney's traffic. I was soon close to vomiting, and while the threat was enough to slow the driver, I still arrived at Olympic Park looking like Ozzy Osbourne after a bender.

This may explain the looks of pity I received as we made our way to the stadium, although the sense that I was being stared at may well have been in my head—a projection of my own insecurity onto the faces of others. A lady wearing a pair of Bono-lookalike, blue-tinted sunnies had at least enough sympathy to invite us to jump the queue to purchase merchandise, and I picked up a mauve U2 jumper. It will come in handy. SCI leaves me perpetually cold.

The sold-out concert was held in the stadium that had been built for the Sydney Olympics, apparently accommodating over 90,000 people; it felt like the whole world was present, an eclectic mix of old-time 80s fans, such as Elly and I, along with rockers from every generation since. With the stage constructed as a futuristic temple, the band played underneath the four claws of an alien hand, ringed by giant a 360-degree video screen and sound system, and topped by a spire that reached into the heavens. The show opened with a transcendent "Beautiful Day," reached its heights with "I Still Haven't Found What I'm Looking For," and connected "Amazing Grace" to "Where the Streets Have No Name"—a twenty-first century worship service, conducted by the Edge and the band, with Bono at the altar as priest and/or god. Together with the crowd, we were able to lose ourselves for a couple of hours. I was reminded that the world was bigger than my hospital prison, and felt a new sense of hope and possibility. This may seem to be giving too much credit to rock stars, but it wasn't the band so much as the experience of transcendence; of being taken beyond myself.

Afterwards, there was another taxi ride, more sickness, and the discovery that the hospital is locked at 10:00 p.m. We eventually broke in through accident and emergency, put up with the surgical dressers telling me off for being late (God forbid I interrupt their game of midnight chess), before they put me into bed. It was after midnight, and I'm pretty sure I was asleep even while in the hoist.

Elly made her way to the unit on her own, facing the challenge of the city at night without the protection of her tall, strong husband.

December 19, 2010 (Saturday)

Elly Clifton Journal

I have always loved Christmas time, and although this one is tinged with sadness, I'm finding myself a little excited and even weirdly happy. I've forgotten what that feels like.

Today, we had the Clifton family Christmas gathering, with the whole lot of them tripping up from the south coast to join us for a picnic at Coogee beach—Olga and Ken, Kurt and Emma (plus four), Troy and Kristine (plus three), Shane and I (plus three), with only Daniel and Bianca (plus two) missing.

The event had taken quite some organization and I found the whole thing quite stressful, partly because I'm still getting used to doing everything on my own. Shane was always pretty useless when it came to planning and organizing parties, but he could at least run errands and control the kids. Now everything falls on me.

Of course, it all came together in the end, and was made even more special by the gift of a beautiful sunny day, along with a light southerly breeze that kept the temperature down. The kids had the space to run riot, yelling and screaming, to swim and get dumped in the beach break, to play touch football that turned into tackle (and the opportunity to beat up on Troy and Kurt), and to stuff themselves silly with lollies, junk food, and fizzy drink.

Their laughter was infectious, and I was tickled pink to see that Shane was smiling; in fact, I was so delighted that I had a little cry. He was dressed up with a spectacular red Santa jacket and a whirligig Christmas hat that he kept on for most of the day. With his permanent lap tray, he made a convenient coffee table, so we piled him up with food and he became the center of attention; where the food is, the Cliftons will congregate.

Family tradition demands we come together and listen to a reading of the birth of Jesus. Shane did the honor, with the kids, big and small, seated on the grass before him, and us adults standing in a semicircle behind. He has a rich voice, and although it has lost some of its power without the strength of abdominal muscles, he read the account with an animated flourish that gave the ancient text life. It's a story of promise and hope, set in the context of fear and sorrow, and listening to Shane tell it fed my soul.

December 25, 2010 (Saturday)

Shane Clifton Journal

Sid's Mary is staying at The Center for Spirituality, a boarding house owned by the Catholic Church. It sits on a hill with views to the city, and we were invited to enjoy Christmas lunch with them. There was a small crowd; Sid and Mary had one of their twin sons, Simon, and daughter, Hannah, along with their partners, and Elly and I were accompanied by the boys, our two sets of parents, and our good friends Rowena and David. Some other friends (Peter and Angela) arranged for us to be given a stupendous hamper from Life Without Chains in Newcastle, so we tucked into its spoils: wine, cheeses, dips, and other naughties. We exchanged presents, and the most memorable is a white T-shirt from Rowena emblazoned in red lettering with, "I envy your fully functional sphincter." She insisted that I have to wear it to work. We shall see.

Over the course of the last month, Sid has been gaining more movement and is now able to spend time out of his chair. He walks with a rigid stiffness, but has recently managed to negotiate stairs. Today, he walked the kilometer and a half from the hospital to the boarding house, with Mary riding in the chair. She is a friendly soul, and on the way she found herself talking to an older gentleman who ended up accompanying her up the street, sympathizing with her disability!

Provided adequate cushioning is available, Sid can sit at the table on an ordinary seat. This gave Simon the opportunity to steal his wheelchair, and we ended up laying out a course and racing. My boys joined in the fun, and I managed to win every race—not so much the advantage of experience as the benefit of a slightly newer and faster chair. At one point it dawned on me that I have made some progress from my first tentative "steps" outside the hospital only a month or so ago.

December 26, 2010 (Sunday)
Elly Clifton Facebook

Jake and Lochie are shooting innocent passers-by from our balcony (third floor in Randwick unit) with their new super soakers . . . They are giddy with excitement . . .

December 31, 2010 (Friday)
Shane Clifton Journal

Christmas rolls into New Year and there is nothing going on in the way of rehab. Once again, we partied at The Center, enjoying champagne on the assumption that I cannot get done Driving Under the Influence (DUI) on a motorized chair. It was a beautiful, balmy night, and we had prime seating to view the Sydney fireworks. I only had the energy to stay for the 9:00 p.m. spectacular, heading back to the hospital for bed soon after.

I left Elly at the entrance to her building (the unit is on the third floor and there is no wheelchair access), and while making my way to my room I ran into an obviously distressed Clint [not real name], so I invited him into my room for a chat. We shared a lubricating scotch and talked through some of the hardships of 2010, and the losses we will have to deal with in 2011.

"I'm nineteen, and my sex life is screwed," he says, choking down tears. "It is so f*@&ing unfair."

What on earth can I say to that? Sometimes the F-word says it all. Clint is only a few years older than my son, and I would hate to be having this discussion with him. I allow the silence to have its way before showing him the books I've been reading, *Is Fred Dead?* and its companions. "They say it's not the end, that we can have fulfilling sex lives," I observe, but as the words come out of my mouth, I know they ring hollow. "But you're right; it is f*@&ing unfair," I add.

We decided more whiskey was in order, and as we sipped he told me about his girlfriend, who is sticking with him. "It depresses me when I see her naked, when we cuddle." He says, virtually whispering. "She is gorgeous, but 'it' is soft and useless and I can't feel a thing."

I have met his girlfriend and she is pretty, and I wonder about her. She is nineteen, and I worry about the potential obligation the accident places upon her—SCI spreads its tentacles to family, and especially to partners.

He continued, a conversation that was starting to make me feel like a priest hearing a confession from a penitent, "I watch porn on the Internet. I can't help it, and I know it's a stupid thing to do. I so desperately want sex and so I watch these videos. And of course it makes everything worse, reminding me of everything I can't do."

I was completely out of my depth as a counselor, and it didn't help that this discussion was bringing my own loss to the surface. I know that my friends would say that I should've offered a prayer, but I just didn't have the faith, nor any idea how to pray without it sounding like a meaningless platitude. I suggested that he schedule a time to see the psychologist, Annalisa (who I'm sure would be better at dealing with this than I).

We had a third (double) shot of whiskey (is this a spiritual counseling technique?), and we talked about the horror of SCI—catheters and PR's and the like. I tried to find reasons for hope, for a 2011 that might better than

2010. We poured out our hearts (an oddly intimate conversation between people from different worlds and different generations—I was more than twice his age), sharing about our partners, our families, and all of those other people with SCI who seem to do okay in life. In the face of my doubt, I finally asked Clint whether he would like me to pray; he did, and so I did.

"Dear God, help us to live well, to make something of our lives with these stupid bodies. Help us to be able to love and to enjoy loving, and to have meaningful sex lives. Bless Clint in 2011. Surprise him with the joys of sex, Amen."

[Editorial note: It strikes me that some of my Christian friends might find it surprising that I prayed for the sex life of an unmarried teenager. If that is your view, then it seems that your religiosity has trumped your humanity.]

With the conversation and prayer reaching their maudlin limits, I wanted to go to bed, but Clint refused to be left alone and insisted I go hunting with him to find somewhere to watch the midnight fireworks. We made our way to the tenth (and top) floor and emerged from the lift to a darkened corridor. Whatever this ward was, it had clearly shut down for the night, but Clint's depression had been replaced by a manic determination, so he headed off into the dark looking for a way to the balcony. It was now 11:55 p.m. and, seeing us, a nurse crankily demanded we return to the spinal ward. Clint simply ignored her. Spying an exit to the balcony, he opened the door, and against the nurse's increasingly shrill protestations, we made our way outside. Less than a minute later, the fireworks exploded, and we were treated to a million-dollar viewing. Hospital security guards turned up soon after, but they allowed us to watch the last of the rockets before escorting us from the ward. I loved being a rebel, and I thought this an appropriate way to finish a hellish year.

CHAPTER 5

The Problem of Pain

A Digression, 2011 New Year Theology

Outside of direct kin, there are so many people who regularly visit, and who provide amazing support to my family and I. Among my regular visitors are three theologians, Stephen Fogarty, Kate Tennikoff, and Neil Ormerod, who drop in once a week, sometimes more often. Stephen is the principal of the college at which I teach (Alphacrucis), Kate has been my associate for years, and Neil is a professor of theology at the Australian Catholic University, supervisor and co-author of my PhD. Our conversations are as wide-ranging as that of any friends, but among other things, we have explored the *problem of pain*, most famously summarized by C.S. Lewis:

> If God were good, He would wish to make His creatures perfectly happy, and if God were almighty, He would be able to do what he wished. But the creatures are not happy. Therefore, God lacks either goodness or power, or both.

The *problem of pain* is the stuff of theology textbooks and not private journals, but given my situation, I am going to take the opportunity afforded by the journal to clarify my current thinking on this most complex of problems, especially as it applies to my situation. I certainly have the time, as the hospital seems to shut down for Christmas and into January, and with no rehab (Grrr), I have the opportunity to think and write.

Pain

The *problem of pain* isn't about pain, *per se*. Pain serves a purpose, which is to warn us of danger. This is obvious when it comes to spinal cord injury, where half of the trouble of the injury is the inability to feel certain types of pains. By way of example, one of my fellow inmates at POW was watching a DVD on his computer, unaware that he was sitting on the power lead transformer. The subsequent burn (that he couldn't feel) gave him an ulcer that forced him to spend two boring and uncomfortable months lying on his stomach.

The problem, then, is not pain, *per se*, but suffering; prolonged pain that serves no meaningful purpose. People normally imagine SCI as the loss of all sensation and movement, but in fact, normal sensation is replaced by nerve pain (that feels like burning skin), and the ability to decide what and when to move is traded for spasm, and uncontrolled bladder and bowel activity. The body still moves, but just in stupid ways. As you can well imagine, it's a disability that impacts every aspect of life: work, recreation, family relationships, and the myriad of social interactions.

I don't write this because I want people to feel sorry for me. While, looking from the outside, many assume that the paralyzed person would be "better off dead," most people with the injury want to live (and flourish), even those with high-level quadriplegia. As I hope to be able to show (if I ever get out of his hospital), I can live a good life as a quadriplegic. It's also the case that every life involves suffering, which is inevitably incomparable, so that one person's burden cannot and should not be weighed against another. The brute fact is that life begins and ends in dependency (both youth and old age are a form of disability), and at every point in time we are vulnerable to affliction and death.

Our vulnerability has two fundamental aspects: first, our fragile bodies (including our brain); and second, our social embeddedness. Like any disability, spinal cord injury is a medical and social problem. In disability literature, there is a tendency to focus on one or the other, but both are significant. We suffer our bodies and we suffer our fitting into society with these bodies, and in the context of suffering the inevitable question arises: "Why, God?"

Sin

The most common answer to the *problem of pain* is to note that the cause of the problem isn't God, but human sin. It's a response, though, that needs to be handled with care. It's true that some suffering, even some permanent disability, is the result of a person's own sin, such as a drunk driver who incurs a spinal cord injury.

Often enough, a person's suffering is a consequence of someone else's sin; a drunk makes a quadriplegic of an innocent person walking along the sidewalk. In this case, human sin is the cause of the disability, but the injured person is still entitled to ask the question, "Why, God? If you love me and are almighty, why didn't you keep me safe?"

I could give a theological answer. Suffering is a consequence of the fall, and sin, by its very nature, isn't fair, except that we're all sinners, and so whatever happens, we get what we deserve. Rubbish! No one deserves to suffer—no one deserves a disability—no one deserves to suffer the consequences of another person's sin, and the gospel promises grace rather than retribution.

In fact, as often as not, disability has nothing to do with sin. My own quadriplegia, for example, is the product of dumb luck and the constitution of the human neurological system and spine. I broke my neck and destroyed my nervous system because I landed badly when jumping a pushbike—an admittedly regrettable decision, but not a sinful one. I'm a quadriplegic because to be human is to be fragile, and to run the risk of injury and even permanent disability.

Many people are born with disabilities, and to say that birth defects (a horrible phrase, by the way) are a consequence of the fall is not only theological and scientific nonsense, but it's insulting to both God and the disabled person.

The point is that talk of disability and sin are best kept separate, unless, that is, we're talking about disability as a social phenomenon. It is sinful when a disabled child isn't afforded access to appropriate education. It is sinful when people in wheelchairs are excluded from venues. It is sinful when vital translation services are not offered to the deaf community. Too often, sinful society is disabling.

Thomas Reynolds, in his excellent book, *Vulnerable Communion*, notes that when his autistic son asks him, "Why did God make me this way?"

> I am compelled to inquire into the social conditions and theological premises that bring this question to his lips. Perhaps in another family, another society, his condition would be seen as a gift, a strength, and not a liability.

Spinal cord injury, though, is not primarily a social problem—it's an embodied one.

The Good

The second category of response to the *problem of pain* is to assert that an experience of suffering, a disabling condition, is caused or allowed by God to serve a greater "good."

Once again, there is some truth here. I've met quadriplegics who say that even if they could have their life over, they wouldn't change a thing—that their disability has contributed good and beautiful things to their life. Many in the deaf community have come to a similar conclusion, understanding their seeming impairment as a gift. Indeed, it's probably true that any person who's lived with a disability for a lengthy period would be able to identify some good that's resulted from their condition. In my short time of living in this chair, I've experienced staggering generosity, deep love, heartfelt compassion, courageous determination, and exemplary care. I've also learned a few things about myself, and I've developed new skills.

Indeed, depending upon how we respond to it, a case can be made that disability enriches society. Almost every human virtue arises as a response to hardship, and this is nowhere more obvious than in inclusive communities. The fruits of the spirit—love, joy, peace, forbearance, kindness, goodness, faithfulness, gentleness, and self-control—are potently manifest in communities enriched by diverse abilities. This is not because disability provides able-bodied people with the opportunity to be charitable, or because people with disabilities are especially virtuous, but because virtue is best worked out in groups where the chaos of diversity reigns.

However, the fact that good can come from hardship doesn't justify its troubles, or excuse God. Personally, I can't imagine any future blessing sufficient to explain the losses I suffer. There is a world of difference between saying God did this to me for a reason, and God can bring good out of hardship. The former is pious nonsense; the latter is an expression of hope and faith. To tell a victim of abuse that their suffering was caused by God for some future good is to forget that God explicitly condemns abuse; but to say to a victim that God can bring good into this situation is an encouragement—a source of hope.

Fragility, Vulnerability, and Flourishing

The difficulty with this whole topic is working out what we mean when we say, "God is sovereign," or, "God caused this." We tend to think of God as a cosmic puppeteer, pulling the strings of creation in a magical and sometimes scary performance. In fact, Christian theology, in affirming God as creator, understands God as the ground of nature and natural laws—so that God works not as a magical puppeteer, but in and through natural processes.

This is vital, because it establishes our expectations. In answer to the question, "why, God?" we have to face up to what it is to be human, to be a creature of the earth—to be born, to grow, to break down, and to die—to be limited in power, strength, and knowledge—to be fragile and vulnerable—to be constituted by DNA and imperfect genes, bones that flex and break, muscles that tear, and blood that spills.

I broke my neck because I'm human and our necks break when twisted badly, and I landed my pushbike upside down. To look for a deeper cause of my quadriplegia is silly, since it is to lose sight of who and what I am; a forty-year-old male who wishes he'd stayed off his bike, but who is incapable of going back in time.

One of the problems of modern society, with all of its medical wonders, is the implicit assumption that we'll live forever in perfect health. We keep our dead and dying out of sight, we abort babies that don't match our ideals of normalcy, we worship a photo-shopped image of beauty, and in consequence, suffering, disability, and fragility come as a complete and utter shock. In terms of SCI, we focus our attention and resources primarily on cure, but pay scant attention to the fact that most people will have to learn to live with a broken body.

The Christian equivalent is the Pentecostal faith preacher who assumes that God always rewards faith with perfect health (whatever that is). This view of faith is not only idiotic, it's an evil, since it leaves people with disabilities feeling guilty for lack of faith, and worse, unloved by God. In fact, if we are not careful, prayer for healing can exacerbate the social problem of disability, by highlighting the fact that disabled people don't belong.

Don't misunderstand me. I am all for prayer, which is a wonderful expression of love and compassion. But we must be careful when and how we pray. Please don't be shy praying for me, but rather than focus on healing, pray for my well-being.

Well-being: Fragility and Flourishing

In CS Lewis's statement of the *problem of pain*, he makes reference to happiness. He's not talking about the "here today, gone tomorrow" emotion of pleasure, but a deeper concept of happiness, understood as lifelong flourishing. "If God were good, he would wish to make his creatures perfectly happy"—i.e. he would wish that they might flourish, and he'd be able to bring that about.

And God is good (I say in hope, with faith), and he can help us to flourish. What, then, might this look like? I'm still trying to work that out, but I do know what it won't be:

- The absence of trouble and suffering.

- Perfect health, perfect bodies, high IQs.

- Clean, tidy, quiet, peaceful (at least not often).

How then might we (and more particularly, I) flourish? Any answer to this question begins with a realistic understanding of what it is to be human. Life is an adventure story, involving ups and downs and swings and roundabouts. Its endpoint is always deterioration and death, and so the story of our life is set in the context of fragility and vulnerability. From this perspective, our goal is not impossible perfection or perfect health, but rather, to tell a meaningful story, or to be a part of a meaningful story. We can flourish, even though we sometimes suffer, if our lives can be invested with meaning.

What will constitute meaning will be different for different people. In terms of my Christian faith, I'm coming to the view that the theological virtues—faith, hope, and love—are the key. Where society assumes that the quadriplegic life is not worth living, faith in Jesus helps me to know that God has not forsaken me, that my life has value, and that I have a part to play in God's story, the good news of the kingdom. Likewise, hope in God helps me to persevere when things get tough; hope is a powerfully resilient force when I'm trapped in bed at night staring at the ceiling. The love of the Spirit is also a transformative force, helping me to exercise the virtues that can enable me to transcend my circumstances—to develop the patience, courage, and self-control that I will need to flourish with this body. Finally, as St. Paul says, "the greatest of these is love," since it is only in the gracious support of my family and friends that I have any chance of getting through the hard months and years that I know are still to come.

Chapter 6

Another Day in Paradise

February 18, 2011 (Friday)

Shane Clifton Journal

I have not been keeping up my journal, but it is worth noting that my hard work is at least paying some dividends. I have had some further recovery in my right hand and arm (triceps), and along with endless exercise and hours of training in occupational therapy, this is giving me at least some level of independence—much more than I might have imagined in the early weeks and months of hospital. I can at least feed myself, if not a little messily, and this makes a huge difference when I am out and about. Indeed, I can access a man-bag and wallet and pay my way. The chair continues to give me freedom and I am taking the opportunity to get away from the hospital whenever I can.

It's now been over four months since the accident and life in spinal rehab is *Groundhog Day.*

- 7:00 a.m. to 9:00 a.m.: Bathroom, grooming, and breakfast.

- 9:00 a.m. to Midday: Exercise with physiotherapists, life skills with occupational therapists.

- Midday to 1:00 p.m.: Lunch, bland food.

- 2:00 p.m. to 5:00 p.m.: Exercise and other *ad hoc* activities (e.g., psychologist, coffee, et cetera).

- 5:30 p.m. to 8:00 p.m.: Dinner, night-time: visitors, etc.

- 8:00 p.m.: Put into bed.

This schedule is interrupted by any number of medical problems and interventions, so it turns out that routine is better than novelty, since anything out of the ordinary is likely to be nasty, slow recovery, and keep me in the hospital longer. Prince of Wales is living up to its nomenclature as a POW camp. Its regularity and control of our schedule, its bureaucratic, stodgy inflexibility, its complete disregard of privacy, its smothering ugliness—and above all—its prison quality food, have turned us SCI patients into inmates.

Indeed, the impact of hospital food should not be underestimated, as it might be by those whose stay in hospital is brief. But we are captive for months on-end, and the parlous state of the mealtime has come to symbolize our sense of entrapment. Sue, the ward dietician, tells me that economies of scale have led to meals being prepared in a factory in Wollongong (two hours south), then shipped to various hospitals, including our own. The difficulty is not only that it's lukewarm when it arrives, nor is the problem that the menu never changes—that the same meals are presented with such monotonous regularity that I've come to hate certain foods (I have even started to wonder whether the hospital owns shares in a watermelon farm, given the fruit is served for every lunch and dinner). The fundamental issue is that the entire menu tastes like the plastic it comes wrapped in. It's worse than simply bland. It looks, smells, and tastes like the inhuman process that has brought it to our table. There is only one way to survive "another day in paradise." Whenever possible, we eat out.

This afternoon, I managed to convince Sid to come for coffee—any excuse to leave the ward. Nowadays, his recovery is such that he normally walks, but Mary is away, so he took the opportunity to use the powered chair. As we scooted along the footpath like two go-carts in a dodgem derby, we earned more turned heads than usual. Inevitably and without self-consciousness, children stared, wide-eyed. I told Sid of a video posted on YouTube by the "*can't*-stand-up" quadriplegic comedian, Chuck Bittner (http://youtu.be/kqVMhq2-5fA). He suggests that when children stare at him, he stares right back and says, "If you don't eat your vegetables, this is going to happen to you!" Ha!

Over coffee, we explored the reactions of people to our disability. As I spend a little more time out of the hospital, I am surprised by how often people ask, "What happened to you?"—or some variety of the same. I am not sure what to make of it. Is the questioner being polite or nosy? I usually presume the former and proffer a brief (if noncommittal) explanation, "I had an accident on a pushbike." I need to come up with a more creative response.

This discussion sparked what we thought to be a brilliant plan: to go into a cafe, order a coffee and food, and when it is served, ask the wait-person to feed us. Would they be willing to say "no" to two quadriplegics (what sort of a cold-hearted bastard does that?), or instead, set aside their work and join us at the table? I don't think we have the chutzpah to try it out, but we enjoyed playing with the idea.

February 21, 2011 (Monday)

Shane Clifton Journal

Today is Jeremy's sixteenth birthday (although it is a school day, so we celebrated with cake and presents yesterday). A few weeks ago, Jacob turned fourteen. Both boys have been admitted to a new school, William Carey, and Jeremy has started his HSC studies (year eleven this year, and twelve next year). All of this is going on without me and Elly is functioning as a single mother, although she is getting great support from our two sets of parents. Jeremy just called to say that he passed the test for his L-plates, and under Elly's supervision has gone for his first drive. I was excited for him, but also reminded of another thing I cannot do—teach my sons to drive. When I hung up, I felt bloody useless and lonely.

March 8, 2011 (Tuesday)

Elly Clifton Facebook

Shane has gone to the college to lecture today. I'm sure it will be a thrill for him to get back to his first love for a day. I just hope he listens to his body and doesn't overdo it.

Shane Clifton Journal

This has been a momentous day. I have given two lectures at college, the first at our Chester Hill campus and the second at Baulkham Hills (Hillsong). This was my first tentative step back into the workplace. For the sake of taking you on my journey, I might try to write this journal entry in the present tense:

Class starts at 9:00 a.m., so I am up early for the usual rigmarole; toileted, showered, dressed—none of which can be rushed. At eight o'clock, I make my way to the hospital entrance where I am loaded into the taxi. As per last time, I can see nothing but the road and I am nauseous well before I arrive on campus. As I get out of the taxi, there is a crowd of well-wishers, but I am in no state to respond to their greeting. Instead, right there in the car park, I tip my chair back (the tilt function rocks back a full ninety-degrees, which normally gives onlookers a shock—time and again people come and ask me if I am okay) and shut my eyes. Breathe easy. And a few minutes later, I am okay to continue.

The class is full, as students and staff not normally enrolled in the unit have come to hear me speak. The topic is (surprise, surprise) the *problem of pain*, and I start by telling my story and giving some insight into life with SCI. Telling it makes me emotional, and describing some of my very early experiences causes me to catch my breath. Things are easier when we move into theory and work through some of the issues connected to the *problem of pain* (the product of my conversations with Neil). With a combination of lecture content and question and answer, the allocated three hours goes by in a blink. It is a thoroughly enjoyable and cathartic experience, although exhausting. Students and staff come and wish me well, and I get a few kisses and hugs, but they are smart enough to know that I need some space.

I eat some lunch, take a hit of caffeine, and then another taxi ride across the city to Baulkham Hills. I steal another ten-minute tilt-back rest to recover from nausea, and then give a replay of the lecture. I'm not sure it works as well the second time, but the students seem sufficiently engaged. I am dead-tired when I finish, but don't have long to mope about because the taxi is already outside and waiting.

Annoyingly, a mistake has been made with the booking and a Tarago van arrives to collect me—a much smaller vehicle than the bus-like taxis that I have used thus far. I drive into the back, but my head hits the roof and I need to lie sideways to fit. I decide (stupidly) that I will be okay, but ten minutes into the trip and I am not only uncomfortable, but also desperately sick. There is simply no way I can travel like this for the hour it will take us to get to POW. I ask the driver to pull over, but we are in the middle of traffic with nowhere to stop.

Breathe.

I determine to hold down the bile and make for the train station at Parramatta—ten minutes away. When we arrive, I get out of the car, lean over the side of my chair, and puke. People look on, and a couple of older ladies (grandmas) put their arms around me and offer to help. I thank them, but there is nothing to be done, and anyway, there are few things as healing as a good spew. In a few minutes, I feel strong enough to go and catch the train.

Nearing the station, I discover I have a problem; my catheter is full-to-bursting. When organizing the day, my wife had asked whether I needed her to accompany me, but confident as a teenage P-plate driver, I assured her I would be fine, with friends and students who could help me out at both campuses. What I forgot was my forgetfulness. In my rush to leave Hillsong, I have not emptied my piss. So now I am alone in Parramatta with a full catheter and the risk of autonomic dysreflexia (a medical emergency that occurs when something goes wrong below the level of injury. Because pain signals that would otherwise make their way to the brain are interrupted, a reflex is triggered, and this causes a spike in blood pressure and risks stroke and even death. Bladder and catheter malfunctions are the most common cause).

I make my way to the Westfield toilets and work up the courage to ask for help. Imagining that a woman—someone old enough to have kids—is most likely to be helpful (is this sexist?), I ask a passing lady for help (late twenties, slightly overweight, I think she looks motherly but I'm not really sure how to judge). She looks at me like I am a sexual predator, and hurries away. It takes me a few minutes to get over the embarrassment, but I try again, this time gambling on a middle-aged man. Again, a disgusted look, no comment, and he quickly walks away. And now my catheter is full-to-bursting. I don't know whether to cry or to scream, but since neither of those is likely to help, I hope for third-time lucky. I look around and spy a portly gentleman wearing a State Rail uniform.

"Sorry to have to ask this," my tone obsequious, "but might you be able to help me with my catheter? It is full, and I just can't empty it on my own."

He responds immediately and generously, "No worries at all, mate. What you want me to do?"

If I could, I would jump up and give him a bear hug, but I just want to get the whole thing done and dusted. We make our way to the handicapped toilet, and he empties the bag without any self-consciousness. My faith in humanity is restored.

It is now about 6 p.m. and I was expected back at the hospital by now. I make my way to the train station and ask the guard for help getting on the train. There is two minutes until its arrival, and as he waits with the ramp, he turns to me and asks, "What happened to you?"

"I broke my neck in a parachuting accident," I say. The look on his face gives me the energy to cope with the train to Central and then a bus to POW in Randwick.

Arriving after 7 p.m., I am utterly spent. I have learned an important lesson. I need to be realistic about my capacity, and two lectures in one day is just plain silly. Nevertheless, there is reason for pride. I have traveled on my own. I have given lectures and taken questions. I have solved problems and faced up to embarrassment. Not bad for a cripple who, only a few months ago, was too scared to travel on the footpath outside POW.

March 9, 2011 (Wednesday)
Shane Clifton Journal

After breakfast this morning, I took a train to meet Elly in Ingleburn, where she had just taken possession of the keys to our new home—my earlier prediction that I had seen the last of Narellan Vale proved correct. Other than pictures online, this was the first time I'd seen it. Although she has had help from my parents, Elly has taken on herself the gargantuan task of selling and buying a new house—legend.

We have moved to Ingleburn for the sake of access to public transport—in particular, the train station. The result is a downgrade in the snob value of our location, Ingleburn backing up against Macquarie Fields to the north and Minto to the south, two suburbs known for the trouble that comes with housing commission residents. We now really are bogan Australians.

The house itself is beautiful (or at least big). It is situated on a large block, with a backyard pool and gardens with enough potential to satisfy Elly's ambitions. To the surprise of some, the house is two-storied with bedrooms upstairs that are, self-evidently, beyond my reach. But there is space aplenty below: wide-open corridors easily traversable in the chair, as well as a generous kitchen, dining room, and two lounge rooms, enough to host a circus. Our goal is to steal the front lounge room, which will become a bedroom large enough to accommodate two beds, allowing Elly and I to hear the sound of each other's snores. There is work still to be done, ramps and automatic door openers installed, and a bathroom gutted and rebuilt. But my brother Troy is a builder, and this work can be accomplished in time for my expected release in April or May. Bring it on.

March 10, 2011 (Thursday)
Shane Clifton Facebook

Elly is leaving the hospital again. Five months in this prison is just about enough, I reckon.

March 11, 2011 (Friday)
Shane Clifton Journal

I don't know what to journal today, but for what it is worth, here is a description of my night-time spasms.

I woke up at 4 a.m. with my legs in spasm, crossed, and jumping around.

Technical explanation: Apparently, spasm is an exaggeration of normal reflexes. As part of the body's defense mechanisms, when skin is stimulated, a reflex signal is sent through the spinal cord to the brain and assessed. If judged as unlikely to be injurious, an inhibitory signal is returned that prevents the reflex movement of the muscle. On the other hand, if the sensation is adjudged as potentially dangerous (e.g., burning hot), then no inhibitory signal is sent and the reflex is triggered, moving the muscle away from danger (try an experiment—lay the back of your fingers on a boiling jug!). In a person with an SCI, the damaged nerves at the level of injury block and confuse the signal, and so the reflex triggers spasm at odd times. In other words, paralyzed people are not always paralyzed; sometimes the muscles below the injury shake and dance.

I first experienced this a few weeks before Christmas. Initially, I was abuzz with excitement, as it seemed as though I was regaining movement in my legs. Movement, perhaps, but to no advantage. From that time, the spasms became more frequent and intense. I experience spasm in my hands and arms if I move suddenly or speedily. When I am put into to bed, my body arches and my legs shake. It is not painful, and I enjoy the reminder that I have muscles that move. It is quite often funny, as nurses trying to transfer or dress me are forced to struggle with my shaking limbs. There are, however, two issues. First, shaking limbs interfere with exercise. Second, bouncing legs wake me up at night—and if they end up crossed, the spasm continues until they are put back into a more natural position. This affects my sleep.

So it was 4 a.m. and my bouncing legs had crossed, and I couldn't do anything about it except hit the buzzer and wait for a nurse. Tonight it was Joan, an out-and-proud lesbian. I confess, I don't understand why people conform to stereotypes, but she is butch with shaved head and all. But whatever her style, she is a great nurse. Tonight, she pulled my legs straight—more shaking—and we chatted away. We have had regular nighttime trysts, with conversation the best antidote to the sense of entrapment that is the reality of being a quadriplegic in bed. Before long, Joan moved on and I drifted back to sleep.

March 14, 2011 (Monday)

Shane Clifton Journal

It was mid-morning and I was on my back again, being transported by a surgical dresser who looked far too old and fat to push my bed. I attempted civility—"how are you?"—and he grunted a reply—"okay"—which meant; "don't talk to me, I'm busy," and then I had to put up with his labored breathing and his stink, past more dirty ceilings to the urology waiting room. I was there for a procedure to replace my urethral catheter with a suprapubic catheter (SPC). While paraplegics normally learn to perform intermittent catheterization (inserting a catheter when the bladder is full), this is not possible for those with limited hand function, so up until now I have had a permanent catheter accessing the bladder through my penis. Surgically inserting it directly through my belly is said to be easier to manage and reduce the incidence of bladder infection. Most importantly (at least so far as I am concerned), it is said to make sexual activity easier.

Some indeterminate time after arriving (I am well-past bothering to watch the clock), Professor Millard bounced into the room, flirting with his harem of nurses (seriously, these nurses were competing for his attention). Taking my file from the bed, he asked me whether I knew why I was here.

"To free Willy," I said.

He laughed and went on to explain the procedure. "To insert the suprapubic catheter, I will inject a needle just above the pubic hairline and into the bladder, to be followed by an incision and the insertion of the catheter. Do you have feeling below the level of your injury?"

With some alarm, I interpreted this question as a hint that he was contemplating performing the surgery without anaesthetic. "A little," I said. "I can't feel needles or hot and cold, but I can tell that I'm being touched. For the sake of you drilling a hole in my stomach, let's assume I feel pain. Knock me out, please!"

"Fair enough," he said compliantly. "We will give you a general anaesthetic. Dream away, and it will be over in a blink."

Soon after, the anaesthesiologist put me to sleep, and then I awoke in recovery with that weird realization that a lot had happened in seemingly no time at all. I was groggy, but nothing felt any different. I asked the attending nurse whether the operation had gone ahead, and apparently it had been completed without a hitch. So there we have the advantage of SCI; that I can have an operation like this and not suffer the pain of recovery. Of course, without SCI, I would not need an operation in the first place.

March 21, 2011 (Monday)
Shane Clifton Journal

I woke up last night with the clock projected onto my roof telling me it was 3:30 a.m. As usual, my legs were shaking, but I also had a strange sensation in my groin and bladder, which I can only describe as being something like a urinary tract infection (it is difficult to describe the sensation when I have such muted and inconsistent feeling). It turns out that what I was sensing was bladder spasm. The problem is that since Willy has been freed, he has also been leaking.

I could tell by the smell that once again I was lying in piss. This time my legs remained uncrossed and had stopped shaking, so I decided not to call the nurse. After a week of early-morning clean-ups and changed sheets, I was tired and needed sleep. Even though the thought of lying in wee left me a little queasy, the fact is that I don't feel the wet, or the warm or cold, so I fell asleep and left the hassle till the morning.

At 11:00 a.m. I was again in urology with Professor Millard. The goal was to see what was going on in the bladder, and to that end, he performed a urodynamic test. What once might have been the stuff of nightmares is now ho-hum, and so I chatted away as a pressure gauge was inserted into my anus and a catheter into my penis (I could sense their presence but felt no pain). Filling my bladder with water, Professor Millard triggered the spasm and measured the reaction of the bladder. I have no idea what his measurements meant, but apparently the solution to my leakage will be an injection of phenol (or Botox) into the nerve endings of the bladder. To be honest, I'm not really sure how this works, but have no choice but to trust that the experts know what they're talking about.

The nerve block will require another procedure and general anaesthetic. To prevent leakage in the meantime a nurse reinserted the urethral catheter, and as the SPC remains in place, I am now double-bagged.

March 23, 2011 (Wednesday)

Shane Clifton Journal

In our afternoon session, Ally (occupational therapist) forced us to play a game of Ping-Pong. Sid took charge of one end, standing tall and stiff, his bat in his right hand, able to move enough to follow the ball across the width of the table, provided the return comes gently. There is no fear of anything else, since I sat at the other end, rooted to the spot (the hand that would normally hold the joystick needed to hold the bat), with a hitting range of about one meter. It is certainly not a bet worthy contest, since, for a rally to get past the initial serve, Sid had to direct the ball directly at my right shoulder and within the limits of my swing range—any variation and the ball was through to the keeper. Ally had the job of collecting our many miss-hits, and she ended up doing more exercise than either Sid or I. We managed a few rallies and played on till laughter had its way, the absurdity of our jerky and uncoordinated movements making it impossible to continue. Ally had a trophy at hand (constructed of Ping-Pong balls and bric-a-brac), and we awarded it to Sid, the spaz-pong champion.

I'm struggling to face up to Sid's imminent discharge next Wednesday. Taking the opportunities left to enjoy each other's company, we decided to take the girls out to dinner. On the way to the restaurant, Mary turned to Sid and chided, "Stop walking like a spaz, Sid, or I won't walk with you." Harsh, perhaps, but he does move weirdly, shuffling steps and arms locked by his side. It can be hilarious, and Mary's teasing adds to what has been a funny day. Most people don't know how to react to disability, but laughing at our playing spaz-pong and walking seems to be the best way forward.

In this mood, Mary later recounted a story from Sid's earlier days in the chair. Apparently, they were at dinner with friends and found themselves in a restaurant with no disabled toilet. No big deal. Bottle in hand, Mary stooped down to the bottom of Sid's trousers and emptied his catheter bag at the table. Without hesitation, their friend observed, "Wow, Mary, you never told me Sid's dick was that long."

March 28, 2011 (Monday)

Shane Clifton Blog

I spent the day in bed, my second since the discovery of a small pressure sore on my bum. Pressure sores are caused by unrelieved pressure on the skin, most commonly from the weight of the body pressing through the bottom and against the seat of the chair. Unrelieved pressure reduces the blood supply, causes cell death, and thereafter, the breakdown of the skin. In the initial instance, pressure sores appear as seemingly innocuous red marks, but if not allowed to heal, they can become open sores and, ultimately, debilitating ulcers (if you have a strong stomach, search "pressure sores" on Google images). Prevention is better than cure, so people with SCI are given special seating and encouraged to relieve pressure, in my case by regular tilting of the chair. If (or when) marks do appear, the hospital requires that we take a conservative approach, which means taking the bum off the chair until the mark disappears. I have experienced this twice before, and each time it took well over a week to return me to the freedom of the chair.

So, I am in bed (again). I must have needed the rest since I slept most of the day, keeping teenager hours and waking at 3:30 p.m. I was woken by a visit from Sheree and her care dog Jade. Sheree works for the Spinal Cord Injury Association and spends her Mondays at POW for peer support, a service intended to provide advice and to encourage us about what can be accomplished by people with SCI. Sheree had a motor vehicle accident thirteen years ago, which left her a C5 quadriplegic with functionality similar to me. She lives on her own and works full time, accomplishing this with the help of morning and evening carers, as well as the twenty-four-hour assistance of her remarkable dog, who opens doors, carries things, and even folds clothes (I find this hard to believe). Her visits are a godsend.

March 29, 2011 (Tuesday)

Shane Clifton Facebook

I spent most of today in bed, but was allowed out for an hour. I took the opportunity to stroll around Randwick. At one point I passed a little girl (perhaps four) who asked Mum,

"Why is that man in that chair?"

I thought it was a reasonable question. Her mother, obviously embarrassed, hurriedly replied,

"Because he needs a rest."

I wasn't sure whether to laugh or run the mother over.

March 30, 2011 (Wednesday)

Shane Clifton Journal

It's been some time since the lease on the unit in Randwick ran out, so Elly is again stuck with the trip backward and forward from home. At this point in my rehab, she visits a little less often, but twice last week she decided to camp over in my room. We stole an old mattress that we found lying about and she crashed on the floor. It was a little like being teenagers again (staying at each other's home and stealing away when our parents went to sleep, to share a room and cuddle and talk the night away). A hospital camp-out is not as romantic, but after months apart it was nice to be able to talk one another to sleep. It made me realize how much I have missed this small intimacy.

Last night was our third sleepover. After lunch today, when Elly had gone home, the nursing unit manager came to my room for a chat (I'm still trapped in bed). It was like having a visit from the school principal. Like a naughty little boy, I was told that it is strictly against hospital policy for Elly to sleep in my room (How does she know? Somebody "dobbed" on me!). I was trembling with pent-up rage, but I tried to give a measured response. I could list any number of hospital policies that are glossed over in the ward, and so asked what possible harm could result from a sleepover. She had the gall to suggest that, in the event of a fire, an extra body in the ward would confuse the evacuation. This is a laughable rationale—the ward is solid concrete and unlikely to burn, and if there was a fire (by some miracle of physics), Elly would be more help than hindrance. But talking to a bureaucrat is, of course, useless. She told me that she had instructed the night staff to ensure Elly does not sleepover and ended our conversation with a threat. "If it happens again, you will be moved from your private room to a shared space."

After she had left, I felt a satanic rage. My mind was abuzz with the countless grievances I have with my imprisonment. I felt like punching someone; I felt like smashing my wheelchair into a wall; I felt like taking off and never coming back. But I was stuck in my bed, unable to move, and all I could do was shout obscenities at the ceiling. Apparently it had heard it all before and stared back at me indifferently.

March 31, 2011 (Thursday)

Shane Clifton Journal

Utterly depressed. In addition to my fight with the NUM, Sid was discharged yesterday, and this pressure mark is not going away, so my planned weekend leave is under threat.

Damn, damn, poo-bum, s**t-face, damn.

April 1, 2011 (Friday)

Shane Clifton Blog: The Elephant in the Room (Prayer)

I am struggling to stay "up." I have spent the last seven days in bed, since the discovery of a seemingly insignificant pressure sore. I'd been planning a weekend release: my first overnight escape from prison and a chance to sleep a night with my family in my new house. A week ago, I was confident this tiny little mark would clear up in time, but here it still is, and so here still am I, lying in bed on my side, with my bum in the air.

Annalisa has been to visit me twice; thank God she's here. I'm not sure what it is a psychologist does—it's not as though she leaves me with a sure-fire solution to any of my issues—but it's nice to have someone I can complain to since I try to avoid being too negative with Elly, who has more than enough to deal with. Annalisa has left me some notes on meditation and mindfulness, along with a CD of contemplative music, so we'll see how that goes.

Before bed last night, Elly and I prayed together. As she asked (pleaded) for healing for the sore on my bum, I couldn't help thinking of the elephant in the room. Was there any point in praying for an insignificant pressure sore when the bigger problem—SCI, the very cause of that mark—had been prayed for endlessly without an obvious answer? Of course, it may be that I'm being ungrateful at this point. After all, things could be much worse—I have movement now that was unimaginable in the early months of hospital. But if I'm honest, this improvement is explainable without prayer, as the natural progress of an incomplete SCI. My friend Sid, an atheist, started as an immobile quadriplegic, yet now walks. In fact, if prayer has been effective in my case, then it seems pretty mean-spirited of God to do such a half-arsed job of it. Movement in my hands and arms—big deal. How about the more important parts of the body?

Of course, the theologian in me could give you various reasons why we should keep on praying. We should never presume prayer is about twisting God's arm; rather, it's about what it does in those of us who pray. Further, it is also true that just because our prayer has not yet been answered, that doesn't mean it never will be (although six months does leave me asking, "How long, oh Lord?"). Perhaps, also, our prayer has been answered, just not in the way we had expected (although I'm not sure what that means). All of this, though, sounds like theological doublespeak.

Now, it may be that the SCI has fried my brain so that I have missed more profound insights as to why my prayers have gone unanswered. Perhaps I will be able to dazzle you with some profound explanation when and if my intelligence returns (and I reduce my drug intake). But for now, given that I'm forced to use this mushy brain, I cannot think of a response that is adequate. What is the point of my praying?

The answer may be none at all. Yet I suspect Elly and I will keep praying, however tentatively and uncertainly. We don't have any other choice. We pray because we have to. We cry out—even feeling like we are shouting into the wind—because we have no alternative. God help us. We need you.

Lee-Anne Bryant Responding to the Blog Post:

[Lee-Anne is one of my former students, and she lived with severe scoliosis. Lee-Anne passed in February 2014 due to complications resulting from her disability.]

I can relate. It really is the elephant in the room, particularly in Pentecostal circles. Someone once said to me that Paul had a thorn in his side, and I have a thorn under my bum. Still, twenty-three years leaves me wondering, too. Sometimes it's a great blessing; it presents unique opportunities. Other times it's a source of massive frustration, as you'd know.

In any case . . . *carpe diem*. Get out there and terrorize. It's fun. You'll leave many Christians baffled.

This is especially fun—I can move my legs; so when people start yelling and grabbing and casting who-knows-what demon of lameness and whatever out of me, I take great joy in extending my feet and wiggling my toes in gratitude before threatening litigation and a kick-box to the head.

I visited a smallish church once, and the pastor asked if he could pray for me. I said sure, why not? Ensue fifteen-plus people surrounding me, casting things out of me, telling me to repent and be healed. Two of the ladies and one of the guys picked me up by the arms and made me stand. I had bruised biceps for three weeks and strained back muscles from being stretched, standing straight with scoliosis. It went on for around fifteen minutes, and every time I yelled at them to let go of me they yelled back at my "demon" to shut up.

After this adventure, they gave me a copy of Joni Eareckson Tada's book—totally contradicting themselves.

So I never visited again.

I'm nervous around conferences and prophetic stuff, because I don't want that to be repeated. I hate being made a fuss of at the best of times, and crazies just seem to enter their element when they see me coming.

April 10, 2011 (Sunday)
Shane Clifton Journal

While I'm on the topic of healing, I have just finished reading Joni Eareckson Tada's *A Place of Healing: Wrestling with the Mysteries of Suffering, Pain, and God's Sovereignty* (2010). Eareckson Tada is perhaps the most famous Christian quadriplegic. She is now in her sixties, having injured herself in a diving accident when seventeen years old. She has thus survived—in fact flourished—more than five decades with SCI.

In comparison to Eareckson Tada, I am a mere infant—both in terms of the time spent as a quadriplegic, and in respect to the level of our faith; where I am plagued by doubt, she has complete trust in God. In this light, it's probably the case that I have no right to criticize her, but the truth is that her book has left me feeling agitated. Perhaps this is because her story frightens me, since it was written during a period in which she was suffering from severe and unrelenting pain. Pain is now a permanent part of my life, and Eareckson Tada's black testimony has me fearing the possibility of enduring months and years—not just of loss, but also of pain. My real problem with her argument, though, was the way in which it celebrates the spiritual benefits of suffering and pain. But before outlining this criticism, there were some things I liked about her book.

As is apparent in the title, Eareckson Tada's book is an exploration of healing and miracles, suffering, and the sovereignty of God. It starts with an affirmation; she has no doubt that God can heal and that he does heal, citing both the scriptures and countless testimonies to the miraculous from around the world (I have some doubt about much of this testimony, but that is a discussion for another time). Having made this statement of faith, she does go on to add the important corollary that miraculous healings are not the norm—that suffering is as much a part of Christian life as is healing—that the latter is intended as a sign of the wonder of God, and as a "sign," a miracle is precisely that; miraculous (and so, rare). I would take Eareckson Tada's conclusion further. Indeed, I am increasingly skeptical about the way in which the Church—and Pentecostalism, in particular (my denomination)—"testifies" about the miraculous. It claims things for the supernatural that are easily explained by the normal progress of nature and almost never puts its "testimony" up to scrutiny. Aside from so-called miracles of the everyday (healing of the flu and the like), substantive miracles (e.g., long-term, complete quadriplegics walking) seem more like Chinese whispers than verifiable supernatural events—something everyone has heard about but no one can pin down with any certainty. What is worse is that the very fact of my raising these questions would itself be seen as a lack of faith (so I write in my journal and not on my blog). But now I am ranting, and anyway, thus far, Eareckson Tada and I are close enough to being in agreement (she just expresses the point more politely).

So what is my complaint? It's that she spiritualizes pain, arguing first that suffering is caused by the devil, and second that the sovereign God causes hardship to bring people closer to himself. Apart from the fact that these explanations are contradictory, her argument is another version of the "suffering serves a good purpose" view that I addressed earlier in my discussion of the *problem of pain*. There's no point in repeating my criticisms, except to say that my disability in and of itself does not make me more spiritual or bring me closer to God (as the pages of this journal make clear).

But what has this got to do with prayer? Should we pray for a miracle?

Of course we should. Prayer is an expression of the heart, of love and compassion, and I would love to experience a miracle. I want to walk, run, surf, and have sex, so up until now, I've prayed for healing. But I am realistic enough—honest enough—to recognize that a miracle is unlikely. And so there comes a point where enough is enough, where hoping and praying for a miracle needs to be replaced by my facing up to the fact of my disability; to its permanence. It does me no good to continue to hope for the impossible when what I really need to do is to make the most of today. I've stopped praying for healing, and instead I ask for grace, so that, despite the brokenness of this body, I can find joy and meaning in life.

[Editorial note: In Growing Sideways *(published in December 2011), Jay McNeill describes his attitude toward faith and healing following the birth of his daughter, Sunshine, who suffers from cerebral palsy:*

And my "faith position?" I don't really have one. Some people would like me to have a more refined position on faith because it would make them feel more comfortable, but the only thing I know how to do is to keep asking God to do something. Praying that the cerebral palsy will go away seems a ridiculous idea. I feel better accepting reality than to live in a deferred state of hope. I wrestle with my responsibility as a Dad to pray, but I can't allow myself to be distracted with the idea that something magical could happen.

My reluctance to pray for healing has gone hand-in-hand with an ongoing conviction that Sunny is wonderfully complete. Some people of faith may criticise me for not being more consolidated in my resolve to pray, but in reality there are very few people who have a child with cerebral palsy and still have the energy to believe that God will bring complete healing. When life-changing events like cerebral palsy enter your world, you are confronted with a truth that leaves no room for nonsense. It confronts the Western notion that we somehow deserve everything to be perfect, despite the sufferings in the rest of the world.

I am always grateful for people's prayers and encourage them with expressions of deep gratitude, but once everyone has finished praying for healing, the reality remains that Sunny is still barely able to hold up her head. People would do better to pray the way Helena and I do: to give us strength and teach us to take delight in who Sunny is.

These words sum up what I was trying to get at in this lengthy journal entry.]

April 11, 2011 (Monday)

Shane Clifton Journal: A Dummy Spit

All this pious contemplation on the weekend turns out to have been so much hot air. My complete lack of spirituality—the gulf that exists between Joni Eareckson Tada and I—was on show today as I went from Bruce Banner to the Incredible Hulk (with the anger but without the muscles) before the entire ward.

It was mid-morning, after I had finished my daily round of physiotherapy, when I ducked into my room to grab my phone, only to discover a nurse unpacking my cupboards and stacking my things haphazardly on the bed. I knew instantly what was happening, but I couldn't believe they would start moving me without the courtesy of even a day's advance notice (or any notice at all).

I knew the answer, but I asked anyway:

"What the hell are you doing?" my voice quivering with the effort to stay in control.

"You need to see the NUM," (nursing unit manager) she responded, not looking my way and clearly embarrassed.

So I stormed off, chair in top gear, crashing into a commode on the way up the corridor and earning the attention of the whole ward. At her office the NUM was in a meeting, but I wasn't in a patient mood so barged in—

"What are they doing with my stuff?" I demanded, fiddling with my joystick and moving my chair backwards and forwards, in unconscious imitation of an agitated person pacing the floor.

She replied calmly and deliberately, "We need the room for an infectious patient. You will be moving into bed fourteen and sharing a room with three other gentlemen."

Any remnant of self-control I had managed to retain melted away. It wasn't only what she said, but that she said it so calmly, without the barest hint of apology. I exploded, yelling and screaming. To be honest, I can't remember what I said—I did accuse her of plotting revenge (over the dispute about Elly's sleepovers), and demanded she come up with an alternate solution. At some point it sunk in that the decision had been made—that nothing was going to change—so I shut my mouth, turned around, and headed out of the hospital and into Randwick for a much-needed coffee.

Later, I barged into Annalisa's office (psychiatrist), and she graciously listened while I complained. But what could she say?

I've calmed a little, and decided to focus on the light at the end of this dark tunnel: my discharge. I suppose I can survive another month or so.

I'm writing this journal entry in the computer room adjacent to occupational therapy. The reality is that, from here on in, an open-plan room is going to make it hard to use voice recognition software. I guess I can accept the idea that cutting down on my writing is probably a good thing (a spiritual benefit even?). As this last entry makes abundantly clear, the journal and blog have become a little too mawkish (and cynical). Too much thinking in a place like this is a recipe for insanity.

So, I may stop by from time to time, but, dear journal, for now it is probably *adieu*. Perhaps I will see you on the other side.

May 9, 2011 (Monday)

Shane Clifton Journal

I woke up at 5 a.m., more than two hours before the attendants were due to get me up. While I'd wake up my neighbors if I used voice recognition software, I'm taking the effort to one-finger-type this brief Journal entry on my iPad:

I'm to be discharged from POW today. Thank God!

[In these journal entries it seems as though I'm ungrateful for the care I received in the hospital, although that couldn't be further from the truth. The POW doctors, nurses, physiotherapists, occupational therapists, and psychologists were not merely knowledgeable and skillful, but they also gave me exemplary and generous care. During the course of my stay in hospital, again and again they went out of their way to support me and I owe them my life. It is true that I came to hate living at the hospital, which kept me from my family and locked me into a routine that became stifling—that felt like imprisonment. This is not an indictment on the hospital and its staff but, rather, recognition of the fact that we are better off at home.]

PART 2

Home

CHAPTER 7

Smashed

May 9, 2011 (Monday)

Shane Clifton Journal

Elly, accompanied by Mum and Dad, turned up to the hospital at about 9 a.m., but after packing up my belongings, along with the bureaucratic formalities of discharge, we didn't get away till after midday. Leaving the hospital was surprisingly emotional. Of course, I was giddy with excitement, but saying goodbye to the staff and my fellow inmates was much harder than I thought it would be. It wasn't only the sadness of saying goodbye—although I was going to miss this eclectic (and dysfunctional) family—but that I suddenly realized I was leaving behind a powerful network of support. How would I cope without doctors, nurses, physios, OTs, and psychologists within shouting distance? I felt like a toddler on the first day of school: "Mummy, don't leave me." But this feeling didn't last long since, after seven months, I think I can say, "I'm a big boy now."

Parked at the back of the hospital was a Mercedes Vito van, which Elly had purchased the previous week. This sounds ritzy ("we own a Merc"), but the Vito is a courier van: a 2.2 L, four-cylinder, turbocharged diesel. It's a strange looking vehicle, with a standard front cabin and an elevated roof that rises from over the back seat to a height of three meters. No one will ever be able to wash the roof, and it'll be challenging to park in shopping centers, but it leaves plenty of room for my tall chair. When Elly picked it up, it was floor-to-ceiling stodgy white, and because she can't abide "boring," she placed two-meter stickers on each side. So it now appears as if massive dinosaur claws are ripping open the doors! I can't say how proud I am of her. She's had fantastic help (the Mums and Dads), but she's taken prime responsibility for purchasing a house, and now a car; two of the most stressful transactions there are. More than just buying a car, she tried to make it look fun.

Eventually, we arrived home and I entered a house bedecked with balloons and streamers, to the cheers and tears of my wife and children. We were all excited, but although we didn't voice our concerns, we were also a little nervous—like newlyweds on a honeymoon, in love, but tentative. Not long after I arrived, Elly looked my way, smiled, and wrapped her arms around my shoulders. Looking on, the boys joined in spontaneously, a five-person hug that expressed our love and constrained our fear. There was one problem. I had forgotten to turn my chair's power off, and with Jacob accidentally leaning against my joystick, we were propelled like a rugby scrum into the kitchen table, which in turn smashed through our rear window, spraying shards of glass in every direction. It put an end to our cuddle, but did give us something to laugh about.

[What we didn't realize at the time was that this event would turn out to be symbolic, representative of the fact that my homecoming would not be the end of our challenges, nor the panacea for the mounting unhappiness that I had attributed to being trapped for seven months at POW. If you are in hospital for long enough, it starts to eat away at the soul. In my case, this focused my attention on discharge, but after a seven-month build up, my homecoming was never going to be able to carry the weight of the expectations I had heaped upon it. I suspect that, unconsciously, I had assumed getting home would bring back my former life. In fact, it was only at home that I really came to understand what the acquisition of an SCI had cost me—had cost us as a family—and this realization was crushing. One of the consequences was inconsistent journaling, so the narrative that follows has some big gaps and jumps around a bit. In truth, the routine of home life is not very interesting to tell, so it is no bad thing that I've spared you some of the boredom.]

May 10, 2011 (Tuesday)
Shane Clifton Journal

It's oddly creepy, being woken at seven in the morning by strangers staring down at you. They introduced themselves as Parvene and Clare, two surprisingly short, middle-aged women, tasked with manhandling my long and floppy frame and getting me up and ready for the day. It did my confidence no good at all to realize that they were both shaking with nerves, an uncertainty exacerbated by the second-language English skills of Parvene (a Hindi-speaking, Pakistani Christian, dressed this morning in a nurses uniform with an incongruous but invitingly warm beanie on her head), and the dense, Irish brogue of Clare. The morning proceeded along the following lines:

Me: "Right, let's get started. Barin . . . is that how I pronounce your name?"

Parvene: "No, Parvene."

Me: . . . pause, none the wiser. "I'm sorry, it's early in the morning. You'll have to spell it to me."

A few minutes later,

Clare: "Parvene, cen yer nip over and grab me them there sling?"

Parvene: —nonplussed—

Me: "She asked whether you can you get the sling."

Parvene: "Ah, this what you want, no?"

Me: "No—I mean, yes."

Of course we soon came to understand each other and it wasn't language that slowed us down so much as that this was all very new, and each one of us was tentative. In the hospital, I was looked after by nurses and dressers experienced in caring for people with SCI, but Parvene and Clare have worked in nursing homes, but not with paralysis. Much of it is similar—a body is a body—and it's only really the toilet that had me nervous. I suspect it must take some courage to stick your finger up someone's bum and extract poo the first time you do it, but what they lacked in expertise they made up for in determination, and eventually things seemed to work their way out (so to speak).

The shift was meant to finish at 9:00 a.m., but for the first morning a 9:30 a.m. wrap-up was tolerable. No doubt, things will get more efficient with time and practice.

The rest of the day was spent acclimatizing to my new environment. It was good to be home, but truth be told, I was at something of a loss to know what to do with myself. The routine of hospital had kept me busy throughout the day, but there wasn't really much for me to do at home. I felt like an old man the day after retirement; free at last, but newly oppressed by an empty calendar.

No matter. Before I knew it, it was 8:00 p.m. and Clare and Parvene were back to put me into bed. That complete, I watched *Doctor Who* on my iPad (Jeremy thinks I look like a Dalek), and the day was done.

May 11, 2011 (Wednesday)

Shane Clifton Journal

It's great to be home in time to celebrate Lachlan's eleventh birthday. He came bounding into the bedroom at some ungodly hour (before the carers arrived), and then refused to listen to our suggestion that he open presents tonight. While Elly went to collect them from their hiding place, Lochie headed upstairs to wake his brothers, and a few minutes later there was the five of us in the bedroom and wrapping paper spread from one end to the other. I'd missed the birthdays of Jeremy (February) and Jacob (January), which made today extra special.

Tonight, we went out for dinner. Lochie had requested Chinese, but when we arrived at the restaurant we discovered a single step at the entrance—enough to keep me outside. There were two other Chinese restaurants in the vicinity, but these also weren't accessible. For the sake of Lochie's birthday, we managed to hold on to our good humor, and solved the problem by sending Elly back home to collect a portable ramp. Not too much later, with fervent and embarrassed apologies from the waiters, we made it into the restaurant. The food was ho-hum, but better than the plastic meals of hospital; and the quality of the company is always more important than the meal itself.

May 12, 2011 (Thursday)

Shane Clifton Journal

Another day and another 7 a.m. wake-up, followed by the same routine. It was Parvene and Rachelle this time—a third stranger in my house. She is young enough that it didn't seem rude to ask her age (twenty-two), and although she moved with confident speed, her nervousness was expressed in endless unnecessary apologies. She appears to have a European background, but is now a second or third generation western Sydney local. A first-year nurse without any practical experience, Rachelle impressed me by attending to the intimacies of the role without hesitation (other than "sorry" . . . "sorry" . . . "sorry"). I like her. She has a contagious energy that enlivens the spirit.

Not much worth writing about today, except to say that I'm struggling to know what to do with myself. I realize this complaint is sounding repetitive. Part of the problem is that I feel a little like an interloper. It's not just that I've spent so many months away. It's that my return home hasn't been to the family routine that I remember so vividly. I'm just not sure how I fit in. This mob has functioned without me for three-quarters of a year, and now that I'm back, what is my role?

I did take the time to explore the house today, and while I gave a basic description on March 9, a bit more detail might help. The first thing you notice when you pull up at our driveway is that it sits on quite a slope, with a driveway steep enough to make me as nervous as a two-year-old on the slippery dip; although, as far as I can tell, my chair is unable to be tipped. When you enter the front door, the lounge room that has been converted into my bedroom is the first on the left. It's a massive open space, which accommodates a small lounge that's nestled into the bay window at the front, our (I should now say Elly's) queen-size, four-post bed, and my single, hospital bed, along with a hoist, commode, and my chair. At the back of the room is a newly installed, built-in wardrobe. Opposite my bed is a thirty-two-inch flat screen TV, which gives me something to look at for all the hours I spend in this room. I also have access to an over-bed table, on which I keep my computer (so I can write this diary) and other junk I might need during the night. So a formal lounge has become a bedroom, designed for function rather than fashion. It feels a little bit like we've taken the hospital home with us, but while it is next to impossible to make my equipment look elegant, Elly has done her best to add some style; hanging purple curtains and sprinkling the walls with art and pictures. My favorites are two black and white glamour shots taken when Elly was pregnant with Lochie. In the first she is naked, looking down at her stomach, which she is supporting with cupped hands. She is wearing the barest hint of a smile, absolutely secure in her sublime beauty and divine-like status as mother. In the second, her breasts are covered, but the exposure of the rose tattoo on her hip and the fact that she's smiling and staring directly into the camera is invitingly sexy.

Now, as I write, I'm staring at these photos and trying to remember our lives when they were taken. It's not merely that it seems a lifetime ago. It's that they seem to represent the narrative of altogether different people.

Perhaps there is some truth in the Buddhist concept of no self; that the changing reality of our bodies and minds from moment to moment is such that the concept of personal identity, of "self," is a mere illusion—the self of the moment has no real connection to the self of the past or the future. For me, at least, October 7, 2010 seems to constitute the death of one self and the birth of another. As Edward Norton asks in *Fight Club*:

"If you wake up at a different time, in a different place, could you wake up as a different person?"

But that's enough gloominess. The good news of this set up is that Elly and I now get to sleep in the same room. After seven months apart, it's delightful to share my dreaming (along with my illusions) lying near my girl. I sleep on a hospital bed with an articulating air mattress that pumps air in and out of separate cells to help avoid pressure marks. And because I spend so much time there, my bed goes up and down and tilts at the head and the tail, thus setting me up so that I can do more than simply stare at the ceiling. An over-bed table holds my computer and iPad, and if I tire of these I have a remote to the TV.

At the end of a day, I do love my bed, but it costs me the opportunity to sleep right next to Elly. It wasn't until last night that I really thought through the implications, which are that a quick snuggle, a holding of hands, along with all the other things that are the reasons couples share a bed, are not going to be so straightforward for us. It's been months—forever—since we made love, but it's one bridge too many to face up to that now.

May 13, 2011 (Friday)

Elly Clifton Journal

It's such a relief to have Shane home. For a start, it means I don't have to drive those torturous two-plus hours in gridlocked traffic to Randwick and back. It also means that I have my man back in the world of our family. I'd almost forgotten how nice it is to eat together, sitting around our own dining room table. Lachlan was inspired to sing grace, which is something we haven't done for years and years (sing it, that is).

> (To the tune of the *Superman* theme song)
> Thank you Lord, for this wonderful food.
> Thank you Lord, for this wonderful food.
> For the people we meet.
> And the food that we eat.

Thank you Lord, for this wonderful food.

It's a relief to have him back—the months in hospital were starting to feel permanent—but it's not without its challenges. I especially hate having people coming into my bedroom early in the morning. Shane might be used to it, but I'm finding it a horrid invasion of privacy. The bedroom is the one area of the house where I should be able to be completely myself, but that is undone when strangers wake me up. What am I supposed to do while this goes on? Do I force myself out of bed, or lie still pretending to sleep? Gone is the freedom of night-time nudity. And worse, I now feel guilty about the tangle of clothes on the floor and the unmade bed. In fact, I find myself caught in a bizarre loop; I feel compelled to clean up my bedroom so that I'm not embarrassed when the carers come, even though part of their job is to tidy and clean the room.

May 15, 2011 (Sunday)

Shane Clifton Journal

If you Google "best things to do in Sydney," up pops a tab that lists points of interest: Sydney Opera House, Bondi Beach, Sydney Harbour Bridge, Taronga Zoo, Hillsong Church. I'm not kidding. According to Google— and their algorithms don't lie—Hillsong Church is the fifth most popular place to visit in Sydney! It's above Sydney Tower, Darling Harbour, the Sydney Cricket Ground, and Sydney Olympic Park.

I mention this because we attend Hillsong church. Well, sort of. We attend the Southwest campus—a label used to hide the fact that it's in Campbelltown. The mother church is a massive auditorium built with glass frontage and stylish curves, and located in the upper-middle-class suburb of Baulkham Hills. It boasts a shopping center and a (man-made) lake on the one side, and double-story, brick McMansions on the other. In comparison, Hillsong Southwest is a square, cream-brick warehouse in an industrial zone, adjacent to a pet barn, and within a stone's throw of the railway.

After an eight-month absence (our holiday and then accident), today was our first day back. We arrived just before the commencement of the 10:30 a.m. service, pulling into the handicapped parking at the front door of the church. While it was pleasing that there was a spot available, as Lachlan manned the hoist to get me out of the van, it felt like I was on show. It wasn't only the goggle-eyed stares of a few small kids—"Mum, why does this strange man need a crane to get out of the car?"—which I don't mind anyway. Rather, I simply wasn't used to being out in public, in the "real world" of the able-bodied, and this added to the tension I already felt. It was stupid really. I wanted to be welcomed back to church, but at the same time I didn't really want to be noticed.

In terms of the latter, I needn't have worried. We were greeted at the door as though we were new visitors, with a gushing welcome and introductions. Inside the foyer we were left to ourselves, and soon after ushered into the auditorium, which I guess I should describe. As I mentioned earlier, it's just a square box. It has no windows, and the walls and ceilings are painted black. When we arrived the lights were off, so the space was dark (you needed to allow your eyes to adjust before you attempted to find seats). This focused the attention on the stage, which was lit by spotlights and decorated with neon † = ♥ symbols—the Hillsong equivalent of the traditional crucifix. The band was on the stage; six singers, three guitarists, a drummer, two keys, and a choir—all so young and trendy that I felt like an old dag (which my kids say I am). Behind them were three massive screens that projected concert-quality live video of the band. If this description isn't making any sense, think of any modern, stadium-based rock concert (U2 at the Olympic Park) and you'll get the idea.

The singing was followed by on-screen church news (three minutes of professional advertisements for upcoming events), and then the pastor welcomed the crowd to church. We must have remained out of view because nothing was said about our return, and I didn't know whether to feel relieved or disappointed. The pastors hadn't visited us in hospital (I guess it's a big church), but was I so egocentric as to need to be noticed, fawned over, patted on the back; "you poor man, you're so brave, it's so wonderful to see you back in church."

Maybe . . . but nothing was said, and then it was time for the sermon. It was video streamed live from Baulkham Hills—I know this sounds weird, but the technology actually works seamlessly. I suppose it's because we live in an age where the screened image is reality; we're just so used to the pixelated faces of virtual friends that a video-streamed sermon feels as authentic as the face-to-face alternative. Today the reading was from Psalm 92:

> Those who are planted in the house of the Lord shall flourish in the courts of our God.
>
> They shall still bear fruit in old age;

They shall be fresh and flourishing.

—Psalm 92:13–14

The key point was that God's desire is for us to flourish, "to succeed in every area of your life—in career and business, in finances, in relationships." For obvious reasons, it was a topic that sat uncomfortably with me. I've sometimes been asked what our family is doing at a church like Hillsong? After all, this is the sort of positive-thinking, prosperity-preaching that other churches crucify and the media savages, and it hardly seems to be the sort of church that the person revealed on the pages of this journal seems likely to attend. Certainly, our reasons are complex. The church is full of life and energy, and it's populated by a circus of young people; so it attracts families like ours. It's also a fact that the senior pastor, Brian Houston, is a relentless encourager. The basic message is that God loves you, that you are more powerful than you've been taught to think, and that you can and should live a happy and meaningful life. Hillsong gets mauled for this seemingly materialist message, but if faith is just about the spiritual—about heaven and hell—and if church does nothing other than leave you bored, depressed, and guilty, then it's pretty darned useless.

Of course, the church isn't perfect, and this message was tough to take today. When successful people talk about triumph over challenge, I'm not sure that they really understand that not everyone wins, that life often isn't fair, and that suffering is inevitable. I'm reminded of a scene in the Princess Bride, when Buttercup is rescued/stolen by the rider in black (an undercover Wesley):

> *Buttercup*: You mock my pain.
>
> *Man in Black*: Life is pain, Highness. Anyone who says differently is selling something.

Obviously, this is a sermon that was hard for me to hear today, because it cut to the marrow of my problem. Is it really possible for me to flourish with this broken body?

I hope so, but I'm not convinced.

May 17, 2011 (Tuesday)

Shane Clifton Journal

I woke up this morning in a panic, my heart racing for no obvious reason. When I calmed myself down enough to think, I realized I felt vulnerable— deprived of the ready access to the experts of the hospital. Fear is a baffling emotion. It can rise out of the blue, for no obvious reason, and seems to defy logic. Why does a forty-year-old adult act as scared as a toddler with monsters under his bed, just because he's a few minutes away from the hospital? Even so, I spent the morning in a tizz, like a nervous puppy unable to concentrate; but since I couldn't run around and jump up and down (or chew tennis balls and piss on the furniture), I instead did circles about the house in my wheelchair, channel surfed the TV, and pestered Elly.

May 22, 2011 (Sunday)

Shane Clifton Journal

I am starting today's journal with a description of my body. I know this is a weird thing to do, but it sort of makes sense in the context of my day. So bear with me.

Following my shower in the morning, my commode is pushed into my room in front of the mirror, ready for me to be dressed into a shirt and my hair combed. Before this is done, I'm faced with a full-sized view of my birthday suit. I realize it's vain to say it, but I used to be relatively proud of my body. I was tall, and slim enough, and running, swimming, and surfing had left me with definition in my shoulders and chest, so that on summer days I could get away with a tight T-shirt and shorts. My wife, at least, *used to* think I was sexy . . . she especially liked my butt—or so she said. Now, however, it's much harder to look in the mirror. What I notice first is my ungainly neck, which projects forward, making me look like a mutant ninja turtle. Below, my shoulders are shrunken and my chest has disappeared altogether, muscles replaced by shapeless, jellied flaps of skin. I could put up with this, since clothing covers a multitude of sins, but it can't hide my tummy. When I'm nude and in front of a mirror, it's hideous—a massive beer belly: a near-term, pregnant tummy, but hairy. Clothing hides the hair, but not the lump. I'm told it's the result of the absence of stomach muscles, which has caused the internal organs to fall forward. At least, that's what I say to myself (and others), since it sounds better than the more straightforward admission, "I'm a fat slob." As for my bum, it goes pretty-well unseen nowadays, stuck as it is on the chair. Well, not altogether. It gets studied morning and night by carers, ostensibly looking for pressure sores, but Jacob says that they are admiring my butt-beard.

Having scarred your brain with this description, I can now tell you what bought it to mind. We went to church this morning and, following the singing, our pastor began his sermon by telling the congregation, "you're all looking spectacularly good today. You must be the best-looking congregation in the city."

Don't tell my boys (who I'm always badgering to pay attention in church), but I'm forced to confess that this is the only thing I remember about the sermon—the memory of my body reflected in the mirror distracting me.

After the service, Simon Bartlett raced his chair over my way for a chat. Simon was—is—a student of mine. In his second year of study—four years ago now, when age twenty—he was at Wollongong beach with his mates when he broke his neck diving into the surf. This seems to be a common cause of injury; at least one other of my fellow inmates at POW broke his neck the same way. Simon had told me previously that it was a scary experience because when his face hit the sand, his head was underwater and he couldn't move. He had to hold his breath, resist the panicked urge to scream, and hope that one of his friends would notice that something was wrong. Just when he thought he was going to drown, he was dragged out of the surf and onto the beach. That action saved his life, but it probably also exacerbated the damage to his spinal cord. Simon is now a C6 (complete) quad. He has very little hand movement, but his arms and shoulders are strong. Girl's would say he's buff, and with his long, wavy, brown hair, good looking.

Most importantly, his injury hasn't kept him down. In fact he is proof that you can make something of your life with SCI. He gets around in a manual wheelchair and has learned to transfer. He drives a Subaru station wagon modified with hand controls, and does so with the (over)confidence of the young. He visited me a few times in hospital (not sure why that didn't make my journal), and again today he went out of his way to encourage me, giving me tips on the setup of my wheelchair and promising that life will get easier. We headed out to the car park and watched him climb into his car with the effortless ease of an orangutan. It was an impressive feat, and Elly was inspired by the possibilities.

"If you can learn to transfer, you'd have so much more independence. It'd make both of our lives so much better."

I could hear the hope in her voice, and trying to sound confident I replied, "True." Inside, though, I was skeptical. I'm not Simon. Although my injury is incomplete, my break is one level higher than his, so I don't have triceps; and as the mirror reminds me daily, my arms and shoulders are embarrassingly weak. I'm Jar Jar Binks next to Simon as Luke Skywalker.

Even so, I sense that behind Elly's hope is a hint of desperation.

May 25, 2011 (Wednesday)
Shane Clifton Journal

Emma, from the Spinal Outreach Service (SOS—seems appropriate), visited me at home this morning. My guess is that she's mid-to-late twenties, but who can tell a woman's age? She's a Kiwi, blonde, tall and fit, and seemed amenable to answering my (no doubt, inappropriately personal) questions. It turns out that she has represented New Zealand in netball, playing for the Silver Ferns, before a recurrent knee injury ended her sporting career. I wasn't surprised to learn that she's a physiotherapist. SOS is a transition service, an effort to bridge the intense supervision of the hospital and the isolation of being home. It's staffed by physios, nurses, and occupational therapists, and while Emma is to be my case manager, I can call on others if I face a problem that needs particular expertise.

From the moment of her first "hello," Emma exuded a joy and confidence that was impossible to resist. We spent our time today working through a goal sheet, identifying needs and putting strategies in place to meet them. She gave a rating against each goal, "1/10" indicates that nothing has yet been done to accomplish the goal, "10/10" indicates completion. Much of it was mundane; find a local GP, schedule the community nurse for my monthly catheter change, arrange scripts for my pills, etc.—and I achieved an average rating of about four out of ten. There are goals for equipment needs; door openers, ramps, exercise equipment, and so on—an average rating of three out of ten. Finally, we talked about sex. We failed (1/10), and so spent the remaining time exploring ways forward. I'm not sure whether or not it should be weird discussing sex with a young, blonde physiotherapist at the first meeting, but such is the strange life we're leading.

Time flew, and after two hours Emma had to leave. On the way out, I asked, "will you be my permanent case manager?"

"Yes," she replied, "although SOS is only an eighteen-month service." Damn. I didn't know that. As I watched her leave, the fears from last week returned, welling up in my gut like a rising tide that threatened to overflow. How would I cope in eighteen months time? An absurd question really, illustrating again the irrationality of fear.

May 29, 2011 (Sunday)

Shane Clifton Journal

Elly was exhausted today and didn't feel like going out, so I decided to take the opportunity to visit a couple of local churches. St. Barnaby's Anglican was first on the list: a 1950s red brick church with the typical, tall, A-frame roof and stained glass windows. With the front entrance blocked by a flight of six stairs, the wheelchair access took me around the side and toward the back of the building. Given the reversed internal orientation, this left me parked—and exposed—in the front row of the service, and put me on edge right from the beginning; "look, everyone, there's a new guy in church, and he's a cripple."

This journal is not a church review, so I'll simply say that St. Barnaby's—with its 1970s-style, off-key music (gratingly magnified in that reverberant building) and long exegetical preaching—was not for me. After the service, I spent some time talking to the rector; but when he learned I was Pentecostal, he launched into a critique of Hillsong and this got my hackles up (only I can criticize my church!). We ended up discussing (politely fighting about) female ordination, and when I suggested his view was sexist, it was apparent that I would not be coming back.

Tonight, with the optimism of second-time lucky, I wheeled myself down the street for the six o'clock service at Ingleburn Baptist Church. I arrived a few minutes late and discovered a fenced-in property with a closed gate, which I couldn't reach to open. Fortunately, I didn't have to wait too long before a young woman helped me access the property, only to discover that the auditorium had a stepped entrance and no wheelchair access.

I wonder . . . did Jesus have an accessible building when he invited the lame and the crippled to the banquet?

June 3, 2011 (Thursday)

Shane Clifton Journal

Today was my first visit to Burn Rubber Burn (BRB), an exercise program set up to help maintain the health of people with SCI or a similar physical disability. In moving out of the hospital where exercise was part of the daily routine, I've become a couch potato. I don't even get the benefit of unplanned everyday activities; walking about the house and climbing the stairs, working in the garden, or performing the myriad of physical tasks that make up even the laziest person's day. Bending my wrist forward to steer the chair doesn't really get the heart pumping! So Keira has drummed into me the importance of regular exercise, not only as a tonic to the tiredness that goes hand-in-hand with my injury, but as a means of beating the odds of quadriplegic life expectancy. Other than skin breakdown and related complications, apparently heart failure—caused by the twin problems of poor fitness and weight gain—is the main killer. I may be crippled and life mostly sucks at the moment, but I still want to live as long as I can. I'm sure I've said this before, but I just don't buy into the idea that "I'd rather be dead than paralyzed." Of course, I'd rather not be paralyzed, but surely there are better alternatives than death?

BRB operates on Monday, Thursday, and Saturday mornings, times that are likely to be impossible for me when I go back to work in September; aside from midweek busyness, I have kids' sports on the weekends. There is a prevailing assumption that people with disabilities don't have a job—we are helpless, pitiable souls, living on a pension—and so have time in the middle of the day to make medical appointments, have catheters changed, and attend exercise programs. In fact, it's beginning to frustrate me that a system that's supposed to support me actually entrenches my disability, by making it harder to get on with a normal life.

The gym is in Minto, only three kilometers from my home. I hunted for directions on Google maps and worked out a route that would enable me to get there on my own. Elly was nervous, though, and wanted to give me a lift. Part of the journey traverses a section of road without footpaths, and so would require me to scoot along on the verge.

"Shane, it's not safe. I'll drive you."

"I'm not ten years old. I'm an adult and I'll be fine."

"Cars and trucks fly along that road, and seven months in hospital is long enough."

"Darling, it'll be fine. I'm driving myself."

This declaration was calm enough, but said with an icy determination that gave Elly little choice. I'm treated by everyone—especially Elly—with perfect care, but it's hard to be constantly worried over, so I feel the need to fight for independence when I can.

Accordingly, I made the trip, but I'm glad Elly wasn't shown a video. The journey was mostly straightforward, except for one section of the road that narrowed at a bridge over a small creek. As I made my way across, I almost jumped out of my wheelchair (a miracle) when a passing truck blasted his horn in protest at my situation. I resisted the urge to give him the bird, and made the rest of the journey without incident.

BRB is housed at the Minto Police Citizens Club. Minto is a derelict suburb, made up of housing commission units and falling-to-pieces fibro homes, and Police Citizens Clubs are never ritzy, so it was no five-star gym; a red brick shed with a tin roof, containing a basketball court and a gym, which was dark, dingy, and freezing cold. But Simone, the exercise thera-pist, was welcoming and energetic, and the workout proved invigorating. Unfortunately, I didn't manage to strike up conversations with other clients, most of whom had a brain injury to accompany their SCI. Truth be told, it was pretty depressing, although it did leave me grateful about my own con-dition. It's one thing to lose physical function, but another thing altogether to suffer brain damage.

When I finished my exercise, I decided that discretion was the better part of valor, and called Elly to pick me up. I mean, it is winter, and it was cold outside . . . and she doesn't need to know the real reason.

June 9, 2011 (Thursday)

Elly Clifton Journal

It's been a month now since Shane came home, and I'm finding myself caught between compassion and frustration . . . but mostly the former.

Yesterday, I walked into the study and at first Shane didn't see me, but the look on his face almost broke my heart; his eyes were nests of sadness. And then he looked up, saw me, and smiled, but it looked Jim Carrey-fake. It was as though he was trying, for my sake, to pretend to be happy.

When the carers eventually leave him alone, and when he's not waiting at the doctors or going to the gym, he's either staring at his computer or sleeping—or both. It's a tragicomedy, and I don't know whether to laugh or cry. He'll be typing away (using his voice recognition software), when things will go quiet, and I'll look over to see him slumped forward, head in hands, out like a light. Other times, he'll be near a window soaking up the sun, with his chair tipped back and his mouth open wide, fast asleep; he looks like Homer Simpson drooling for a doughnut. The television can be on, and Lachlan and Jacob fighting and screaming, and Shane will be completely oblivious. Last week, Jacob took the opportunity to draw stick figures on his exposed belly (which he can't feel, so he didn't wake up), which had all four of us laughing uproariously.

But while it's funny, I can tell that he's struggling, both in frustration and with boredom. He doesn't seem to know what to do with himself. He spends most of his time on the computer, although I'm not sure what he's doing. As far as I can see, he hasn't been working on his journal. When I asked him about it, he said that he has nothing to say. I think he's doing some preparation for classes next semester, but mostly he seems to be reading. This morning, he told me he's been working his way through Aristotle's Nicomachean Ethics. He tried to explain it—something to do with the search for happiness—but he didn't make much sense. If joy is his goal, I reckon that Aristotle is a pretty stupid place to look.

If Shane's bored, then I'm overwhelmed. I feel like a single mother of four children. I'm a taxi driver, a chef, a cleaner, a nurse, and a servant. I'm coping, but only because I have no choice. If I'm honest, every now and then, while I'm slaving away and I glimpse Shane doing nothing, resentment wells up within me. I'm not really annoyed at Shane, though. Maybe it's God I'm angry at, or this uncaring universe. It's just so unfair.

There has to be a better way to live.

June 12, 2011 (Monday)
Shane Clifton Blog: "Tethered"

One of the things about SCI that is difficult to get used to, is being tied to a fixed location. I have carers in the morning and night and, generally, this provides a structure to the day. I'm woken at 7:00 a.m., hoisted into a commode, taken to the bathroom where I am toileted and then showered, returned to the bedroom to be lifted back into bed, dressed, and then hoisted a third time into the wheelchair; a game of musical chairs that sets me up for the day ahead. At 8:00 p.m., carers return and I am lifted back into bed and settled for the evening. There is something healthy in a routine of this type. My body and soul appreciate the rhythm, and I generally sleep well and awake relatively refreshed.

The real challenge is the fact that this routine keeps me tethered. It feels a little bit like being strapped to an elastic band. I can move around and have a certain amount of freedom, but I can only go so far before the elastic drags me back home. I am a forty-year-old living under the constraints of a ten-year-old boy whose mother is keeping a tight rein. My boys think it's hilarious that my bedtime is before theirs.

While I can't cut the elastic that binds me, I can stretch or untie it if I am organized. I can defer night-time care, "please Mum, can I stay up late tonight?" I can also cancel it altogether and ask my wife and children to put me to bed. The morning is more problematic, but with months of planning I can arrange for carers in a different location. And if you're wondering why Elly can't manage my care on her own, you just haven't thought about it enough. Aside from the pressure of running a family (she is virtually a single mother who now has a fourth child), there are just some things a spouse should not be asked to do! Elly is amazing and cares for me throughout the day, but I'm not sure our relationship would survive my bowel care, nor the relentless cycle of getting me in and out of bed.

June 21, 2011 (Tuesday)
Elly Clifton Journal

Shane and I have been talking about the ways in which he is imprisoned by SCI, but it's not just him, it's me also. Shane wrote a blog about it, and I've been inspired to do some art. I'm normally a painter, but this time I've used black ink pen, I think because it feels like some of the color has drained out of life. Okay, so the picture has a gum tree, representing my passion for the garden, but hanging off the main branch is a cage with two cockatoos trapped inside: Shane and I. On a smaller branch, immediately above the cage, are two more cockies, Jacob and Lachlan. They are free, but still hanging around. Jeremy is on top of the tree, testing his wings—we can see him, but he's about to fly away. I've entitled it, "Living with Quadriplegia," and I think it sums up our life at the moment.

July 12, 2011 (Tuesday)

Elly Clifton Journal

Shane has taken himself off to an outpatient's appointment at POW today; it's a good thing, too, because I feel like slapping him.

In recent weeks, the seeds of tension have been planted by Shane's inaction and my exhaustion. I'm starting to think he's being too passive. In the hospital, he was doing what he could to improve his function, to wring every possible movement out of his broken body, but since coming home he seems to have given up. I can't help but compare him to Simon Bartlett. Simon seems to be able to do pretty well everything for himself. He plays sports, drives his own car, works part-time, involves himself in church, and seems to have boundless enthusiasm. Shane, though, sits at his computer and does not much more. He's James Stuart in Rear Window, sitting still and watching life happen around him.

I think his whole world would be transformed if he could only learn to transfer. If he didn't need a hoist, he wouldn't be stuck in his bed or in his chair. He could sit in the passenger seat of a car, join me for a cuddle on the lounge, or go to bed when he chooses. Imagine how much difference this would make to his life.

Imagine how much difference this would make to my life.

In hospital, I'd investigated a post-discharge, intensive rehab program called Walk On, described on its website as:

> An individually designed intensive activity based rehabilitation program to assist a person with a spinal cord injury to improve and maximise their functional ability and lead a more independent life. The program involves repetitive, task specific activities and intense, dynamic, weight-bearing exercises all performed out of the wheelchair one-on-one with a qualified Exercise Physiologist or Physiotherapist.

When I first brought it up, Shane's physiotherapist was dismissive, so I let it slide. It had been on my mind again lately, and then on Sunday night, Channel 9 aired a 60 Minutes special on SCI, focused specifically on Walk On. I asked Shane to watch it with me and I thought it gave a pretty convincing case, including some encouraging testimonies. But I knew from the outset that he was agitated. When it finished, I turned the TV off and tried to talk to him.

"I think you should enroll," I said, trying to keep my tone friendly and encouraging. I went on, "There's nothing to lose and so much to gain, and it's got to be worth a try. Just think of how much freedom you'd have if you could learn to transfer. I think you'd enjoy it, exercising again and spending time with motivated trainers."

I waited for him to reply but he wouldn't look at me, and for more than a minute he just sat there, staring at his hands. I tried again.

"I need you to think about this. I'm not sure I can keep living this way. If you can't do it for yourself, do it for me."

More silence, but eventually he answered.

"I don't like living this way either, darling" (I hate it when he uses endearments at times like this), "but the fact is, we need to accept that this is the way life is. Walk On offers false hope; even its name is an oversell. And even if it is worth a try, we can't afford it."

I gave up at that point, and turned on the TV to drown out my frustration. To say that we can't afford it is nonsense. I'd mortgage the house—I'd sell the damned thing—for even a chance that he could learn to transfer. But if his heart isn't in it, then what's the point?

On Monday it was tense at home, and today he's gone out, thank God.

July 12, 2011 (Tuesday)

Shane Clifton Journal

I hate TV reports on spinal injury. They almost always celebrate the "miracle" of people with an SCI walking, whether by robotics or the latest trendy exercise regime. Rarely do they mention the difference between a complete or incomplete injury, or the fact that neurological recovery may well be out of a person's control. And who cares about walking when a wheelchair can get you from A to B? Walking is not the issue. It's all the other rubbish that goes with the injury: the bladder and bowel, the spasm, the nerve pain. If they get my penis working, then I'll really join in the celebration (although I doubt they'd show that on the national news). More to the point, when will they air a special report about a quadriplegic who has had no physical recovery, but has gone back to study and earned a degree, or succeeded in the workplace? Instead, every month or so, we get another vignette on disabled sports or miraculous walking.

Sunday night they were at it again, this time touting the supposed successes of the Walk On program. I'd seen the advertisement a few days before, and I'd been praying that Elly hadn't noticed. But of course she had, and we watched it together, and it opened old wounds; Elly's desperate hope for my recovery, set against my need to accept my condition and stop chasing a mirage.

I'm as motivated to do the Walk On program as Peter Griffin (*Family Guy*) is to diet. I've spent seven months in hospital working my hardest to gain what function I could, and I've had enough. Every moment of exercise with this broken body is tedious and often painful, and the thought of spending my days at Walk On fills me with cold dread. All the more because its promises are almost certainly hype, preying on the vulnerability of the newly injured and their hopes to "walk on." As my doctors and physiotherapists said to me, Walk On operates on the assumption that the exercise of muscles left paralyzed by neurological damage is capable of repairing the neural pathways impacted by injury; i.e., that passive exercise rewires the injured nerves. The problem is that there is no scientific evidence proving that this is true. Of course, there are all sorts of non-evidenced based treatments that claim to repair neural pathways—the injection of stem cells by Indian or Chinese doctors, acupuncture, prayer from a healing evangelist— but I intend to follow the evidence.

At least prayer is relatively easy to obtain, and free (depending on the persuasive power of the evangelist). Walk On requires a person to be engaged in three intensive, two-hour training sessions per week. At a cost of $80 per hour, this adds up to more than $30,000 a year, not funded by the government. To this cost needs to be added the fact that travel to and from the gym, along with the exercise itself, would take the better part of the day, three days each week, during which time I would be unable to work to earn a living. Altogether, the program would cost me more than $60,000 a year. Aside from the fact that I don't have this sort of money (perhaps I might fund-raise, but the reality is that disability reduces income and adds costs, and so is inevitably impoverishing), it's also the case that I'd rather be at work than at the gym. And even if I gain some additional function while enrolled in the program, any benefits obtained are likely to be lost when the intensive exercise ends, as it surely must.

All of this, of course, is a justification, and probably a biased one—an excuse for my unwillingness to enroll in the program. From Elly's perspective, any potential for increased capacity—especially if it made possible the ability to manually transfer—and so reduce the pressure on her, has to be tried, regardless of the costs. Better to have tried and failed then not to have tried at all, and so my reluctance is judged by her as a capitulation.

We are at an impasse. The stakes are high, and the tension in the house is palpable.

[Editorial note: This post records my attitude to Walk On at a particular time in my rehabilitation. It says much more about me (and my weaknesses) than it does about the efficacy of the program. Indeed, many participants swear by it, testifying that it has transformed their life. People interested in the program should do their own investigation.]

July 22, 2011 (Friday)
Shane Clifton Journal

At last, a resolution. Emma, from SOS, visited yesterday, and we worked through my goal sheet. It was mostly administrative, and we spent much of the time discussing the Walk On program. Emma seemed to share my perspective about the long-term effectiveness of the program (and its cost), but was also sensitive to Elly's important concerns. In response, she proposed an alternative; that I work with the outpatient physiotherapist at POW, focusing specifically on determining whether I can develop skills to transfer. My enthusiasm was sufficient that she made a booking for me there and then, with weekly sessions starting on August first. This means I'll be able to work with people that I trust, and it has the additional advantage of being free (to my US friends, this is one of the countless advantages of Australia's universal health care system). Also, it'll only steal one day a week of my time.

Elly seems genuinely pleased, and it feels to me like some of the tension between the two of us, which has been quietly but insistently bubbling away under the surface, has already faded away.

August 1, 2011 (Tuesday)
Shane Clifton Journal

It was a surprisingly emotional experience to go back into the POW gym today. I arrived a few minutes before my 11:00 a.m. appointment, and the room was relatively empty. Two paraplegics were chatting while working out on the arm crank, and a lone quadriplegic had his hands strapped to a set of pulleys and with some difficulty was lifting his arms up and then down; a stupidly easy exercise made painfully hard by SCI. He was wearing a set of ugg boots with cut-out toes, and he had a vulnerable and shell-shocked expression, which suggested he was new to rehabilitation. It was all too familiar, and I felt a mix of intense compassion and grateful relief. Life is hard now, but I wouldn't trade places with that poor soul for any amount of money. It made me realize something that I hadn't thought about until now, which was that in the space of less than a year, I'd come a hell of long way. After all, I'd made my own way to POW today. So who knows, maybe a transfer won't be out of the question.

In the midst of this reminiscence, Keira noticed me and bounded over to give me a hug. It was good to see her, looking as fit and pretty as ever, but our brief conversation was interrupted by the arrival of my new therapist, Fernanda. As required, she was dressed in the standard, red-shirt physio uniform, which seemed intent on obliterating individuality, but it had no chance of containing this "take-no-prisoners" Argentinian. Indeed, she lived up to the stereotype; determined, fiery, direct, and talented. I have said previously that I am unreasonably nosy, but for the most part Fernanda kept me in my place, taking a focused and no-nonsense approach to my rehab. After only one session, I could tell she was going to be exactly what I needed, teaching me skills, encouraging, cajoling and chastising me when necessary, pushing to see what could be achieved within the constraints of my injury.

While Walk On promised to concentrate on exercising muscles below the level of injury, Fernanda's strategy was to work with the muscles I had that functioned, and to focus on technique rather than strength. We spent much of the time in this initial session talking through the goals and strategies that she intended to employ in the weeks and months to come, which could be broken down into three stages. To affect the transfer, I was going to need to be able to get my bum in the air (stage I, the goal of the first month), slide sideways, (stage II, the goal of the following months), then drag my legs over, before repeating the process until I had moved from A to B (stage III, no fixed time commitment at this point). The whole thing sounded implausible to me, but apparently it could be achieved by utilizing the strength of my shoulders and biceps.

After a lengthy conversation, we had about a half-hour to do some practical work. I was hoisted out of my chair, sat on a plinth, and with Fernanda in front and an assistant behind, challenged to raise my bum. For most people, this is easily accomplished by bending and then straightening the arms, but such a movement requires triceps, which I don't have. Instead, Fernanda placed my arms straight down beside me and locked my elbows in place, like a backward boomerang, impossible to bend when bearing weight. With the arms locked in, I could then (apparently) raise my bum in the air using the strength of my shoulders. All I needed to achieve was a millimeter's clearance. That, at least, was the theory. In practice, I struggled to keep the arms locked in place, especially the useless leftie. Each time I tried to raise myself up, it gave way and I flopped down, to be caught by Fernanda. I'd forgotten the intimacies of the physio/client relationship, with the session involving plenty of wrestling and cuddling. With the addition of a video recorder and overdubbed background music, it could have become a YouTube hit; an awkward and clunky, spastic dance.

By the end of the session, I didn't think I'd accomplished anything and I was feeling pessimistic. Fernanda must've noticed my hangdog expression.

"Why are you looking like that?" she asked.

"Like what?" I said. "My face always looks like this."

"Don't be a ninny. You've done great. Lift that chin up and show me you've got some grit. I'll see you next week."

Appropriately chastised, I made my way home on the bus and then train, a journey of about two hours. Arriving home, I told Elly about the session, and in response to Fernanda's closing encouragement, she made me laugh with a quote from George Costanza (*Seinfeld*):

"Yeah, I'm a great quitter; it's one of the few things I do well . . . I come from a long line of quitters. My father was a quitter, my grandfather was a quitter . . . I was raised to give up."

I'm sore and my muscles are aching, but I'm not George. I look forward to next week.

August 22, 2011 (Monday)

Shane Clifton Journal

This week was my third working with Fernanda, and today I got my bum off the plinth—only by a few millimeters, but it's a first step. I'm proud and sore. Too tired to write more today.

PART 2: HOME

September 9, 2011 (Friday)
Shane Clifton Journal

I started back at work this week. The college has moved premises, from
Chester Hill to Parramatta, so the semester started late. The move is a boon
for me, since the old campus was in the suburbs near a non-accessible train
station (sometimes it doesn't seem like we live in one of the richest coun-
tries in the world). Parramatta, though, is Sydney's second central business
district, and the new venue is only 400 meters from an accessible station.
To get there, I drive my chair straight down the hill from my house to Ingleburn station, a 1.9 km journey, which takes about twenty minutes. From
there, the stationmaster gets a ramp to help me onto the train to Granville,
where I change for the final leg of the journey to Parramatta. All told, on
Tuesday it took about one hour and twenty minutes. On Wednesday, I had
an off-site class at Baulkham Hills, which added a bus ride to the adventure,
which then took two hours (a trip that would have taken forty-five minutes
in the car).

This probably sounds like I'm grumbling, but I have no complaints.
Elly has offered to drive me, but I know she doesn't need the extra burden. I
could catch a taxi, but that would cost more than $100 each way, compared
to a $2.50 disabled rail pass. And the truth is that I like doing the journey
on my own. It's empowering, not having to rely on carers. It makes me feel
like an adult. And whether I stay at home in front of the computer or get out
and about on the train reading my iPad, I'm sitting on the same chair doing the same thing, so a short or long trip makes little difference. Plus, I'm
well looked after by rail staff, and I'm becoming adept at asking for help if
I need it. If I'm feeling especially needy, I simply add some spasticity to my
movement and this show of helplessness seems to generate the compassion
needed to encourage people to open toilet doors, or adjust my clothing, as
the case may be. On the trip home on Wednesday, the weather turned icy
cold, and a young and beautiful African woman wearing a striking orange
and black hijab wrapped a blanket around my legs and dressed me in my
beanie and mittens, and we then spent the rest of the journey in a delightful
conversation about Ramadan, which had ended in the previous week with
a celebration of Eid. As she got off the train, she handed me a small box of
baklava. Grace is sometimes found in surprising places, and disability can
be a potent social lubricant.

As to work, the new premises are perfect, with the college going out of its way to ensure that I'll be comfortable. The accessible bathroom opens automatically with the push of a button. Likewise, the entrance to my second story office is automated, and my workspace set up for disabled access. The office itself looks a little sparse, with a window looking out to the concrete wall of the neighboring building, a desk without a chair (I carry my own), and newly painted, but utterly desolate, white walls. Missing were my four bookcases, which would normally have been packed tight with my collection of theology and philosophy texts, built up over the course of fifteen years study. I've decided to give my collection of books to the library, a hoard with a second-hand value of more than $7000. There's not much point in keeping paper books that I can't read, merely for the vanity of an office that makes me look like a scholar. Books deserve to be read.

I taught two classes this week—one in Parramatta and the other at Baulkham Hills—and so went to work two days. I enjoyed myself, which is noteworthy, since I can't think of many times in recent months where I've been able to say as much. It's wonderfully stimulating to be back in the classroom, and a reminder that I should count my blessings. Indeed, I'm fortunate to be able to return to work that I enjoy, unlike many with SCI.

It's been a full week, although it has slowed again today. As I write, I'm in bed waiting for a community nurse to come and change my catheter. She was supposed to be here at 8:30 a.m., before my carers finished their shift, but I'm still trapped in bed three hours later. Once again, it's assumed that because I'm disabled, I must have nothing better to do than wait in bed for a nurse.

Nevertheless, in the light of what's been a positive week, I'm not going to allow this trivial incident to steal my enthusiasm.

September 13, 2011 (Tuesday)
Shane Clifton Journal

I left home for work today a little before 9 a.m., making my way along the footpath with my headphones on, playing an audiobook; Orson Scott Card's *Ender's Game*. About a third of the way along, past a series of well-kept townhouses and down to the local high school, is a relatively steep hill that adds a little excitement to the trip. Although my chair is limited to 10 km an hour, the slope allows me to clock up an impressive 11.5; it's not Formula One, but it's faster than walking. When I reached the base, distractedly engrossed in Ender's slaughter of the buggers . . . *"crunch."*

It turns out that I'd failed to notice a black Audi exiting the school driveway, and without slowing, I'd crashed into its side.

I was shocked, having almost been thrown out of my chair, but as far as I could tell, I was undamaged. Of course, it might have been the case that I'd broken bones without feeling it, but on inspection it seemed as though my steel footplates had absorbed the blow. They were a little bent, but my feet didn't seem to have moved.

And the car? The motherly looking driver was a little distraught, and seemed to be caught between wanting to tell me off and worrying about whether I was hurt. The Audi itself was unscratched. It turned out that I'd ran directly into the right, front tire.

I think this is another story I'd best not tell Elly.

September 23, 2011 (Friday)
Shane Clifton Journal

I am not bloody Christopher Reeve (may he rest in peace)!

There, I've said it—or at least I've written it. It's something I've felt like shouting at people over the last couple of weeks. As I've said, I've been back at work, and so I've been renewing acquaintances with people that I haven't seen since before the accident. The initial meeting inevitably goes something like this:

"Shane, it's so nice to see you."

At this point I'm scratching around for a name, since the spectacle of my injury has given me a certain degree of fame, which leaves me at a disadvantage. So I normally go for something generic.

"And you. Life treating you well?"

"Sure, I'm doing fine. I certainly can't complain—to you, of all people."

Another silly assumption; that troubles are comparative and need to be weighed, after which the trouble measuring least is rendered invalid. This is nonsense. Troubles are troubles, whether great or small, and an SCI doesn't undermine my capacity for empathy. But while I'm thinking this, I'm being observed, and the conclusion reached is almost always the same.

"You're looking so much better than I expected. You've got much more movement than I imagined."

"I'm not bloody Christopher Reeve," I feel like replying, but instead I again go with the generic.

"Thank you, I'm doing well."

Of course, that's rubbish, but white lies are the essence of renewing acquaintances.

You might be wondering, then, why these conversations annoy me. The reason is utterly egoistic—the sort of thing you admit in a journal that will never be read. My issue is that, when people imagine quadriplegia, they assume complete paralysis of everything from the neck down and have an image of a paralyzed Superman in their mind. Then when they see me, they are surprised by my movement and I feel like a fraud because I've been claiming to be a quadriplegic but have more movement than the Man of Steel!

At this point, since I haven't done so for some time, I guess it might be helpful if I give an update on my injury and subsequent recovery. I should start with a justification of the label "quadriplegic," which refers to:

> A person who has a spinal cord injury above the first thoracic vertebra (T1), paralysis usually affects the cervical spinal nerves, C1 to C8, resulting in paralysis of all four limbs. This may result in partial or complete paralysis of the arms as well as complete paralysis of the legs." (http://www.apparelyzed.com/quadriplegia. html)

So I'm not Christopher Reeve, but I am a quadriplegic. As I said, my break was in the fourth and fifth cervical vertebrae (C4/5), and from relatively early on I had function typically available to those with a C5 injury (biceps, shoulders, partial chest and above). Because I'm an incomplete quad, I've had further recovery. While my left side has changed little, my right side has regained awkward and weak, but useful movement in my triceps, wrist, hand, and fingers, which have provided me with the ability to eat and drink (I need help cutting), perform basic grooming activities, use a computer mouse, move pieces on a chessboard, pick up and replace objects, and throw food at my children (inaccurately).

In fact, it is not neurological recovery that matters most, but having the determination, patience, and creativity to learn the techniques that enable independence. A YouTube search on the term "quadriplegic" reveals any number of manual and mechanized tips, from every day advice on how to open doors, put on clothes and shoes, exercise, and empty a catheter, through to more radical examples of quadriplegics who shoot guns, paint with their mouth, ride motorbikes, traverse rapids, scuba-dive, and sky-dive. Of course, the ability to perform any activity depends upon the level and nature of the injury, as well as the priorities and resources available to the person with the SCI.

So yes, I'm doing okay, and I'm moving more than I did in the early days. But I remain trapped and lost. While I'll keep repeating the white lie—that I'm doing well—for the sake of a speedy conversation, underneath it all, I'm pretty pissed-off with life.

October 15, 2011 (Friday)
Elly Clifton Journal

I love spring; it's not too hot and not too cold, so my garden can explode with color, without the harshness of the summer heat. My garden is full of my favorites: roses, daylilies, bromeliads, hellebores, and loads of bulbs; hence the explosion. I don't remember where I've put all the bulbs, and I love the surprise that it creates. I love bringing the color and fragrance inside. I feel like I've shared in their creation with God.

Out the back, my pride and joy is my turtle pond. It was only about a month before the worst day of my life that Shane used a bobcat to dig me a pond at Narellan Vale (that must be about the last bit of labor I got out of him). Not long after we moved to Ingleburn, my Dad helped me dig another, this time with a couple of shovels—a task that almost killed us. But the turtles were appreciative, and after hibernating through winter, they've now been awake for about a month and are getting fat on fish and mealworms.

This afternoon, I stole Shane away from his computer, dragging him outside to get some vitamin D and watch the turtles feed. What we forgot were the lunatic dog's "barkers eggs," which were hiding in the grass. Of course, Shane managed to get the stuff on the wheels of his chair, after which I spent a joyous forty-five minutes scraping dog-poo out of the tread.

November 3, 2011 (Thursday)
Shane Clifton Journal

It's been a difficult month . . . six months, in fact, since I left the hospital. I feel like this journal has become a tedious catalogue of woe. I write sporadically because what on earth do I say? Got up, fiddled around, went to bed. Boring to live, boring to write, boring to read.

I almost hesitate to write on, because I've got another complaint. I'm lonely. In hospital, I was surrounded by friends who shared my experiences, and flooded by visitors who kept up the flow for seven months straight. When I first got home, it was something of a relief to get some privacy, but the flood has become a desert, so much so that I sometimes find myself longing for POW (I can't believe I've admitted that).

Part of the problem is that most social activity occurs at night, but it's then that I'm in bed. Last week, we decided to attend a Tuesday night church fellowship meeting, organizing the carers to put me to bed later than normal. I discovered, however, that I just don't function well in the evening. Tiredness and night-time headlights seem to exacerbate my car sickness, and halfway there I threw up. I then struggled unhappily through the meeting, before facing the dreaded return journey. I'm pretty sure we won't go again. I don't have the fortitude and the payoff doesn't seem worth the vomit.

Then there is the dilemma of inviting visitors to our home. Elly is already worn out, and if friends come over she is left to deal with the additional stress of preparing the house and, when they leave, cleaning up. She seems to be incapable of leaving things as they are; I tell her "people won't care if there's a bit of mess," and she looks at me like I'm an alien, and then proceeds with her cleaning. As a result, I'm reluctant to issue invitations, and unlike at hospital, people don't just "drop in."

Going to bed at eight also separates me from the family. They might come in periodically, and occasionally someone will sit with me and watch TV. But mostly I'm in my bedroom alone. Sometimes that's fine. I read and write, and I often enjoy the imaginative freedom that comes with being by myself. Yet family life is built on time spent together. Not forced conversation, but the unimportant chitchat that goes with sharing everyday life.

Also, I'm worried about my boys. Prior to this bloody accident I could wrestle with them, play soccer, and on the weekends take them to the beach or the skate park, or any number of shared sports and games. But now I can't drive and I can't play. I am precisely the Dad that I never wanted to be: the boring, housebound, old fuddy-duddy. My boys compensate with computer games, and that worries me most of all.

So many of my acquaintances tell me how well I'm doing and praise my virtues, which are apparently helping me to be victorious over SCI. Real life is always messier than people suppose.

At least my kids seem to have retained their sense of humor. Earlier today, Elly asked Jacob, "Son, can you make your Dad some lunch?" His reply, "but Mum, I've already fed one animal today"—referring to our dog!

November 7, 2011 (Monday)
Shane Clifton Journal

After three months working with Fernanda, today I got my bum in the air and then moved myself sideways. Admittedly, my five-centimeter shuffle was a long way from a transfer, but this small movement felt like an athletic achievement of Olympic proportions. The key to this success has been focusing not on strength (which I don't have), but on the techniques employed under Fernanda's guidance; locking in my elbows by angling my shoulders, and moving my bum by ignoring it altogether and swinging my head in the direction opposite to my intended target.

After a solid, twenty-minute workout, Fernanda allowed me to rest, placing my chin on her shoulder. I found myself looking down her back and staring at pink undies, which were showing through the top of her shorts. Most of the exposure of SCI is one way. It's our bodies that have no privacy, so it was slightly gratifying that this display was reversed. In fact, nothing really was exposed—a bit of cotton—but I thought it best to try and direct my gaze elsewhere. I certainly wasn't silly enough to say something to Fernanda, although she probably wouldn't have minded. As I've said, the physio/client (I no longer think of myself as patient) workout is intimate.

December 14, 2011 (Wednesday)
Elly Clifton Journal

Shane's been stuck in bed for a few days now, trying to heal up a pesky little pressure sore. It's hardly a sore, actually. The nurses would class it as grade one and it's a tiny thing, only a pink mark about the size of my thumbnail. Nevertheless, to prevent it from growing, he's stuck in bed with his bum in the air. It looks downright uncomfortable to me, but he seems to cope okay.

Actually, he's become a remarkably patient person, a virtue that he never exhibited prior to the accident.

For morning tea, I made him a coffee and tea cake, and when I carried it into his room, I discovered him watching surfing on the TV. I looked at the screen, then back at him, and my heart just broke. Even now, thinking about it, I can't help but cry.

"How can you watch this show, my love?" I asked.

He responded, almost nonchalantly, "It's okay, I was never as good as these blokes anyway."

I jumped into his bed and put my head on his shoulder, and we watched the rest of the program together. I cried on and off from beginning to end.

December 14, 2011 (Wednesday)

Shane Clifton Blog: The Spirituality of Surfing

Elly and I have just finished watching the surfing documentary, *Lost Prophets: Search for the Collective*. It's the story of a group of surfers trying to escape the commercialism and aggressive competition of modern surfing (represented by corporate brands and immensely wealthy sports stars) in the pursuit of a more spiritual and prayerful surfing culture. It is the idea that surfing is about the joy of connecting with the ocean, of enjoying adventure, and of appreciating both the solitude of nature and the sharing of one's passion with other surfers.

My childhood is filled with rich memories, many of them related to surfing. I discovered my first surfboard lying under a caravan while camping at Currarong (South Coast, New South Wales); a beaten-up, single-fin emblazoned with the brand name "Shane," obviously waiting for me to claim it. With my brother Daniel and our friend, Cameron Long, we spent hours in monstrous waves at the local beach break. Of course, "monstrous" is relative, but I was ten years old and whatever the actual size of the waves, I had discovered my lifelong passion.

When we weren't camping, we lived in Berry, a small rural town 15 km inland from the South Coast beaches. We surfed every chance we could. When we couldn't persuade our parents to drive us, we would catch the 5:15 a.m. train to Werri Beach at Gerringong, where we had a twenty-minute walk, lugging our boards up and down the hill to the beach. These were the days before swell and wind information was available on the net, so we had no idea whether or not we would get any waves. We normally arrived at the beach when it was still dark, and we'd try to guess what was in store for us by listening to the roar of the breakers. If the sun rose to reveal a perfect wave—big and glassy—we would hoot and holler as we launched ourselves into the water. Even the disappointment of small surf didn't stop us getting wet.

If the wind direction was wrong for Werri, at about 6 a.m. we would wake up the local taxi driver and cajole him into taking us to the neighboring Gerroa Beach. The poor bloke was amazingly generous to us teenage hooligans, who had forced him out of bed and piled into his car, surfboards on our laps and sticking out the window.

One weekend, in celebration of the end of the school year, I went camping at Caves Beach with Matthew Wright, Shane Murphy, and Mark Mulverhill. Mark was not a surfer, but came along for the ride, taking to the waves with a boogie board. The swell was savage, and we surfed alongside a fast-running rip that flowed from the beach out to the point. The rip was hunting prey, and while those of us on surfboards could negotiate its current, Mark was swallowed up and dragged out to sea. Before we had a chance to respond, he was dragged around the headland and pummelled by waves, perilously close to the rocks. We watched on in mute horror, sure that he was going to die. Even now as I think about it, three decades later, the adrenaline rush of panic hits me in the gut. Thankfully, Mark lived to make this a story worth telling. Dragging him on, the flow of the current eventually carried him around the headland to a neighboring beach, a journey that Google Earth tells me is only 700 meters, but that seemed interminable at the time. When Mark emerged from the surf, we embraced like long-lost lovers. Later that night, we celebrated by getting drunk on Passion Pop; a cheap and nasty wine that we'd managed to get someone to purchase on our behalf.

I could rant on endlessly about escapades in the surf, but here is my last story. The day before my wedding, I went surfing with my brothers. We returned to Currarong to be greeted by world-championship quality waves that I counted as a wedding present from God. The session ended that day when I fell and smashed my back on the fin of my board. I still have the scar as a mark of the day—much better than a tattoo.

My surfing adventures slowed when Elly and I moved to Sydney. I lived in the western suburbs, and the travel to the beach hardly seemed worth the fight for waves with the mobs of surfers who controlled the line up. In recent years, though, I took to the sport again with vigor. For the sake of my "old man" body, I purchased myself an easy to paddle long board (a 9-foot-2 Jackson Mal), traveling down to Wollongong at every opportunity. I purchased some additional boards and started to teach my boys to surf. We were a bunch of Sydney kooks in the water, but we loved it.

Watching the documentary and thinking of surfing as a spiritual adventure was gut wrenching. Elly watched, cuddling me. When it was over, she didn't speak. What was there to say?

I desperately miss the surf. Looking back, I am stung with regret. Why didn't I make the most of my opportunities? Why did I give it up for all those years? Why didn't I immerse myself in the spirituality of the surf, or take a hold of the sublime; the revelation of God in the ocean?

Looking forward . . . well, I don't know that I have the fortitude to face in that direction.

This passage of Scripture speaks for me, Ecclesiastes 11:7–10 (The Message version):

> 7Oh, how sweet the light of day,
> And how wonderful to live in the sunshine!
> 8Even if you live a long time, don't take a single day for granted.
> Take delight in each light-filled hour,
> Remembering that there will also be many dark days,
> And that most of what comes your way is smoke.
> 9You who are young, make the most of your youth.
> Relish your youthful vigor.
> Follow the impulses of your heart.
> If something looks good to you, pursue it.
> But know also that not just anything goes;
> You have to answer to God for every last bit of it.
> 10Live footloose and fancy-free—
> You won't be young forever.
> Youth lasts about as long as smoke.

January 6, 2012 (Friday)

Shane Clifton Journal

We've just finished our first post-injury family holiday, returning to my parent's home in Callala Bay. Since I deliberately stayed away from the computer, it's only now that I'm back home that I can put pen to paper (mouth to microphone) and update the journal.

I should start by noting that getting the holiday to happen required serious planning and the whole event turned into something of a production; so much so that I suspect Elly is in need of a holiday to recover from our holiday. This was not only because nursing care had to be arranged, but also because taking me anywhere is a little like moving house. I need a bed, commode, hoist, medical supplies, and a seemingly endless array of paraphernalia. All of this had to be organized and packed, and I was of almost no help at all.

Now this might be seen as one of the compensations of SCI; you get to dodge the chores. As a husband and father, however, the inability to take the lead in the business of family life is thoroughly emasculating (and I say this as a raving, male feminist, not to imply that Elly should not also lead). Our roles and responsibilities frame our identity—our sense of self—so loss of the capacity to carry them out eats away at the soul. This, of course, is less of a burden than that carried by Elly, who takes on the responsibility of all that extra work, in addition to fighting the understandable urge to punch me for doing nothing to help.

Because of my tendency to get car sick, we decided that I would catch the train and meet Elly in Nowra (the end of the line on the way to Callala). While this turned a two-hour car ride into a five-hour journey, I had Lochie for support and we enjoyed a relaxing and romantic trip, the train snaking its way through forests, under mountains, and past beaches along the Illawarra coastline. We passed some of my old surfing haunts, running so close to Bombo Beach (near Kiama) that I could smell the salt and vinegar flavor of the ocean breeze, and soon after, looking from the crest of a hill down on Werri Beach, its crescent shape a sandy smile with white-water teeth. I was surprised to discover that the memories that burst forth were joyous; of early-morning anticipation, of the chill of the first dive under the water, of the derisive encouragement of friends ("grow a schlong kook"), of the golden rule, "do something to your mate that you wouldn't want done to you," of barrels and wipe-outs. And as they tumbled into my consciousness, the barrage of memory didn't unmask even a hint of the emptiness I feared might accompany this sighting of the surf.

The pleasure of the journey might also have had something to do the company of my boy. He's not only a helpful lad, but he can be cheeky-good fun. We played a couple of games of chess (he has some natural talent, actually) and he took great delight in teasing me by stealing my iPhone and taking over my Facebook account; he announced that I loved my youngest son more than the older two, that Vegemite, lemon, and chocolate on toast is my favorite food, and that I'd fallen out of my chair onto the platform (I managed to convince him to delete that one quick-smart so as not to give his mother a heart attack).

Later, when Lachlan and I had been collected at Nowra and driven to Callala Bay, we enjoyed a family get-together; my parents, brothers, our troop of kids, and the unadulterated pleasure of relaxing with people you love. We spent the time crowded around a table on the patio, with the Dads attending to the sizzling and smoky barbecue that projected the smell of burnt meat and beer-soaked onion like incense over our communion, while the girls sat together making fun of their husbands. My brothers and I told tall stories of surfing and fishing, and the kids crashed into chairs and screamed and cackled an off key hymn in the background. It's in sacred times like this that disability fades into the background and is rendered irrelevant. I imagine that even Jesus, before his melancholy resurfaced at the breaking of the bread, was able to set aside his burden and live unafraid in the ecstasy of the Passover fellowship on the night of his betrayal. Indeed, it is no surprise that the pinnacle of the church is the supper, since all human life finds its meaning at the table.

But I am rambling, if only to hide the fact that disability refused to be kept quiet. It was sometime after dinner that I started to feel queasy. What began as a dull ache quickly became a stabbing neck pain that sliced its way up to my head and triggered a brain-shattering migraine. Nothing I did relieved the throbbing—lying back, sitting up, massaging the neck, crying . . . I was descending into hell and couldn't see a way out.

Not sure how to help, Jacob went to find Elly, who came running and realized immediately that I was having an episode of autonomic dysreflexia (AD). AD occurs when something goes wrong with my body below the level of the SCI. For a "normal" person, the autonomic nervous system sends a signal to the brain—pain—to indicate the location and extent of an issue (extreme pain equals big problem). For an "abnormal" person with a SCI, these pain signals are blocked and, instead, a reflex is activated that causes a narrowing of the blood vessels and an increase in blood pressure (http://www.sci-info-pages.com/ad.html). This manifests itself in headaches, a rash on the face and chest, as well as other symptoms, which provide the vital message that an issue needs to be addressed, but don't help locate the problem (it could be any number of things). More significantly, the increase in blood pressure creates a high risk of stroke. AD is thus considered a medical emergency, and I get to wear a pretty silver bracelet as a result. This is a long-winded way of saying that it felt like my head was about to explode.

In cases of AD, it is recommended that you don't mess around, but call an ambulance—which Mum promptly did (with enough nervousness that it took her some time to remember her home phone number). Seeing their Dad in so much pain, Jacob and Lachlan were crying, but Elly, cool under pressure, set about investigating the issue. First, she measured my BP, which registered a confronting 240/179 (an average BP is 120/80, and for a person with an SCI 100/65). Since this confirmed that what I had was more than a mere headache, she administered a dose of captopril, a tablet placed under the tongue intended to reduce the blood pressure (by relaxing and widening the blood vessels). She then went hunting for the problem and discovered a small kink in my catheter line, which she repaired.

By the time the ambos arrived, things were heading toward normal. My head still throbbed, my face was still a beetroot red, but we all felt a little calmer. Obviously, Elly had fixed the problem, which turned out to be nothing at all, so I didn't need to spend a night in hospital. Thank God, I hate hospital food.

This was my first experience with AD. I had learned a thing or two and will be able to react better next time—hopefully without the need to call an ambulance. The experience had given us all a shock. In case we'd forgotten, we had been given a grim reminder of my vulnerability.

Kurt complained wryly, "You always make yourself the center of attention!" This gave us a good laugh before I was put to bed. And thus ended our first day on holiday.

I woke the next morning to be introduced to Kirra. She was tall and lean, but powerful, with a strong jaw-line and large, almost masculine hands—perfect for the job of manhandling my body. She was immaculately dressed, wearing a tight skirt that needed constant readjustment—an odd choice. It was nerve-racking, dealing with a new carer and an intimate routine, but Kirra was a willing learner and, in due course, I was in the chair and ready for the day. When she left, Elly came over conspiratorially,

"Did you notice?"

"Notice what?"

"The beard, shaven, but obvious under the make-up, and the Adam's apple."

"Well, that explains the hands."

I later claimed I was too guileless to notice such things, but Elly just thought I was dense. Of course, it was nothing more than trivia anyway. Kirra was good at her job and friendly, a gracious presence to wake up to.

The rest of the holiday went on as holidays do, with boating, fishing, surfing, and golfing. There was only one obvious difference; I was excluded from it all. I struggled to work out how to deal with this. On the one hand, I was pleased to be staying at a place where my brothers could take my kids on the adventures that were now beyond me. As I noted in this journal last year, it had started to bother me, the fact that they were missing out on the activities that I had once encouraged and facilitated. On the other hand, none of these locations were accessible to me. Wheelchairs don't cope with sand, and South Coast beaches don't have boardwalks. Boating and bush-walking were also beyond my reach. Once, I did follow Dad and my brother Dan around the golf course, but watching them play made me long to stand and take a swing (for posterity's sake, I should note that Dan kicked his father's butt, winning seven of the nine holes). I spent most of the time at my parents' home, churning my way through novels (Raymond Chandler and John Green), trying to keep my rising frustration in check. We were on holiday, after all, and my family deserved a good time. Only my contented-ness would make that possible, so I tried to smile and remain jovial, and at least some of the time managed to convince people that I was having fun. Mornings were hardest, looking to the hours that stretched ahead, not knowing what to do with myself, or how to pretend I was happy.

As the days stretched on (we were down for ten) it got so that I could taste my frustration. The problem wasn't the holiday, since I liked be-ing with my family. Rather, it was a deepening sadness, a growing sense of hopelessness that I was unable to resist. Was I trapped in a lifetime of boredom? Would I ever find something that would enable me to be happy? What can I do for fun in this broken-down body?

Then, on the morning before we left for home, Dad arranged to take me sailing. Callala Bay is home to a chapter of Sailability, a club set up specifically to enable disabled people to enjoy the sea-spray and saltwater. I arrived at the clubhouse with an entourage made up of my extended fam-ily, and when the equipment had been set up, Dad, Troy, Kurt and Jeremy lifted me out of my chair, carried me down the beach and placed me in the sling-seat of the sailboat. This is easy enough to write about, but in real life it was no easy task,

"I've got his arms, Kurt, you pick up his legs."

"Jeremy, get your hands under his bum. Come on put some effort in."

"Lift him higher over that side, Troy, you short wad."

"Dang, Shane, you're a heavy lug, and this floppy, dead-fish body of yours isn't making things easy."

Despite all the complaining, the boys manhandled me into place in relatively quick time, and then pushed us out to deeper water. The boat was a two-seater, Access 303, with Dad managing the ropes and sails (mainsail and small jib) and me in control of the lightweight joystick rudder. To my eyes, it looked absurdly small, with our large, lanky frames (195 cm / 6-foot-5) making it a toy, surely vulnerable to the merest whiff of breeze. But while, for safety's sake, we were wrapped-up in sunflower-yellow lifejackets, I'd been assured that the weighted centerboard and low center of gravity seating position made it "almost impossible to tip." Fortunately, the relatively mild, early-morning breeze wasn't going to put that claim to the test.

Callala Bay is the smallest corner on the northern shore of Jervis Bay, which is a massive body of water encircled by more than 100 km of shoreline. We sailed close to the shore and kept within sight of the clubhouse, but still experienced that humbling sense of wonder at the immensity and power of the ocean. The sound of the wind on canvas and the motion of the bow through the waves reminded me of surfing, and the feeling was one of freedom.

An hour went by in a minute, and for the sake of avoiding pressure on my bottom, we headed back to the beach. Dragged, lifted, and shoved, I was returned to my chair, and in due course, we made our way back to Sydney. The sadness that had built over the course of the week remained, but there was also a seed of hope. Since we lived inland, sailing might not be an every day or every week experience, but in enabling me to glimpse freedom, the morning spent on the water had left me with the promise of more to come.

February 11, 2012 (Saturday)

Elly Clifton Journal

At 2 a.m. this morning Shane woke me up:

"Wake up. Get your bum in the air . . . comma . . . and slide it across . . . full stop . . ."

"Shane, what are you talking about? Are you okay?" I replied, nonplussed.

"Wake up. If you don't get your arse in the air then go home . . . full stop . . . go to sleep."

I thought this was pretty rude, until I realized that he was talking in his sleep, presumably dictating to his voice recognition software. He does this sometimes when he's wide-awake. Last week he was giving me a compliment:

"Sweetie . . . comma . . . you're looking pretty sexy with your cleavage showing in that smoking black dress . . . full stop."

It is oddly endearing, this pronounced punctuation. Although it does make me wonder whether he needs to take a break from the computer.

February 13, 2012 (Monday)
Shane Clifton Journal

I went to work today wearing a charcoal-grey suit, white shirt, and brand new lime-green tie. This is definitely a new image for me. Prior to the accident, I was a slovenly scholar, perpetually dressed in jeans and a T-shirt, normally with an absurd slogan ("To be old and wise, you must first be young and stupid," "Jesus is coming, look busy," "Silence of the lambs— Story of an Aussie barbecue," "Stop using Jesus as an excuse for being a narrow-minded, bigoted asshole"). I have discovered, however, that clothes make the disabled man, and I'm treated with much less pity when dressed up. This was important today, since I also resumed my position as Chair of the Academic Board of Alphacrucis College.

At first the meeting went smoothly, although about an hour in, I noticed the tangy, acidic smell of urine. It was only a waft, and I thought it must have been caused by a small spillage, nothing to worry about. I went on with the meeting, and it wasn't until we were nearly finished that I realized there was more than the mere hint of the smell of urine, but a suffocating stench; I was clearly leaking, a fact confirmed by a glance at my legs.

"Shane, did you hear the question?"

The board was looking at me, expecting a response, but in the last few minutes I had lost the flow of the conversation.

"No," I said, followed by an awkward pause.

What do you say in these situations? I thought for a bit and decided there is nothing to be embarrassed about, so took the straightforward approach.

"I'm sorry, but it seems I've wet my pants" I said, heading toward the door.

"I'll keep that out of the minutes," the secretary observed, and it was enough to draw some welcome laughter as I left the room.

Outside, I wondered what to do to fix the situation. I knew I needed help, and decided the best person to ask was Narelle; she teaches Old Testament, but had once been a nurse—actually a midwife, but close enough—so I figured she'd have the guts and good humor to face my mess. I made my way into her office.

"Here's a request you don't get every day," I said with a wry smile. "Are you game to stick your hands down my pants?"

Narelle laughed, and bent down to open my button and zipper. She hunted around for the issue, and it turned out that the tubing between the catheter and the bag had been separated, so urine had been pouring out directly onto my lap. The reconnection was easily made, but while Narelle could zip and re-button my pants, there was no getting rid of the wet stink.

I thanked her, returned to the Academic Board to give my apologies to the meeting, and wheeled off to the train station to make my way home. Altogether, the journey took more than an hour and a half. I felt like a drunken old man, and I tried not to look at passers-by and fellow commuters, who I imagined turning up their noses and hurrying away. By the time I was showered and dressed, I'd been sitting in wee for about seven hours. Elly had the *pleasure* of washing it from the nooks and crannies of my chair.

April 1, 2012 (Sunday)

Shane Clifton Blog: Another Blog Post You'll Wish You Hadn't Read (Not an April Fool's Joke)

Troy and Kristine had come from Callala Bay (they live next to my parents) to stay for the weekend, bringing their troika (Aiden, Taylor, and Ameliese) for a corrupting visit to their Sydney cousins. The goal was to spend Saturday in the city, riding the train, exploring the opera house and the rocks, and making our way to the New South Wales Art Gallery to inspect the Archibald prize.

Like the suburb in which it is located, Ingleburn Station is old and tired. It's the only station in Sydney (that I have seen) that retains the pre-digital, yellow, timber, flip-turn timetables, which need to be adjusted by a stationmaster before the arrival of every train. While we managed to keep the kids from confusing passengers by giving these a spin, we weren't quick enough to keep them away from a shiny red button that sat alongside. Ameliese, who was dressed as a princess in a pink taffeta dress, decided it needed to be pressed; after all, for a six-year-old, buttons are there for the pressing. She got something of a surprise, however, when a male voice boomed out,

"Please state the nature of your emergency."

What she had failed to read was the purpose of the button, and the notice warning of a $500 fine for pressing it in the absence of a crisis. While we all laughed, Ameliese was either scared or mortified (or both) and broke down in tears. She was soon pacified by the arrival of a shiny, new looking (no graffiti) yellow train.

We piled on board, with the younger kids insisting on using the ramp that enabled the guard to get me on the train. After fifty minutes of chaos and noise, we departed the carriage and congregated on the platform at central station, waiting to change trains. It was then that I heard my tummy rumbling and noticed the unmistakable smell of flatulence. Or so I thought. A minute or so later my hands, after wandering around my back, returned to scratch my face when I realized my mistake.

Shit!

(I have recently been in discussion with my mother about whether there is ever an appropriate time to swear. We agreed that swearing was mostly ugly and thoughtless, but I argued that sometimes only a swear word will do the trick. She wasn't convinced. Whether this present usage proves one or the other of us right, I will leave to you to decide).

So, what do you do with crap on your hands and face and making a puddle in your wheelchair? The single handkerchief we had on hand did not do the trick (sorry, Ameliese, but you are not getting that one back), and a trip to the bathroom helped only a little. I can't get out of a chair without a hoist, and we had no spare clothes in any event.

It's moments like these when you wish you could disappear, or jump backward or forward in time, or swap bodies with someone else, or do anything other than sitting in the wheelchair. But you don't have a choice, so you do the only thing you can; grit your teeth and take the next step, and the one after that, no matter how damned mucky. In fact, that is the only way to deal with SCI as a whole. People sometimes call you an inspiration, "you're so brave," they say. But that's rubbish. All any of us can do is to play the cards we're dealt, and if that means sitting in crap, then what choice do you have?

Leaving the kids with Troy and Kris, Elly and I waited twenty-five minutes for the next train and headed for home. Our carriage, fortunately, was mostly empty, and Elly was nice enough not to tell me until later of the patrons nearby pinching their noses and rushing to move on. I wished I could have joined them.

After another monumental clean up by my amazing carers—who must sometimes wish they had trained as accountants—I was fresh as a daisy and back in bed.

I probably don't say it enough, but carers are remarkable people. Parvene is a Pakistani Christian, my age, with dark skin and black wavy hair that carries a streak of grey where the new growth has not yet been colored. Together with her family, she immigrated to Australia thirteen years ago, and while her English is improving, she often struggles to understand and to be understood, and this has its moments of frustration (and hilarity). She has her own ideas about the way things should be done, and can stubbornly ignore me when she thinks she is right (for example, she likes to save on washing, so she has me wear socks two days in a row, despite the vigor of my complaint when I catch her out). But she treats me like a relative rather than a client, and when she saw the state I was in today, she immediately started on the horrendous clean up. She was accompanied by Angeline, a beautifully gentle and sweet-natured Indian-Fijian. This is her second week on the job—one hell of an initiation.

So here I am again, another lazy, layabout Sunday. A morning of meaningful conversations with Troy, watching surf videos in preparation for the world championship tour (WCT) at Bells Beach, and deciding whether or not to hit the "publish" button on this blog. Do I really want to inflict this story on the world?

April 27, 2012 (Friday)

Shane Clifton Blog: The Strangeness of Prayer and Providence

Life is all a matter of perspective. Let me tell you the same story in two ways—don't worry; I will keep it short.

On Thursday, I had a class to teach in the afternoon at Hillsong in Baulkham Hills (feminist theology—one of my favorite subjects). I woke up feeling a little uncomfortable, but nothing serious enough to keep me from taking the journey to class. Just as I was about to leave, however, my chair broke down. The challenge with an electric chair is that mechanical problems can leave you stranded. So, I canceled my class, got hoisted back into bed, and went about trying to arrange a repair. About an hour later, I noticed my tummy rumbling and the result, given I have no control of that part of my body, was yuckiness of a sort that cannot be described. Once again, my brilliant carers to the rescue, getting me into the shower, cleaning me up, and sorting out the mess that had been left on my bed.

So what has this got to do with providence? Well, if my chair hadn't broke down, I would've been on the way to Hillsong—perhaps even in class—when my bowel gave way, and the result doesn't warrant thinking about. As things stood, I needed to spend two days in bed (perhaps more—I'm still there), and so the fact that it took two days to repair my chair was of no consequence. All in all, I am able to thank God for his providential care in this odd confluence of events.

Or am I?

Of course, I might also be able to complain about providence, given that both my broken chair and broken bum prevented me from making my class and kept me stuck in bed.

Now if you really want to send your brain in circles, ask yourself what prayer I should pray in this situation? Of course, I have prayed (and I would invite you to pray on my behalf) that this current sickness leaves me. But the challenge of this prayer is that this current problem is subsidiary to a larger one, and God does not seem to have answered the many faithful prayers that I might "take up my bed and walk" (John 5:8).

For many, these are the difficulties that lead to atheism or agnosticism. I understand that. If I'm honest, I am also sometimes agnostic—a Christian agnostic, wondering where on earth God is in this sometimes horrible life. Mostly, though, I see life as a gift, and appreciate that faith is not predicated on my control of God through prayer, or on the assumption that life should be free from crisis and pain. If all of life is understood as a gift, as a wondrous spark amidst the fragility and finitude of the universe, then there is reason for thankfulness, for the small moments of grace.

So, "thank you, God, that my wheelchair broke down yesterday."

What, then, might I conclude about providence? Let me quote an insight I heard from Neil Ormerod during one of his many visits to me in hospital:

"Providence can only be recognized when looking backwards, with the eyes of faith; seeing the care of God in the midst of suffering."

May 2, 2012 (Wednesday)

Shane Clifton Blog: Providence?

Last week I wrote a blog entry describing problems with my bowel and "small moments of grace." As I reread that blog from a different vantage point today, it really does seem like super-spiritual, sanctimonious tripe.

"Look at the man who wrote that; isn't he wonderful? Such a man of faith in the face of hard times." Vomit.

I wonder whether "he" and "me" are the same person. Has an alien exchanged our brains?

Today, I can't see any grace in the midst of this half-life. I spent three days last week in bed, and thought my bowel issues were over. I felt well, chirpy even. On Monday, I went to POW and exercised with Fernanda, no problems. On Tuesday (yesterday), I went to college and taught a class in the morning, no problems, felt fine. But at 2 p.m., I was in my office working on a lecture when my tummy did its thing, and out came the shite.

You'd think it'd get easier, but I don't know how to convey how frustrated and angry I felt. It was like an explosion in my brain, my thoughts an angry whirl of violence; I wanted to jump out of my skin, to run my wheelchair through the window, to smash my computer, to scream and curse and shout out to God: "Enough is enough!"

I'm not sure what I actually said out loud, but it was enough to get Narelle to come running.

"What's the matter?" she said, with a concerned look on her face and her hand reaching to gently touch my shoulder.

I shut my eyes and tried to control my breathing, inhaling and exhaling, slowly and deliberately.

"I have pooed in my pants."

I found this difficult to admit, and was irrationally embarrassed.

This time, though, Narelle couldn't help, so I faced up to the fact that I had no option but to catch the train home. I contemplated the taxi, but no driver would pick me up. I almost called Elly, but it would take her an hour to get to my office, and then there would be the return journey together in a small space, and I couldn't inflict that on her. So off I went to Parramatta station, arriving on the platform as the doors were closing on the train, my call to "hold that door" was ignored by a guard who stared at me disinterestedly.

(You should probably stop reading now, and move on to the next heading. I'm sure you get the idea, and don't need more detail. If you have a strong constitution, read on . . .)

With a sense of *déjà vu*, I waited on the platform for another half-hour till the next train. Just to make sure that I didn't forget why I was there, my bum opened again. What came out was not a small stool, but a flood of shite. And there was nothing I could do about it but sit still and hope it had ended.

After a half-hour eternity, the train arrived. In my whole journey to date, I had not once been suicidal, but for a split-second I contemplated driving my chair onto the tracks. Only for an instant, though, and then I realized that my desire to live was strong enough to put up with the occasional bowel accident.

On the train, the rollicking motion of the carriage caused further rumblings and more crap, which I could now see had made its way down the back of my chair and onto the floor of the carriage. I can't do justice to the smell. It filled the carriage like a rotten-egg, smoke bomb. For fifty minutes I sat on the train as it moved from station to station, doors opening, people stepping inside, then turning around immediately and heading elsewhere; and me, with my head down, not looking at anyone, and praying for this nightmare to end.

At Ingleburn Station, I apologized to the guard, but didn't have the courage to mention the floor. Fifteen minutes later I made it home, but for the sake of my family, I waited outside (for an hour) for the arrival of my carers. They came at 5 p.m., and by then I'd been sitting in a pool of excrement for three hours.

The mess was indescribable—so I won't bother trying, except to say that the clean up took hours.

Wednesday (today), I'm woken, taken to the toilet, showered, and put back into bed. Two hours later, I was on the phone talking to friend when my bowel opened again. Another new experience; a phone poo.

Providence? Faith? Moments of grace? What was I talking about in that previous blog post? Right now those words seem meaningless.

Anyway, I have again been cleaned up and put back into bed. At my wife's instigation, the carers have dressed me in that T-shirt Rowena bought me for Christmas, the one I thought I'd never wear that reads, "I envy your fully-functional sphincter."

Part 2: Home

[Editorial wrap-up: This chapter has been mostly depressing, focusing on how difficult I was finding it to live at home with SCI. I should say, however, that this is not the whole story, and nor is it the end of the story. Not every day was as bad as those I have described, but it is certainly the case that, overall, the first year (and more) out of hospital was full of unhappiness. In fact, I need stronger language; it was soul-destroying. There were moments of hope and joy, and I will say something about this in the chapters that come. But before I do, it is important to face up to the worst consequence of SCI, which is the impact of the injury upon sexuality.]

CHAPTER 8

Sex

[Editorial warning: This chapter explores explicit sexual content.]

Shane

It was at least nine months before we made any real attempt to make love. We had read our SCI porn while in the hospital (*Is Fred Dead?*), but for obvious reasons, did not get a chance to experiment; even private rooms have doctors and nurses in and out all day (and if you interpret that last clause naughtily you have a dirty mind). Then, my return home had not been the romantic dream we had envisaged. Any parent will appreciate the extent to which teenage children make it difficult to steal private time, and this is exponentially worsened when carers spend hours in your bedroom every day. Elly had never been a morning person, so there was next-to-no chance of her getting up before their seven o'clock arrival. During the couple of hours it took to get me ready, Elly would be up and about and going on with her business, as efficient as any mother who, once started on a task, is not easily sidetracked. And if we were inclined toward a dalliance while the boys were at school, I was fully dressed in my chair and not easily stripped. Elly might have hoisted me back into bed and undressed me, but the effort was one-sided and seemed out of proportion, which left only the evening, after the 8–9:00 p.m. shift. By that time, any seed of desire had been buried by exhaustion.

Of course, given the importance of sex for a healthy marriage, none of this really explains the months that it took us to make the attempt. Perhaps the seven months forced absence had established a psychological block? I would make hints and suggestions now and again, but without the enthusiasm that might be expected from a man who'd gone seven months (and climbing) celibate, and certainly without the romantic attentions that would have been needed to get the party started. The fact was that I was nervous; unsure what I would have to contribute to the mutual giving that is at the heart of sex.

Elly

While I have never had Shane's voracious sexual appetite (I'm sure many wives understand what I mean), I have enjoyed a great sex life, one that was getting better as the years went on. I don't understand it when people say that sex with their long-term partner has become ho-hum; for us, the more experienced we became—the more comfortable we were with our bodies and each other—the richer our lovemaking. I'm sure this will embarrass my children, but we regularly had earth-shattering orgasms, and even now I quiver with the memory of the last few times that we made love (it was in the spring of 2010, with the early-morning sun pouring in through our window and lighting up our entwined, naked bodies). I truly felt like this coming decade was going to take us even higher (I'd say deeper, but that might sound crass). I don't know much about Tantric sex, but I had this notion that I was coming into my prime, and with the kids at an age where they could be left on their own, the opportunities that were opening up to us would deepen our sensual intimacy and take us into an experience of ecstatic transcendence.

I don't know. Maybe I'm making more of this because of our loss. Of course, I can still have some relief, and I haven't had to go without orgasm or face the prospect of never having one again, so it might seem as though my loss is not as big as Shane's. But I do ache for him, and his loss is mine, since it is the death (or at least a radical limitation) of my dream.

This raises the question, why did it take us so long to get back on the horse? I'm not sure I have an adequate answer (do any of us really know why we do what we do?), but part of the problem was simple exhaustion. Sex and tiredness don't go together.

Shane

In the early months following my return home we had a few nice cuddles and kisses, but not much more. In August 2011, we decided that if romance wasn't going to come naturally or spontaneously, we needed at least to take the practical step of evaluating the sexual function the injury had left me. It is commonly assumed that SCI makes sex impossible—that was certainly my view on the matter prior to my accident. What you discover when you investigate the issue, however, is not only that SCI people are able to enjoy sex, but that they are at pains to make it clear to the broader community that disabled people are not asexual; that SCI is not the death of sex, that paraplegics and quadriplegics are as horny, as sexually talented, as kinky, and as diverse in their sexual expression as is the broader community. It is an understatement to say that researching the topic of SCI and sex provides one with an education!

The first thing to do was to see whether I could get and sustain an erection and, if I were going to be really lucky, orgasm. Psychogenic erection quickly proved impossible. Like most men, I think the female form is wondrous, so that even the suggestion of flesh (Elly's favorite tease was often played out in public places, when she would lean toward me and force my gaze down her top) was enough to get me hot . . . and hard. If it's not too weird to cite the Bible on this topic, this brilliant passage of Scripture describes my perspective to a tee:

> How beautiful your sandaled feet,
> O prince's daughter!
> Your graceful legs are like jewels,
> the work of an artist's hands.
> 2 Your navel is a rounded goblet
> that never lacks blended wine.
> Your waist is a mound of wheat
> encircled by lilies.
> 3 Your breasts are like two fawns,
> like twin fawns of a gazelle. (Song of Songs 9:1–3)

Now though, even a sighting of "twin fawns of gazelle" has no impact on me (below the neck, anyway). Elly tried her best (and she's talented), but it affected not a hint of movement. Of course, this was to be expected. A good number of people with SCI cannot achieve psychogenic erection. I knew this clinical fact, but the formality of the label (psychogenic erection) and diagnosis did nothing to blunt the hellish torture of this loss.

For a while, I simply couldn't accept it. One night, when I was in bed and Elly was in the lounge room, I found myself looking for porn on the Internet. I flicked through (too easy to find) pictures of naked girls, which sent me to links showing explicit videos. But my penis was spitefully disobedient, and all I gained from this voyeurism was self-disgust at the betrayal of my ideals. Even so, I returned to those websites on and off for a month, driven by desperate hope ("please, Fred, wake up"), compulsive despair, and a perverse self-destructiveness. Of course, this did nothing for my well-being, so I determined to take control of my habits (and for the sake of my children, to find a network-wide content filter). All of this to say, no amount of voyeurism or fantasy was going to help me to stand tall.

Next on the agenda was an attempt to encourage a reflex erection—if the mind can't do the job, what about the reflex response to touch or movement? The literature (both scholarly and informal) gave plenty of hope. According to one study, "Sexual Function Among Patients with Spinal Cord Injury," "9% had psychic erections, 95% had spontaneous erections, 92% had erections from penile stimulation. . . . 25% could ejaculate and have an orgasm" (Comarr A.E., Urologia Int 134–168).

More experimenting was in order, and this was something I could test for myself. As Elly says, "if God hadn't meant for us to masturbate, he would have made our arms shorter." So, put to bed at eight each night, my hand (with the incomplete movement it had regained) did what came naturally, but without the natural response. Sometimes (too many times) when spasm woke me up in the middle of the night, I would imagine making love to Elly—in the bedroom in the sun, in a secluded section of the beach at dusk, on the private balcony of a resort—and my hand would beg for Fred to come to life, but he persisted in his shrunken denials. And because my arm is as long as it is, even as I write (almost two years later), it lands there most nights, in a sad ritual supplication that is resolutely ignored. I need to find a way to move on, to accept its answer—"no"—but memory, encircled by longing, still maintains its tenacious grip on my mind.

I have wondered why, when I've had recovery elsewhere, I have been lumped with the 5 percent of people with an SCI who cannot get an erection. At first, I suspected that the nerve block intended to stop my bladder spasm and prevent leakage had damaged the nerves that control my penis, although my doctors have assured me that the procedure shouldn't have that effect. I have since concluded that the issue is nerve pain. In the months before leaving the hospital I started to feel a sensation that seemed like an intense urinary tract infection. The doctors tested my urine for bugs (an imprecise test, given bacteria is almost always found in catheter bags), and prescribed a series of antibiotics. These made no impact on the burning sensation on my penis and it was concluded that my issue was not a UTI, but nerve pain. So, the permanent burning was a sensation that I just had to get used to, and eventually I learned to redirect my focus; i.e., it is always present to greater and lesser degrees, but most of the time I can ignore it. The burning feeling is exacerbated by touch—it feels a little bit like being scratched—and maybe this is the reason that reflex erection eludes me; the sandpaper-burn of touch mitigates any automatic response.

In September 2011, I was trapped in bed with a pressure mark, when Elly decided to join me after her mid-morning shower. There was the thrill of skin-on-skin, of soft lips caressing the nape of the neck, and then the sinking disappointment of touch that Fred treated with absolute indifference. As I've said in my journal, I have muddy sensation in my body below the level of injury, and that includes my penis. So I could feel the touch—I knew what Elly was doing, but this only added to the frustration. And I was feeling more than just disappointment. I was stupidly embarrassed. There is so much of our sense of self—of our power as husbands and lovers—wrapped up in the potency of our penis. But as Elly persevered, her hands inviting, encouraging, demanding, pleading for a response, the smallness and softness of the reply spoke to me in emasculating whispers. Eventually we gave up, and instead I urged Elly to allow me to try to return the favor. My movement in bed is restricted—I am pinned down flat on my back—so I couldn't cover her with kisses or gift her with the sensual pleasure of a complete body massage, but I had some hand movement that might be of service and a mouth and tongue that worked fine. She was not interested.

Elly

It just didn't seem right to enjoy an orgasm when Shane could not. And he seems to be obsessed with oral sex and cannot get it into his head that I just don't like it. It's not only that I can't escape the memories of abuse that it ignites. The reality is that it just doesn't excite me, and if that is all that is left of our sex life, then God help us (please). I know I can't get back all that we lost, but I long for the feeling of him inside me—for the joy of togetherness. In any event, these early failures didn't exhaust our options.

There were medicinal aids that we needed to try, so I encouraged Shane to talk to his doctor.

Shane

Dr. Swee Ling Tow supervises my outpatient care. It is often the case that doctor-patient relationships are hierarchical, with the patient largely passive. Swee Ling, though, operates as a consultant and friend, and is precisely the sort of person needed to help work through the medical challenges of SCI and sex. She is somewhere near my age, married with a growing daughter, and our conversations about this intimate topic were entirely natural and easy-going. She suggested to us a number of medical options and sex aids that might be of help.

We decided to delay the use of drugs and started with the mechanical, spending $230 on a Vacurect Erection Enhancement System (i.e., a vacuum pump); a bizarre device whose working is best described by specialists:

> The cylinder is placed over the flaccid penis and a pump used to create a vacuum around it, which encourages blood flow. Once the penis is engorged, a ring is placed around the base of the shaft to prevent blood leaking back out. (www.impotent.org.uk)

We got a chance to try it out in November 2011. I felt it had potential, but Elly didn't agree.

Elly

I hated that pump. Right from the beginning it left me feeling cold; even the setup stole sensuality from foreplay. It was more like cooking than sex:

> Step 1: Attach the tension system to the base of the cylinder by pressing firmly. Step 2: Apply a dime-size amount of personal lubricant on the index finger and apply to the glans head of the penis. Apply the excess lubricant to the opening of the tension system. Step 3: Gently rest the tip of the penis in the opening of the tension system. Step 4: Move the sleeve up and down the cylinder to create a vacuum; this will draw the penis through the tension system into the cylinder. Step 5: After creating the erection, remove the cylinder from the tension system, leaving the tension system in place at the base of the penis.

I suppose I should admit that it did have some effect. It gave him a semi-erection, but nothing to write home about, and it deflated pretty quickly. But what really got to me was that the vacuum brought all the veins to the surface—one capillary bled—and the thing looked a hideous, beetroot red (I'm sorry if reading this is making you gag). I can't cope with blood and veins at the best of times and I even feel faint watching a blood test. So when the vacuum pump made Fred look like an angry old man with varicose veins, the last thing I felt was horny.

A couple of times in later weeks, Shane tried to encourage me to have another attempt, blackmailing me into trying to get some value out of the $230 we spent. But if he wants to use that machine he's going to have to do it with someone else!

Shane

Swee Ling had given me a prescription for the famous "little, blue pill." We were under strict instructions, given that Viagra affects blood circulation and interferes with the medication usually administered in the life-threatening event of autonomic dysreflexia. Those instructions suggested we start with the minimum dosage (25 mg), and build up from there. But given my history, we decided to try the 50 mg tablets (another $70 for four pills). While there was nothing of the rigmarole that went with the pump, it at least required some preplanning—to pop the pill an hour or so before the main event to enable it to take effect. I had been reading about Viagra use by people with an SCI. The stories were encouraging, and I was hopeful.

Elly

We had decided this time to try things out in the chair. His carers had dressed him in tracksuit pants and I was able, with only a little difficulty, to pull them down enough to give us access. His chair arms fold back and out of the way, so once I removed his T-shirt, we were able to enjoy a skinny, face-to-face cuddle, and a lingering kiss of the type that had been far too irregular in recent years (it was Rachel McAdams and Ryan Gosling in The Notebook, kissing desperately in the rain after a long absence).

I was a little reluctant to make my way downstairs, with a niggling fear scratching its way into the back of my head, "what do we do if this doesn't work?" I was excited to see that the baking powder had some rising impact (and without the varicose effect), enough that we could have some success. This was a homecoming of sorts, and for a moment it was heavenly, but only for a moment—a half-hearted rise and then a sinking and a slinking away, as though he wanted to be somewhere else.

I sat for a while on his lap and tried to hold back tears. My heart was breaking, and I couldn't imagine what Shane was feeling and how he was coping. He seemed to be trying to stay upbeat, to focus attention on pleasuring me. He didn't seem to understand that his loss felt like mine; that at that moment I was as disabled as him.

Shane

It was months before we made any further attempts. One of the rehab goals that we had been encouraged to set by Emma from the Spinal Outreach Service was to open every door that offered the possibility of taking us on the journey of establishing a healthy and enjoyable sexual relationship. To that end, Emma provided us with resources and support, and she often asked me what progress we had made. There were still things we needed to try—higher dosages of Viagra, alternate medicines, sex therapists—and I appreciated Emma's concern and valued her input, but as the weeks and months ticked over, it got a little embarrassing to reply each time that we had achieved little; that we mostly avoided talking about sex and intimacy altogether. We slept in separate beds. Well—that had been forced upon us because I needed a hospital bed and a power-pumped, alternating air mattress to prevent pressure sores. But while our beds were pushed together, we stayed apart. No goodnight embracing. No lip-on-lip kissing. No flirtatious whispers. No cheeky public flashing. We lived together functionally. She functioned as a carer, and did so willingly and diligently. But we were not lovers.

I was desperately unhappy, and so arranged to see a psychologist. I had three sessions and gave it up. I knew the issues and I knew the next steps, and paying cash for the privilege of sharing just fueled my frustration. The problem wasn't deciding what to do, but having the grit to do it.

I was also coming to the conclusion that, while we should keep trying to resurrect Fred, we needed to redirect our expectations. I was starting to accept that my situation wasn't going to change, and to realize that my pleasure might be found vicariously in Elly, in the intoxication of her orgasm. But she wouldn't respond to me. I tried buying flowers and seeking out cuddles—not as bribery for sexual favors, but to show that I did love her, that there was more substance to this relationship then we were currently experiencing. Even so, every sexual invitation, subtle or direct, was pushed aside. She was too tired, too busy. She wasn't up to it now but would be right tomorrow. She enjoyed a kiss but wanted nothing more. And I couldn't force the issue. Any activity was dependent upon her. She couldn't be passive and have me stir up her passions, but needed to take the lead, to locate the accessories (oil, vibrator, et cetera), to adjust the chair, to do the undressing, to move our bodies into place. And because she didn't want to, I was helpless.

One moment in mid-February that is imprinted in my memory occurred while I was stuck in bed with another pressure sore, and I asked Elly to bring the massage oil and come for a cuddle. I was already naked in bed, and I could see the coldness in her expression as she looked at me. "What's wrong?" I said, "don't you think your nude man looks edible?"

I was joking, but she missed the humor. "To be honest, your body, with a catheter tube puncturing that hole in your belly, along with your spasmodic limbs, is just not sexy."

She was being honest and the truth needed to come out. But it hurt me deeply, and left me wondering if there was anywhere to go from here. Had we reached the point where sexual intimacy was over?

Elly

I felt pressured by Shane, and he didn't really understand the issue from my perspective. The problem wasn't really the way his body looked (he's still the best looking man I know) but the way it worked . . . or didn't work. The biggest issue was that all the responsibility fell on me and most of it was nothing more than work. Preparation replaced foreplay, and when everything was in place I then had the responsibility to get us both aroused. And the truth was that making love to him was like trying to get excited by an inanimate object—a statue. He sat or lay in whatever position I left him, virtually unmoving.

So then (again) he wanted to change focus, to concentrate on pleasing me. But that just created another form of pressure. I still had to do all the work, and then I was expected to have fun. But that wasn't easy because—and I hesitate to write this—he was no longer Casanova. Before the accident, as a lover he was a musician, but now his fingers are clunky on the keyboard. Although his right hand and fingers move, they do so awkwardly, and he has no feeling, so his caress is rough and uncomfortable.

Perhaps all this could be overcome. My biggest problem, though, was memory; every time we attempted to make love I remembered the delights of before, and the present was a wasteland by comparison. And when we finished, I would look in Shane's eyes, and he was just so sad. I felt like I was looking into his soul, and it seemed empty. And I wasn't sure if I could keep doing this to myself and to him.

Shane

Twenty twelve rolled on, and while we were making progress in other areas, sexually, we were stuck. It wasn't until spring that we decided we had to try again. Over the autumn and winter I had allowed myself to fall into a stupor of self-pity, and blamed Elly for her unwillingness to let go of the past. But this judgment was unfair, underplaying her loss and overstating my commitment. I also tried to take my eyes off myself (this accident has increased my narcissism) and pay attention to Elly, to her care for me, her tender support. I wasn't always successful, but I tried to change my perspective. When I looked back I started to see not what only we had lost, but also the deep reservoir of two decades of love. That was something worth fighting for.

It was time, we realized, to lay aside the pressure of sex and orgasm and take hold of a broader concept of intimacy. We made a point of snatching moments of intimacy during the day; we took the opportunity to hold hands, to talk together before going to sleep, to steal a peck on the cheek, neck or forehead, to give each other compliments and express love. When the opportunity arose, we enjoyed skin-to-skin contact, long cuddles, and slow, gentle, heartfelt kissing.

But we also knew that we had not yet exhausted all of the potential miracles of modern medicine. I tried more pills. The maximum dose of Viagra (100 mg) elicited in Fred a lukewarm response—wobbly and short-lived. Alas, the same for Cialis, following dosages of 10 mg and later the maximum 20 mg.

The final option was Caverject, which required an injection. The drug works similarly to Viagra, but its targeted delivery is said to increase the chances of success. This was a procedure that we had left till last, knowing that sticking a needle in Fred was unlikely to inspire Elly. But in November 2012, with all other options exhausted, I decided the way forward was to take my carer, Kristy, to outpatients to learn how to give the injection. Then, with training in place, it was in early December that we took the plunge.

It was preceded by something of a surreal conversation,

"Kristy, I am going to have sex this morning, can you stick a needle in my penis?"

"Yes, please," she replied, laughing (like most nurses I know, she gets a sadistic joy in giving needles, and the location of this one was going to be especially interesting).

I was stupidly nervous watching her prepare the needle, but felt nothing when it was injected, as per the instructions, "into the spongy tissue on the side of the penis."

We waited, and when the allotted time had passed, Elly joined me for a romantic cuddle that was meaningful, regardless of the outcome. And Fred? Diddlysquat.

More months went by, and then another year. We were in love, but we were rarely intimate. We realized we needed to try again. Swee Ling had suggested an appointment with a sex therapist, and so we arranged to attend the clinic at Royal North Hospital. Given our detailed history, this visit was going to be hands-on, seeing whether the experts could do better with the injection than we had done on our first attempt. On arrival, we were ushered into a sterile clinic, replete with white walls, floor, and roof, and a stainless steel sink. A delightfully friendly, buxom, redheaded clinical nurse, and a suited, greying doctor, met us and asked that we flesh out our situation. After fifteen minutes of "tell-all" conversation, I was asked to tip back my chair, whereupon my pants were pulled down, and the doctor and nurse had a look around. Without much ado, the doctor gave the injection (still a scary moment), and asked Elly to massage the area, both to spread the drug and inspire Fred. As her reddening face made clear, it was a mortifying task in front of the nurse and doctor—on the opposite end of the scale of sexy. I didn't know whether to laugh or to scream. There I was, in a room with three people looking on as I received a hand job to see if I'd go hard! It was the least erotic scene ever observed.

There was a modicum of success, but not enough to write home about, so the doctor decided to add some vibration, using a machine that sound like an electric drill. The combination had some effect, at least enough for the doctor to call time on the show. Whether it would work in real life was yet to be seen. Truth be told, Elly and I were just pleased to get out of the room. Life truly is absurd, and all you can do is laugh.

So, did it work at home? On a scale of one to ten, I'd give it a technical five, a comedic seven, and a romantic two. It's not a process that one is going to be driven to experience daily, weekly, or even every month. It contains nothing of the addictive potency of pre-injury sex. But it does enable an intimacy that can be appreciated every now and then, and so instills hope. And hope has encouraged a renewed closeness, physical and psychological.

Elly

Yes, we are not without hope. We are beginning to learn that memory does not need to be an enemy. It can make a monster of the loss, but it can also encourage everyday intimacies that are too easily forgotten, and enrich experiences that might otherwise seem bleak. Who knows what the future might hold for Fred, but Shane and I will learn to grow in our love and to appreciate whatever enjoyment our bodies will allow us.

We are kissing more frequently, and cuddling more naturally, and re-kindling intimacy and love. Sex isn't what it was or what we pray it might be. But we have each other, and we're in love, and that's more than many people can claim.

[Editorial comment: I have wrestled with whether or not I should include this chapter in the memoir. I worry that it leaves Elly and I too exposed, that it provides unnecessary detail, that it indicates a perverse exhibitionism, that it encourages voyeurism, and that it speaks against the sexual potency of others with a similar injury. This latter concern is important to me, because I know that people with an SCI can be extraordinary partners and talented lovers, since their injury encourages them to focus on their partner's pleasure. The challenges Elly and I have faced are ours and ours alone, and shouldn't be assumed to be indicative of anybody else.

In reading this chapter again, I'm finding myself asking why sexual adjustment has been so difficult for us; in particular, why we allowed so many months (and years) to pass between our attempts at lovemaking. I have no ready answer to this question, other than to say that accepting sexual loss and embracing new sexual strategies is the most difficult part of adjusting to an SCI. While I'm sure that many people have coped better with this transition than we have, at least our commitment to each other remains strong. The ecstasy of orgasm is glorious, and I miss it desperately, but it's also true that its pleasure fades quickly (or so I console myself—please don't tell me if I'm wrong). A deeper and longer lasting happiness is found in the type of committed love that stands its ground "in sickness and in health," with or without orgasm. When I'm feeling down, I need to remind myself that Elly and I are fortunate to have such a love.]

CHAPTER 9

Going with the Flow

I know what it is to live with loss and sadness, but as time passes I am learning how to be happy, or at least content. In reality, most of my days are as mundane as anyone's. I work part-time, and the rest is spent dealing with the effects of my injury. The challenge has been to find joy and meaning in the humdrum of life. In the depths of my unhappiness, it was the experience of others with an injury similar to my own that first suggested the possibility that quadriplegics could live "the good life."

May 11, 2012
Shane Clifton Journal

I met John and Pam Trefry while I was in hospital, almost a year ago now. John has been a quad for more than five decades and was recovering in POW after a car crash; a motorist had run into their accessible van while John was in his chair, strapped in the back. The accident had left him bruised and battered, although he managed to remain upbeat. He was a storyteller, with a lifetime worth of experience in the chair. Indeed, his positive attitude made it clear that he had more than simply survived with SCI, but over the course of decades he had flourished.

I thought of him often in the months after I departed from hospital, reckoning that I could learn something from his experiences. In the midst of my struggles, I needed an injection of hope, and John's story offered precisely that: a real life example of a quadriplegic who had lived a happy and full life. I decided to try and track him down. It was no easy task, since he wasn't listed in the phone book, and privacy laws made the hospital reluctant to help out. Eventually, I found a nurse willing to contact John on my behalf, after which we arranged to meet at his house at Sylvania Waters.

With my work colleague Andrew Youd as driver and cameraman, we made our way past the canals and two-story, double garage displays of middle-class wealth to the Trefry's home, which stood out as one of the few modest houses in the area; a modest, square, red brick home, with none of the shallow flashiness of its neighbors. When we arrived, John and Pam were seated on the front yard, soaking in the sunshine, and as Andrew lowered the hoist to get me out of the car, Pam yelled out,

"Good thing you arrived with a disabled person. I don't have much time for so-called 'normal' people."

It was a brusque and typically Aussie introduction, but it was well meant and welcoming. As we made our way over to the house, Pam noticed that my catheter bag was full and hurried off to get a bucket. It's the sort of no-nonsense generosity that sums up her character. Later, I learned that she was seventy years old, but it was hard to believe. She is a willowy redhead with the sort of height that gets taller and thinner in memory, and with energy that says she has decades of life in her yet. John, in comparison, looked his age, but after fifty years living with quadriplegia he had every right to do so. He wore a buttoned-up shirt, long pants, and woollen ugg boots—in defiance of the sunny, spring day—and was comfortably hunched into what looked like a new electric wheelchair with his elbows resting on his lap table, his wrists hanging loose, and his fingers curled over. It was a familiar scene, the hunger for the warmth and the sun, his posture, and his twisted hands. John was an aged version of me, and looking at him with his generous and welcoming smile made me feel like I was with family.

For the next four hours, I asked questions and John told his story. It's impossible to do it justice in this journal, but I can note a few highlights:

On April 2, 1959, at eighteen years of age, John was a passenger in a motor vehicle accident that caused him to break his fifth and sixth cervical vertebrae (C6 quadriplegic, complete). He was to spend seven months in hospital, five of those in traction, a treatment he describes as torture. At that time, quadriplegia was considered terminal, or at the least completely debilitating, so throughout his hospital stay he was given very little help in the way of physiotherapy or occupational therapy, and almost no preparation for any level of independent living. Nothing was said about the possibility of preparing for work. He was disabled, in every physical and social sense of the word.

Upon discharge, he was sent to Weemala Nursing Home in Ryde. The home had been established in 1899 to accommodate patients discharged from hospital without alternate residence, and its entryway still proudly bore the tagline, "Home for the Incurables." Given limited staff, John was rarely placed in a chair and spent almost all the time lying flat on the bed, staring at the ceiling. His most vivid recollection of his time in the home was a question he once asked the matron:

"How long am I going to be in here?"

She replied, "When you come in here son, you don't come to get better. You slowly get worse and die."

John's family eventually helped him escape, and he was given a place in the newly formed spinal rehab unit in Prince Alfred Hospital, where he was able to learn the skills needed for living with SCI. The best teachers, he said, were other injured mates. During his stay, he fell in love with one of his nurses, Pam, and they married in 1963. I asked Pam about the transition from nurse to lover; about whether she was worried about marrying a person who would need lifelong care. She responded,

"I didn't even think about it. I fell in love, and that was that."

In 1964, in the context of widespread prejudicial employment practices, John got a job with the newly formed Paraplegics Association (later renamed ParaQuad). In the early days, the tasks he performed were relatively menial. John recalls sorting buttons, removing those with split eyes from the remainder; another time they removed rusty knobs from batteries; and again they sorted bottle tops. While such work seems tedious, John enjoyed himself. He was working out what he was capable of and developing his skills. He had to determine how to perform jobs with limited function and this required planning and inventiveness. When he was not working he was ordinarily treated like an invalid, incapable of doing anything for himself, but the work gave him the opportunity to contribute to something bigger than himself. Early on, John earned about two dollars a day, which wasn't much more than the cost of the transport to get to and from work, but money wasn't the point.

In the years that followed, John took on different roles and expanded his skills. He wanted to learn to drive, so imported hand controls were fitted to his key car. His wife helped him transfer into the driver's seat, and a friend from work would help him at the other end. Thereafter, ParaQuad added an engineering arm to its offerings, managed by John, who could pass on his love for driving to other people with SCI. Later on, John joined the sales team, answering phones and assisting his fellow injured to purchase various products vital to their care. Altogether John ended up working at ParaQuad for forty years before retiring.

Of course, John's life involves much more than work. Together, he and Pam built a house, adopted two children, Richard and Michelle, and are now grandparents. Their marriage has lasted fifty years and counting.

That's John's story in a nutshell, but what's its relevance to me? Naturally, a person's story is their own, and any straightforward identification—"John did that, so I can also"—is pointless. But spending time with John has reminded me that SCI is not the end of life, but merely the beginning of another chapter. His rich story has challenged me to stop focusing on the past, and instead to be hopeful and look to the future; to see what is possible rather than fixate on what I've lost.

More than anything, it's hope that I've lost in recent months. I've long known that hopefulness is the key to moving forward in hard times, but hope isn't something that can be manufactured. It's a gift; and you need to receive it from others. I've known hope through the gift of faith, and this has stuck with me through the worst of times. John's story, however, adds a concrete basis to my hope, and I'm grateful for the time he gave me.

[Editorial note: John passed away on August 14, 2013. I was thankful that I had recorded his story while it was still possible to do so.]

May 31, 2012 (Thursday)

Shane Clifton Journal: Virtue, Positive Psychology, and Happiness

It's been just over a year since I was discharged from hospital, and during this time I've been unhappy and increasingly depressed. I have been seeing a psychologist, although I'm not sure it's helping. What has been of greater value is putting the one part of my body that still works—the brain—to the task of thinking about happiness; about what the term means and how it might be found. This has led me to explore the philosophical tradition of happiness and virtue, which had its origins in Aristotle (fourth century BC), was taken up by Thomas Aquinas (thirteenth century), and again by contemporary ethicists, such as Alasdair MacIntyre (recall my reading of MacIntyre's *Dependent Rational Animals* in the weeks leading up to my accident—see October 6, 2010). I have also explored the scientific studies of Martin Seligman and the School of Positive Psychology. With all this reading in my head, I have today finished drafting a journal article, "Happiness and Spinal-Cord Injury: A Journey through Traditions of Virtue to Positive Psychology."

Now, I ask you, what sort of a nutcase writes a 10,000-word research paper because they are unhappy?

By way of summary, there are at least three dimensions of happiness: pleasure, gratification, and meaning.

Happiness as Pleasure

From Aristotle through to Seligman, the key insight is that happiness is not principally connected to positive feelings—ecstasy, delight, excitement, amusement, and the like. This is because these are transient—here one minute, gone the next, and easily forgotten. As I well know, they are also out of our control, dictated by circumstances. They also are subject to habituation. The thing that makes us excited today is ho-hum tomorrow, so we need to ramp up our activities in the pursuit of pleasure by going faster, increasing dosages, taking more risks. This is sometimes described as the hedonistic paradox. The pursuit of pleasure as an end-in-itself leads inexorably to boredom. Ultimately, then, pursuing happiness through positive emotions is a dead-end street.

On the face of it, this is good news for me. Part of the torment of SCI is that it takes away many of the things that give delight and excitement. So, conceiving of happiness as transcending the transitory causes of euphoria suggests that I can be happy, even if I can no longer surf, play golf, or orgasm.

Does this mean that all these things and the positive feelings they gave me are unimportant? Not necessarily. Research has shown that positive emotions build personal resources that enable a person to succeed in more meaningful activities. Apparently, temporary emotional happiness encourages our creativity and flexibility, increases stamina, motivates perseverance, and enhances our social skills, all of which contributes to our ability to succeed in other areas of life. Obviously, negative emotions have the opposite effect. Unhappiness can be like a virus that spreads to every part of our life. So, while a life oriented primarily to the pursuit of pleasure (hedonism) is self-defeating, we still need to find ways to have fun!

They say that "savoring" is the key to avoiding the hedonistic paradox and sustaining pleasure. For me, this might involve taking my time to enjoy a meal, or quaff a dram of expensive single malt whiskey. There's nothing like single-malt Lagavulin, sixteen-year-old scotch to warm the heart.

Happiness as Gratification

Beyond mere pleasure is gratification. The virtue tradition talks about a happiness that transcends the moment and is earned over the course of life. Indeed, the term "happiness" is misleading and might better be called "well-being" or "flourishing." Our well-being is connected to the gratification or satisfaction we experience from applying ourselves to activities that we consider valuable—by working hard and making progress in our work, study, art, sport, and the like.

To earn this gratification, we need to exercise virtue. Virtues are habits of character (patience, generosity, courage, and the like), and while there are lists of virtues—some of which might be considered universal and others culturally constructed (even some that are of special importance to people with SCI)—it is necessary for a person to work on themselves, both to learn virtue and to embed the habits that are the grounds of success.

So what has this got to do with me? In the first place, my research and writing on happiness is itself gratifying, as is my academic vocation. Although I struggle to admit it, I should be grateful because my passion for study, writing, and teaching isn't destroyed by my injury—a rare blessing for people with an SCI. In fact, my disability has the potential to focus and motivate my scholarship. In terms of my journal, it is difficult to describe this type of happiness. It often involves the grind of "hard work," which may be gratifying to experience (I like what I do), but tedious to describe. I have spent countless hours (days, nights, and weekends) writing my journal and reading philosophical and scientific literature, but what can I say about any of that time?

Disability itself provides an avenue for exercising the virtues. I need to learn patience to deal with the slower pace of life; fortitude to rise above pain; courage to face the day with the risk of bladder, bowel, and other complications; thankfulness to encourage the many people who help me out; and generosity to contribute what I can to others. Not that I'm especially virtuous—as this journal can attest. But if virtue is its own reward, then I can take some joy from making a go of life with the challenge of my rickety body.

Happiness as Meaning

Finally, the virtue tradition recognizes that pleasant experiences and the activities that provide gratification only enable us to achieve full happiness if we can direct our lives to a larger meaning and purpose. As Martin Seligman notes, "just as the good life is beyond the pleasant life, the meaningful life is beyond the good life."

For me, there are at least two primary meanings to life. The first is faith, which is trust in God (and in others), and which gives life perspective. It sustains hope and helps me to know that I'm part of something bigger than myself—that the limitations of my broken body don't define me. The second is the love of family and friends. A happy life is ultimately about sharing laughter and tears, memory and regret, success and failure, survival and loss. A flourishing life is grounded in deep and sustaining love.

The research and writing that has gone toward the creation of my journal article has been cathartic and gratifying. But it's one thing to construct a theory of happiness, and another thing altogether to be happy. I hope to realize and embody some of these insights, but I am not there yet.

June 8, 2012 (Friday)
Shane Clifton Blog: Cold Call Healing

I was fast asleep on the train on the way home from POW hospital Wednesday, when I was woken by a gentleman offering me a brochure for "Padstow Healing Rooms" and inviting me to a Thursday evening healing service.

My initial thought was to offer him a phone number for Weight Watchers. He could, after all, benefit from their services, and presumably he would be happy for strangers to offer him weight-loss advice.

I resisted the temptation and accepted his card. Later, when I recounted the event to Elly, she didn't understand my aggravation, and to be honest I'm not sure I did either. Was it the approach itself; the out-of-the-blue offer of prayer, which felt a little like a Saturday morning knock on the door by a Jehovah's Witness? Or was it that I just don't like being "that poor man in a chair who needs pity and prayer?" Of course, at one level I am pitiable, and I do need prayer, but aren't we all and don't we all? What I want is to be treated the same as any other person. If I'm asleep on the train, leave me to rest; if I have my head in a book, leave me to read; and if I seem to be open to conversation, then chat away. No topic is off-limits (well, almost none). Talk about the chair and the body by all means—they are a big part of my life. But strangers on a train shouldn't launch straight in with an offer of a miracle. They just don't know enough about me to presume they have the answer to my problem.

July 6, 2012 (Friday)

Shane Clifton Journal

I received the following comment as a reply to my blog post of June eighth:

Hi Shane, I was just checking the Internet and found your comments. It's me, the guy who gave you the card. I am sorry for making you angry and feel any less than "normal." Yes, I am 20 kg overweight, have been battling with it for years; and you are right, why don't I give the cards out to others? I guess you were an easy target. I thought to myself, if I am involved in a healing ministry and just walk away without giving you a card, then where is my faith? I felt God's love for you as any other person. I don't have the courage to go up to most people, and that was new for me. I guess I cared enough to give you a card, and I wasn't judging you; and yes, we don't have a relationship, but I'm willing to make a start. I am not full-of-myself, nor claim to have all the answers, but believe Jesus can heal and just want to help. We have had many incredible healings, but have also had people not healed and die. I don't have all the answers but was just being obedient. Anyway, my name is Harry, and if you do want to come in one Thursday night, it is a safe, gentle place; we are not psyched-up freaks. Thanks for your honesty. I also have a disabled son with autism and he has had degrees of healing, but not yet 100 percent, so I understand pain a little.

Cheers mate, Harry.

Well, that's left me feeling a little sheepish. Lesson in life: be careful what you say on the Internet. You never know who might be reading.

July 7, 2012 (Saturday)

Elly Clifton Journal

I've long thought that Shane is far too cavalier in his chair, but he always ignores my warnings. He screeches around corners, races through shopping centers, and seems to prefer the verge of the road to riding on the footpath. He paid the price today, however.

We were watching Lochie play soccer and Shane needed to empty his leg bag. We were outside and the grass would do, but he figured that at least a modicum of discretion was needed, so he drove up a hill near where we were seated and emptied the bag behind a light post. That done, he discovered the slope was too steep to allow any forward progress, so instead he backed the chair down the slope. It looked like he'd made it, but near the bottom he bumped against the concrete footpath, where the wheels of his chair stuck fast while the momentum of his downhill journey tipped the chair over.

I saw the whole thing happening in what felt like slow motion, but I was too far away to do anything about it. In a panic, I ran over; only to find him laughing, seemingly unhurt. With the help of the nearby soccer Dads, it was surprisingly easy to get him upright. Nothing on the body or chair was broken, and I can only hope that this incident will give him some reason for caution.

When I suggested as much to him, he said:

"If you want to live, you've got to risk."

True, but surely a little practical wisdom wouldn't go astray?

July 23, 2012 (Monday)

Shane Clifton Blog: A Day's Work

It was still dark and felt like midnight when Kristy came in, purred into my ear (she has this weird thing for cats), removed my snorkel, and ripped off the covers with a wickedly excited smile,

"Wakey, wakey."

"Ahh, what the flamingos are you doing? Which idiot said you should get here at this time in the morning?" I shouted in a whisper; it was six thirty a.m. and Elly was trying to sleep in the bed next to mine, so I needed to complain as quietly as possible.

"The idiot quadriplegic," she replied smugly. Kristy is absurdly tiny (she insists on dieting when her weight climbs to 46 kg), especially when you consider that her job is to move my 194 cm, 99 kg frame about. She currently wears her hair black (although I have seen pictures of her as a bottle-blonde) and likes to hide her HDS (height deficiency syndrome) by way of misdirection, wearing tight shirts that cause you to concentrate on her other assets. She is an effervescent personality and brings a mad joy to this otherwise tedious morning routine.

It still took two hours, but when done I headed off to the train station, rolling down Oxford Road in the cold, winter rain. On days like this, Elly would normally give me a ride to the station, but she wasn't feeling well and I didn't want to wake her. I had been tempted to take the day off since I knew that the college would understand and that no one was forcing my hand. But I enjoy work, both the responsibility and the hanging out with friends. Besides, I know that if I don't treat life as an adventure, then I won't live. So I forced myself to head outside into the rain, dressed up in my pink and yellow raincoats, with one covering my head and torso and the other my knees and feet. When dressed like this, I paint an absurd picture:

> I looked like a pink and yellow marshmallow; like a kindergartener on their way to school; like a little girl who, against her mother's wishes, selected her own outfit; like a peach and a banana growing old in a bowl of fruit. (Blog: shaneclifton.com)

It took about fifteen minutes to get to the station, and by that time I was a little sorry for myself, wishing I'd stayed at home. Halfway down the hill, the raincoat had come off my legs, and since I couldn't fix the problem I got wet. Of course, it was only water, and after warming and drying on the train I made it to work without further incident.

At work my disability is rendered irrelevant—I'm a theologian and not a quadriplegic—except for one small incident. A secretary made me a cafe latte in a glass cup, and while I'm normally smart enough to ask for plastic or paper, today I wasn't thinking. I picked up the glass, and though I couldn't feel it, my skin was obviously burning. The result was spasming fingers and spilt coffee. Fortunately, most of the hot liquid landed on my lap tray, so no real harm was done.

For lunch, the college had arranged a Christmas in July celebration. The meal was a feast; honey and mustard glazed ham, baked salmon, roast vegetables, pear and walnut salad, and individual plum puddings for dessert. We ate in the college dining room, with its big glass doors looking over the courtyard and a hubbub of voices pierced with bursts of laughter filling the enclosed space. It was succulent and deafeningly enjoyable.

It had stopped raining by the time I went home in the early afternoon. As always, I tipped back my chair to rest on the train, and a mother accompanying two children looked at me jealously. "Would you like to swap places?" she said. Laughing, I answered, "willingly." It had been a big day, and it wasn't long before I was asleep. When we arrived in Ingleburn, I was still out cold and the guard had to wake me. As I drove groggily back up the hill, I remembered my morning trek and was thankful I'd decided to head out in the rain.

July 24, 2012 (Tuesday)
Elly Clifton Journal

Forty-two years old today, but I feel fifty. I'm tired and worn out, like a badly used packhorse aged before its time. I shouldn't complain today, since the boys brought me breakfast in bed and spoiled me with presents; a ruby ring from Shane, a scarf and chocolates from Jacob and Lochie, a voucher for a pedicure from Jeremy and Kate (Jeremy's girlfriend). Even so, my role as a taxi driver continued, taking one to an excursion and the other to soccer training. And I'm just not sure what or how to celebrate.

Lately, Shane's been banging on about happiness. He seems to think that he's turned a corner and he has a new hope for the future. I just can't see it. Nothing seems to be getting any easier. There is so much that I miss; late night dates, holidays—overseas and local (that we just can't afford), walking on the beach holding hands, pride at the sight of my fit, hunky man with a surfboard, spooning in a shared bed, Saturday morning sex, naughty weekends away, two person baths, a helping hand in the yard, spontaneous decisions, sharing the cooking, Shane's laughter, driving something other than a bus, Shane driving (or sitting in the front passenger seat), the top down in our convertible, a private bedroom without carers, watching Shane wrestle the boys, listening to him playing guitar, impromptu dances in the kitchen, our old home and neighborhood, being given a champagne when I'm watering the garden, back massages, sleeping naked (and Shane doing a nude midnight dash when the kids had forgotten to put out the bins) . . .

I've got to stop this. It's not healthy.

July 29, 2012 (Saturday)

Shane Clifton Journal

Stephen, Greg, and I spent the afternoon tasting single malt at World of Whiskey in Double Bay—the decadence of the activity appropriate to the exclusivity of the suburb. Elly, in a sad and sacrilegious concession to her lack of class, left us to ourselves, complaining, "it's flavorless swill that burns the throat; horrible."

I arrived a few minutes after the intended start time, but a place had been kept for me and the tasting had not begun. The shop itself was glass fronted, with a pure white interior and rows of lighted shelves accenting the neatly aligned Scotch bottles, revealing the endless nuance of color that is one part of the mystery of the brew. Taken altogether, the shop is a temple to the "nectar of the gods," the displays acting as the stained glass window that promises an encounter with the sublime.

Our host, David was a surprisingly young man, tall and blonde, with a broad Australian accent that seemed incongruous with the erudition with which he attacked his topic. He began by describing the process of making malt whiskey, which is initiated by the fermenting of malted barley to produce a distillers' beer with an alcohol content of about 5 to 10 percent. The beer is then distilled (normally twice), using a glass kettle to boil the brew and extract the steamed alcohol (spirit), which is then watered down to a strength of about 60 to 65 percent and placed into oak casks for maturation. All whiskeys share this basic process, with a number of elements contributing to the variety and nuance of flavors: distillation and the resulting character of the spirit; the source of water used to mix with the spirit, as well as the climate of the region; the history of the cask (normally, second-hand casks are used, having originally stored sherry or bourbon—a key element of flavor); and finally, the period of maturation.

Does knowing about this process contribute anything to the pleasure of the drinking? Obviously, the brew is the same whether or not you know its provenance, but does it taste the same? Taste is not merely a product of swallowing, but also of conscious attention. To truly savor what we eat or drink, we need to think about it. Assessing flavor is a product of both discernment and comparison, and this is where knowing about provenance helps. We can say, for example, that this scotch has a heavily peated flavor, similar to other whiskeys in the Islay region, brewed in this particular way. The unique and comparative data on the process and location of making the whiskey thus frames our capacity to appreciate its flavor, and taste its shades of character.

If that description sounds like pompous nonsense, of course it is!

In any event, we eventually got down to the tasting. For me, there were two "winners." The first was the Ardbeg ten-year-old, a pale gold whiskey with a smoky nose (David suggested smoked fish, which didn't sit well with me); initially sweet on the palate, but growing into a smooth peaty flavor as it sits on the tongue, with a smoky and long-lasting finish. It is a drink that reminds you of long winter evenings with friends, telling ghost stories around an open fire. The second was a sixteen-year-old Lagavulin. A darker, amber color, its flavor is a sensuous, inviting smokiness with a hint of the sea (this is suggested by David, and I think I know what he means). It has a luscious, smooth peat palate, and a finish that caresses and warms the mouth and throat. It is a drink that evokes reverence; that causes you to close your eyes and realize that there is, after all, true beauty in the world. It was Galileo who is supposed to have said that "wine is sunlight held together by water," but that is only because he had not yet quaffed a Lagavulin.

Again, if that description sounds like pompous nonsense, of course it is!

With our souls pleasantly warmed and expanded by six shots of whiskey, the three of us went out from the tasting and spent an hour discussing philosophy. We dutifully solved the problem of the meaning of life although, for some odd reason, I can't remember our conclusion.

It was a delightful afternoon, one that wasn't spoiled by what turned out to be a long and wet trip home, the result of an afternoon thunderstorm and having to watch three different buses that didn't have wheelchair access pass by my stop.

August 1, 2012

Shane Clifton Journal: SCI and Work

I spent my afternoon in the city, having been invited to join the In-Voc steering committee, established to trial the benefits of early intervention vocational training for people with SCI. While most people have a job before their injury, only about 35 percent return to work afterwards. This has drastic consequences, not only because the disability pension is a poverty-level wage, but also since vocation is an important contributor to happiness.

Involvement in the committee is a reminder that I am fortunate to have been able to return to work; many are not so lucky. It's also helped me to see that I can put my leadership and board experience to use. And I've also written a paper, "Spinal Cord Injury and the Joy of Work," which has been accepted in the Scandinavian Journal of Disability Research. This is satisfying, and provides seeds of hope for the future. By way of a teaser, I've copied out the introduction below:

> The relationship between work and happiness has always been ambiguous. We spend most of our lives either preparing for work or being at work, and so it is an activity that comes to frame our identity. Often, we begrudge the amount of time we are forced to give to our jobs, which can be stressful or tedious, exhausting or boring, too complex or meaningless, or all these things at once. The workplace is nearly always political, and we are never paid enough for what we give or for what we put up with. But where would we be without work? The civil rights movement and feminists have understood the significance of work, of equal access and equal pay. The central place that work holds in our lives is not merely tied to the (false) assertion that money brings happiness, although we do need to earn enough to pay for necessities and the small pleasures of modern life. More substantive, however, is the meaning that work provides. Happiness transcends the ups and downs of day-to-day life in the marketplace and is built upon the story of a life; a narrative made up not only of family and friendship, but also of our contribution to the world. Whether our labour is paid or voluntary, that contribution is generally accomplished in and through our work.
>
> What, then, of those who cannot work or, at least, tend not to? This paper examines the contribution of work to the well-being of people with a spinal cord injury (SCI). It is exploratory in nature, seeking points of convergence between empirical socio-scientific studies, the virtue tradition (with its insight into dependency), and the conclusions of positive psychology. This unusual conflation requires some explanation before we come to the heart of the argument being made—which is that the "happiness" of people with spinal-cord injury is connected to their work and to the virtues (especially virtues of dependency and independency) that frame personal well-being and success.

August 24, 2012 (Friday)

Shane Clifton Journal

Once a month, a community nurse changes my catheter. It's a simple enough procedure, yet it's oddly exciting to watch—I must have masochistic tendencies! It involves a tube being taken out of a hole in my belly (actually, below the belly, above the pubic bone), and another inserted. More than a year after its original insertion, the wound has not yet healed, so as I watch I know that it should be horribly painful, but also that I won't feel it, and it's the war between both thoughts that makes the experience oddly exciting.

You have to get your kicks where you can.

Elly was out and about this afternoon and I was home alone, when a package was delivered, addressed to Jeremy. Since he is almost never around anymore (girlfriend and other excuses), I sent him a text:

"A package has just arrived for you, mate."

"Cool, what is it?"

"I've no idea."

"Open it then."

"I can't. You'll have to wait till Mum comes home."

"Okeydokey. You're useless!"

It's gratifying to discover that I've raised compassionate and well-mannered kids.

September 12, 2012 (Wednesday)

Shane Clifton Journal

Almost every week for more than a year, I've traveled the two-hour journey from home to POW to work with my physiotherapist, Fernanda, with the sole goal of learning to transfer. It's been a long, hard slog, and my accomplishments have been measured in centimeters rather than leaps and bounds. As each week went past, I felt like I'd accomplished little, and given the repetitive nature of the therapy, I almost never bothered to journal my experience. Looking backwards, though, I do have reason to be proud.

As I mentioned earlier in this journal, in the first few weeks I managed to get my fat bum in the air. Thereafter, Fernanda punished my success by making me repeat the task again and again, with the goal of getting me to lift it higher and build stamina. Our sessions lasted an hour, and I left smashed every time.

With stage one accomplished, the second task was to slide sideways. To do this, I had to lift my bum and swing my head opposite to the direction I wanted to travel, which enabled me to inch my way across the plinth.

In stage three, a slide board was forced under my bum, and the lift and slide were directed from the plinth to the chair. To slide across, I also needed to bring my legs with me, and I quickly discovered what my carers have always known; my legs are lead weights.

And so it went, week after week, with gradual improvements—up, slide, drag, and again, and again. Over the course of the year, I have managed to traverse from the plinth to the chair and back again. And so I could transfer! Well, sort of. I need help, with one person standing behind and another in front. And I've only ever managed to transfer on a level surface. I simply cannot budge if confronted with the smallest slope, and in the real world things are rarely horizontal.

Fernanda has been on holidays for the last three weeks, so I'd been allocated to Keira. Working with her again has been like spending time with a sister, but it's also been apparent to both of us that my progress has stagnated. At the end of the today's session, we realized there wasn't much purpose in making another appointment.

I left the hospital unsure whether to count myself a winner or failure. I had persevered and accomplished a task that seemed impossible only a year before. Yet I knew that a more determined person might have continued, might have pushed harder, might have spent the money and time on the Walk On program. But I've had enough. It feels like I have tried to climb Everest, reached the first base camp, and just don't have the goods to climb further. I'm still unable to ride in the front seat of a car, or slide onto the couch next to Elly. This final appointment has an ominous finality about it. It's a resignation, a capitulation to my fate. Without some spectacular intervention (and both Christians and scientists believe for miracles), my physical recovery and functional capacity has reached its limit.

Even so, as I said, I think I can be proud of what I did achieve and the effort I put in to make it happen. I've spent almost four hours in travel every week for more than a year, and pushed my weak muscles as hard as I could. I've learned how to do a transfer of sorts and, provided I have help, I'm sure this is going to prove useful in the future—at least to occasionally get me out of trouble.

I also sense that the closing of one door represents the opening of another. Rather than focus on yet more rehabilitation, I can now devote attention to things I'm good at and that I enjoy. If I'm honest, the overriding feeling I have is one of relief.

November 17, 2012 (Saturday)
Elly Clifton Journal

Shane and I went with the boys into the city today to watch a live performance of comedian Carl Barron at Sydney's State Theatre. We arrived with what we thought was plenty of time to spare, only to discover that the venue was undergoing renovations and the handicapped bathrooms were closed. With the help of an attendant, we were then taken through the construction zone to a second bathroom, which we discovered was too narrow to accommodate Shane's chair. It was then suggested that a handicapped bathroom was available at David Jones across the road, so we decided to send Shane on his own while I took the kids into the theatre to get our seats. Twenty minutes later he still hadn't turned up, and the theatre bells were ringing to warn that the doors were about to be closed. This set me up for a fight with the doorman.

"I just wanted to let you know that my husband is in a wheelchair and has had to use the disabled bathroom across the road. So when he returns, can you please let him in?"

"No, sorry, madam. When the show starts I'm not permitted to open the doors."

"I understand that. In this case, however, my husband is late because your disabled facilities weren't available, and it's now been almost twenty minutes and he's not returned." I said this calmly; confident reason would prevail.

"Sorry, madam. There's nothing I can do."

This left me incredulous. And mad.

"What? Don't you have the sense to realize that there are some situations when rules need to be bent? Or is it that you don't have the arm strength to open the door? My husband is late because your theatre isn't properly set up for wheelchairs. This is discrimination. Do I need to take this matter up with the ombudsman?"

There's nothing like the threat of discrimination to get your way, but before the doorman had the chance to reply, I saw Shane screeching in through the front door (10 km an hour can be pretty fast in tight spaces), and we made it inside as the doors were shutting. I was tense, and not really in the mood for stand-up comedy, but Barron had me laughing before too long. If you've never had a chance to see him perform, he's short and bald, and as the son of a sheep farmer from Longreach (inland Queensland), he has the broadest of Aussie accents. In the light of my recent incident, where I'm pretty sure the doorman was covered in my spit, his first joke seemed appropriate.

"Sometimes you're talkin' and a little bit of spit flies out. You see it floating in the sky and land on 'em. You both see it happen, and you're thinkin', 'Woops, I got him!' He's thinking, 'Woops, he got me!' But no one says anything. Because it's a secret. If his spit lands on me, I don't do anything. I don't wipe it straightaway because I don't wanna embarrass 'em. Hey, I've got his spit on my face, and I'm worried about his feelings. You go, 'sorry, Carl,' and I go, 'nah, nah, it's alright, I love being spat on.'"

The rest of the show was mostly boy humor, and to be honest, not my thing. The kids, however, were re-telling fart jokes when we left the theatre.

Jeremy: "I hate dates. I sit at home all day, and I don't fart once. I go on a date, and I've got twenty in the bank straight-away."

Lachlan: "Do you do those secret farts at the supermarket, and then quickly piss-off to another aisle?"

Jacob: "My Dad was proud of himself when he farted. He sounds like he's strangling a chicken when he farts."

The boys thought this was especially funny because Shane can't fart now. Presumably gas comes out of its own accord, but there's no pressure and no noise. At last, I discovered an advantage of SCI!

Afterwards, we spoiled ourselves with gelato, and then headed toward Town Hall Station for the train home. We were near the station and Shane wasn't concentrating on where he was going, when he almost lost his head traversing under a driveway boom-gate that he hadn't seen coming. I was a little worried, but Shane was unhurt. Jeremy laughed so hard that he almost threw up, and the boys teased their Dad and giggled most of the way home. This cheap entertainment seemed to have trumped Carl Barron.

November 23, 2012 (Friday)

Shane Clifton Journal

Today was pure joy; a sunny spring day spent in the city with Sheree Hurley. I have spoken previously of Sheree and her dog Jade in their role as peer support at POW. We have met up a few times since my leaving the hospital.

She is a great encouragement, and it's refreshing to spend time with someone who understands my day-to-day experiences. What I especially love about her company is her contentedness. She doesn't ignore or deny the difficulties of living with SCI, but neither does she let them keep her down. On the contrary, she leads a full and mostly happy life, and I find her sense of well-being contagious.

We met up at the Museum of Contemporary Art (MCA) at Circular Quay. The day was warm, but Sheree's crip-circulation and thin frame had her rugged up for winter, wearing a jumper and jacket, a purple scarf, and a woollen beret, out of which flowed her shoulder-length auburn-red hair. The MCA cafe is on the top of a modern-styled building, looking over the Quay to the Opera House, Harbour Bridge, and beyond. We ate on the balcony, which today was awash with sunlight. Friendship, conversation, sunshine, and food in such a location, along with a black Labrador that draws the attention of all and sundry—on days like this, life isn't half bad!

While conversation was the real reason for our get-together, the ostensible purpose was watching a film, *The Intouchables*. Sheree was a little reluctant, saying; "I haven't seen a film in years." I found this hard to fathom, but I promised that she would enjoy herself. The French, subtitled film tells the story of Philippe, a C3/4 quadriplegic with no movement from the neck down, and his carer, Driss, a poor, black, paroled migrant—each in his own way "untouchable," the former a pitiable paralytic, and the latter a despised African. The plot is a simple one. The wealthy Philippe hires Driss as a personal carer, even though he is patently unsuited to the task; an ex-con with no nursing skills and no understanding of SCI (is there anyone in the world who doesn't know that paralytics normally have no/little feeling and that, even so, it's a bad idea to pour scalding hot tea onto their legs?). He is hired on the sole basis that, from the very beginning, he responds to Philippe without pity, even without compassion. He jokes, teases, challenges, and questions Philippe in a refreshingly unselfconscious way, with no topic out of bounds (even quadriplegic erotica).

At one level, *The Intouchables* follows a predictable and stereotyped pattern. A wealthy, white man is brought together with a poor, black man, and cultures clash; the white man introduces high culture to the unsophisticated black man, the black man introduces funky dance and lawless joy to the stuck-up white man, and both are transformed. As is typical, it also ignores the obscenity of the white man's wealth in the face of the black man's poverty (and as I've noted elsewhere, without owning up to the fact that disability and poverty often go hand-in-hand). And yet, at another level—and this is what counts—the film is sheer delight. What it has going for it is a number of rich characters, as well as insight into the unique world of quadriplegia from the perspective of both the person with an SCI and his carer.

Obviously, the story resonates with the experiences of Sheree and I, and she left the cinema surprised to have actually enjoyed a movie. After coffee, we said our goodbyes and I thought about the fun that I've had today. I've spent so much time down in the dumps, and I wonder whether I have found one of the keys to pleasure: friends and film.

November 30, 2012 (Friday)
Shane Clifton Journal

I've spent a week in bed with a pressure mark, which I think I incurred during my day in the city last Friday.

Surprisingly, I'm not feeling too frustrated. There is a rhythm about these days in bed. Carers wake me and stare at my bum, looking for improvement.

"The mark is still there . . . not blanching."

"Bummer. It's your fault, you know."

"Why?"

"Because . . . I believe in shooting the messenger."

Even though it's against the advice of my doctors, I usually get up early and go to the bathroom (I just hate pooing in bed). I appreciate the time on the commode, since it affords me the opportunity to sit up and to look at the world from this more optimistic perspective. In far too short a time, I'm trapped back in bed and rolled onto my side to elevate my bum, and then the next ten hours are spent in rambled conversation with the voice recognition program on my computer, until blurry vision forces me to squint so tightly at the bright light of the screen that I call it a day.

In the evening, the carers return to tidy and deal with my mess. I exercise using therabands attached to my bed. Finally, my bottom is re-checked (anyone would think it was worth looking at), normally with the same script. But tonight,

"The mark is almost gone . . . pale, barely visible."

"Excellent, and well done. You fixed it."

As I lie here on what should be my last day in bed, looking back on the week I can honestly say it hasn't been too bad. I've had time to write, and I've enjoyed the opportunity. Perhaps "enjoy" is the wrong term. Being in bed for days on end is challenging—uncomfortable, tedious, restrictive. But perhaps I am learning to find contentment, to build myself a garden in the middle of the desert.

January 16, 2013 (Wednesday)

Shane Clifton Journal

Prior to my accident, our family had an annual booking (January 9–16) for a site at Lake Conjola Caravan Park. In the middle of the fabulous Australian summer holidays, the five of us would steal my parents' caravan and spend a week lazing about. The location is postcard-perfect, with the park nestled against a small hill to the south (offering protection from the occasional, southerly buster winds), alongside a tidal lake to the North (allowing the cooling northwest breeze—and intermittent gale—to moderate the summer heat), and a surf beach to the east. To top it all off, less than a kilometer away is the famous Green Island, home to a spectacular left-hand reef break that holds big swells and offers rambunctious, long-walled waves. We had managed to secure a site in a prime location next to the lake, and when you find such perfection, you never give it up. Consequently, each year we were joined by the same neighbor—the Kesbys, Beddoes, and Poppywells—and in this community atmosphere we lived the high life, playing all day and partying all night (well, till 9 p.m.), sharing cheese and biscuits, beer and champagne, and happily meaningless conversations.

The accident ended our annual pilgrimage, but the boys had started bugging us to return. It was certainly true that we needed an adventure, a break from the monotony of the routine of home, so we decided to book our usual dates in January, opting to rent what was billed as an accessible cabin for five. It was expensive; almost three times the price of a caravan site. But disability makes everything dear, so *c'est la vie.*

On the day of departure, Elly determined that she was going to have me ride upfront, both to mitigate car-sickness, and to include me in the fellowship of the journey—my usual spot in the back of the van meant that I couldn't hear the family chatter. The difficulty was that the Vito cabin sits higher than my chair—too high to enable the use of a slide board—so the transfer was accomplished by muscle-power. Elly, Jeremy, and Jacob lifted me out of the chair and shoved me up and into the front seat, while Lachlan and Kate (Jeremy's girlfriend is joining our holiday, so things must be getting serious) pulled me from inside the van. I'm a useless blob of jelly in these situations, but with a few grunts and groans, they managed to jostle me into position. And it certainly proved to be a much better journey for me.

As to the holiday itself, I don't see the point in writing a travelogue, since the purpose of a vacation is to do very little worth writing about. A few reflections will do. I should admit that I was reluctant about the arrangements for my care. Lake Conjola is in the middle of nowhere (halfway between Nowra and Ulladulla), so we were unable to arrange a nurse. Dad offered to take on the duty, and with some hesitation, I agreed. Aside from the fact that I didn't want to burden my parents, I can't really explain my reluctance. It just seemed weird to have Dad doing these intimate tasks. But the old man has some pluck, and everything worked out well.

The dingy and dilapidated cabin was situated the furthest possible distance from the lake (a marathon journey to the campsites of our friends and family), and it was tiny—among the smallest in the park. It purported to sleep five, but this included three prison-styled, vertical bunk beds, without any spare room for my equipment. Our troop of teenagers ended up deciding to bunk down in a tent on my parents' site. What got my blood boiling was that during the previous year, two spacious cabins had been built lakeside, but with eight steps on entrance, they were inaccessible for anyone in a wheelchair.

But enough whining—well, maybe a little one. It messed around with my head a little, being so near the surf and water, watching others have fun but being unable to join in. But it didn't make me as depressed as I thought it might, and I was at least able to enjoy the fun had by my boys; Jeremy all cuddly with Kate, and Jacob and Lachlan turning girls heads and swimming, wrestling, jumping, surfing, diving, skating, fishing, canoeing—all non-stop, breaking only for a quick bite to eat.

I spent a lot of my time basking in the sun and reading. I particularly loved the strange but oddly profound novel by John Irving, *A Prayer for Owen Meany*. A riveting, but quirky book, it tells the story of a disabled saint—Owen Meany—who accidentally kills his best friend's mother, and accurately predicts his own martyrdom. It's not only a stinging critique of the Vietnam War and the shallow pretensions of modern society, but more profoundly, it explores the meaning and fragility of life, and the mystery of providence for those who suffer. In the context of my own dealings with the past—and the challenge of transcending a loss that is made real in reminiscence—I was struck by its insight into memory:

> "Your memory is a monster; you forget—it doesn't. It simply files things away. It keeps things for you, or hides things from you—and summons them to your recall with a will of its own. You think you have a memory, but it has you!"

February 4, 2013 (Monday)

Shane Clifton Journal

I sent my two research papers on disability ("Happiness and Spinal-Cord Injury" and "The Joy of Work") to a number of academics with expertise in the field to see whether my research and reflection had value. I received feedback from Professor Gwynneth Llewellyn (Professor of Family and Disability Studies; Director, Australian Family and Disability Studies Research Collaboration; and Director, Centre for Disability Research and Policy, Faculty of Health Sciences, University of Sydney . . . Wow, quite a portfolio) and today she came to visit me in my office in Parramatta. It was a worthwhile visit, at least from my perspective; Gwynneth was generous, friendly, and encouraging. Not only has she suggested places to publish my work, but she has also encouraged me with the possibility of further research, suggesting potential grant opportunities.

It's sometimes said that bad things happen for a reason and although I'm not convinced—it seems to me that bad things just happen—it's certainly the case that most circumstances create potential opportunity. I'm discovering that my experience of SCI can coalesce with my academic skills so that I can research, write, and advocate for people with disabilities. To do this would at least invest my day-to-day struggles with purpose.

February 9, 2013 (Saturday)

Shane Clifton Journal

I have taken to watching people. Sometimes this is a circular exercise; I am watching people watching me, as they negotiate the best way to respond to my disability. Children are my favorite. Yesterday, I was perched at a cafe on Wollongong Beach, watching half-dressed beachgoers stroll along the footpath adjoining the beach, when two boys approached, obviously brothers,

"I'm four."

"That's a strange name" I replied. "I'm forty-two, but you can call me Shane."

"That's not my name," he said giggling, "I'm Tim and this is John and he's six." He took a breath and stared at my chair, " . . . Why are you in that?"

"I broke my neck. If you look closely, you can see my scar."

Leaning closer he took a good look at my neck, and the ensuing silence gave his brother the chance to interrupt.

"What does this do?" He said, looking at my wheelchair control panel.

"It does lots of things. For example, it tells me how fast I'm going. Would you like a race?"

He turned to glance at his parents, and they nodded their head, so the three of us lined up along a spacer in the concrete, and on John's shout, took off, heading for a sign twenty meters along the footpath. My chair is fast enough—it travels about 10 km an hour—but it is slow off the mark and no match for two energetic children. They were ecstatic with their victory, and so we raced again, but even my cheeky, false start didn't change the outcome. I offered them a chance to race sitting on my lap, but that was a step too far. Soon after, the food and coffee I had ordered arrived, so I took a break and the boys' parents urged them to give me some peace.

This didn't last long. After a few minutes, Tim stood before me, looking at my bent-up hands that were resting on my lap alongside a dinner tray and half-eaten lunch. He seemed to be psyching himself up to ask a profound question.

"Why have you got that spoon?" he asked seriously, pointing at the plastic teaspoon on my lap tray.

"I'm just lucky, I guess."

This stupendous question—which illustrates the beautiful simplicity of children (and their ability to accept disability as normal)—and my absurd answer left Elly falling over herself in laughter.

March 16, 2013 (Saturday)

Shane Clifton Journal

Elly and I spent the day with Jeremy (I've just discovered that he doesn't like to be called Jem, which makes me sad), along with his girlfriend, Kate, and her family. We were gathered to watch him skydive, with the intention of landing in the park alongside Wollongong Beach. His mother was nervous, but Jeremy seemed to have my attitude to such things—excitement without much fear. He landed safely (of course) and seemed to have a great time. I also enjoyed the spectacle, if not as much as the subsequent lunch at the cafe on Wollongong Beach (we are becoming regulars).

Last year, Kurt tried to organize to take me on the same jump, assuming that a tandem skydive would make that possible. Unfortunately (my wife thinks, fortunately) it proved a step too far, as we were told that no party is passive during the journey up and back down again. There is the need to climb onto a small airplane (without a hoist) and, with limited maneuverability inside, to be able to move toward the door in preparation for the jump. Once in the air, a skydiver needs to be able to control his limbs to direct the flight, and then when nearing the ground, to be able to hold his legs in a position appropriate for landing. Obviously, none of this is possible when your body is made of Jell-O.

I would have enjoyed parachuting, and it was one of those things I had intended to do "sometime" but never got around to. Even so, I wasn't shattered to learn that I couldn't do the jump, and nor did I find myself jealous of Jeremy's opportunity. This insight hit me in the middle of his fall. I couldn't yet see any parachutes, so we were staring at the sky, and I was visualizing what it would be like; the nervous anticipation, the thrill of the jump, the moment when it's too late to back out and you ask yourself, "What am I doing?"; the relief when the parachute opens and leaves you with an unsurpassable bird's-eye view of the beaches and mountains of Wollongong. Now, as I am writing, this brings to mind the terror of October 7, but at the time I simply enjoyed the free-flow of my imagination. And then I realized that I was content. No doubt, it would have been fun to join in, but I could still have fun, not only in the vicarious thrill of my son's experience, but in getting together with friends, in shared anticipation (and relief), in allowing the imagination to run free, in the kindness of the autumn sun, and the beauty of the beach with its mountainous backdrop.

July 15, 2013 (Monday)

Shane Clifton Blog: There's Nothing like Nudity to Cement Friendship

On Thursday and Friday of last week, I was invited to speak in Melbourne at the CBM/Luke14 conference, *Honest Conversations: Disability and*

Authentic Christian Community. Its highlights were too numerous to mention, so let me instead tell the story of my Saturday.

I woke up to the phone alarm of my carer, Lauren, who was sleeping in the bed nearby. A little strange, perhaps (at least that's what her boyfriend thought, although I'm not much of a threat), but it's both cheaper and safer to have someone to share the room. We were staying at the Ibis, Glen Waverley, one of the few motels that could accommodate my needs. But the disabled room was crowded—a single and a hospital bed, hoist, wheelchair, commode, and suitcases—so that Lauren had to play a game of Tetris, moving the detritus around to get me out of bed. My teenage boys call Lauren "the hot carer," and she is short and slim, especially when measured against my lanky and overweight frame; 45 kg to my 100 kg. It beggars the imagination that she can woman-handle my body around, but she's more powerful than she looks, and has proven up to the task on the previous two days.

Today, though, she looked tired—queasy even—but got on with the task without complaint. With the covers ripped off, I was rolled one way, then the other, and the sling was placed behind my back. Then I was hoisted, and Lauren dragged me, straining, across the carpet to the commode. Without warning, she bent over, groaned, ran to the bathroom, and puked.

She returned, and we both knew we were in trouble. We were in another city, on our own with no other carers nearby, and I needed to get up and ready; but how could Lauren struggle on? And then I had a flash of inspiration. Last night, I'd eaten dinner with a few friends, including Jay McNeill. The two of us had formed a unique friendship online, but hadn't met face-to-face until yesterday. Jay is the father a child with cerebral palsy, so I figured he must be used to disabled bodies and bodily fluids. I gave him a call and immediately he agreed to come and help (my thanks to his wife, Helena, who sacrificed a hair appointment to let him come).

In the meantime, Lauren managed to get me to the bathroom and soldiered on with the business of my bowels; I'm sure the smell and her sickness was intolerable, but she is courageous. Toilet, shower, and then Jay turned up, and I could see the look of relief on Lauren's face. He took over the hard slog of pushing the commode and hoist, and helped me get dressed. There is nothing like a little nudity to cement a friendship!

Before long, I was in my chair and ready to make something of the day. Leaving Lauren to go back to bed, Jay and I headed down for breakfast and then arranged to meet his family at a nearby cafe for morning tea. Jay and Helena have beautiful, twin, nine-year-old girls: Jasmine and Sunshine. Jazzy was rugged-up and wearing cat ears, and she was delighted to see pictures of our pet cat, with whom she shares a name. Sunshine (the daughter with CP) was strapped comfortably into her chair, and at first seemed a little overwhelmed by the hubbub of the crowded cafe. She was in constant movement, her arms and head disco dancing, and before long she gave me a full-faced smile that matched her name. We held hands, and I felt like I was in the presence of an angel.

We chilled for an hour, although it seemed like minutes, before Jasmine got justly restless. Helene gave Jay permission to waste his day with me, and we decided to head for the city. I was booked to lead a "fireside conversation" at Fitzroy North Community Church later that evening, so Jay and I had a few hours to kill. We rode the train to Flinders Station, and then made our way over the padlock bridge to Southbank for lunch. It was raining (as it had been all week in Melbourne—surprise, surprise), so we got a little wet, but discovered the cosy P. J. O'Brien's pub, and hunkered down with a bowl of soup and a thick black Guinness for lunch. I noticed a small puddle of water under my chair, which presumably came from our dash in the rain. No big deal.

It's hard to explain the quality of the friendship that has formed between Jay and I via email and blogs, but our conversation was both lighthearted fun and deeply meaningful. We talked disability, parenting, God, work, social justice, and writing. Jay gave me the outline of his forthcoming novels, and his creativity and passion inspired me.

As is my habit, I checked on my catheter and was surprised to find it empty. I then noticed the puddle on the floor had grown. God no! I was soaking in piss. The bloody catheter had come undone at my thigh and soaked my pants and chair. We (sheepishly) left the restaurant, and there was nothing for it but to head back to Glen Waverley. Before jumping on the train, we found a bathroom, and Jay stuck his hand down my pants to reattach the line. Nudity, wee, and hands down pants, all on the second date.

We arrived back at the motel at around four thirty p.m. and found Lauren still in bed. She was feeling a little better, although physically drained, but offered immediately to help get me cleaned up. Together the two of them stripped me off, gave me a shower, and then left me in bed while they washed and blow-dried my seat cushion. Of course, I was a lazy sod while they did all the work, and by 6 p.m., diva that I am, I was in my chair and dressed in my second outfit for the day. God forbid I'm seen in the same clothes morning and evening!

Leaving Lauren again, Jay and I called a cab and headed back into the city. I think I've mentioned it before on this blog, but I hate wheelchair taxis, especially at night. I'm seated high and at the back, with my head above the top of the windows. This means that all I can see outside is the blur of concrete road as we bounce along the tram-bumpy streets of Melbourne. I had no choice but to shut my eyes, rest my head in my hands, and pray for a quick trip.

We got there, eventually, and were met by the engaging Ben, who directed us to the wheelchair entrance. The building, recently refurbished, is fabulous; the main auditorium is enclosed by a high arched timber ceiling and modern stained glass windows, and leads to a smaller room that is hosting the evening's festivities. And "fireside conversation" it was to be, with the cosy room oriented toward a fireplace that I was surprised to discover is gas—it sure looked real to me.

Shane Meyer, who has organized the event, rushed over and gave me a hug. Shane is a Kiwi, and he and I have been friends for years—before my accident. He noticed I was flagging (it'd been a big day, too much travel, and it was nearing my bedtime), and offered cheese, biscuits, and mulled wine (have I mentioned this church is spectacular?), while he sent Ben off to scrounge us up some food. Before long, he returned with a chicken roll, and I managed a few mouthfuls before it was time to start.

I was chuffed to learn that the event had "sold out" (they capped the numbers at thirty), and the room was full of energetic and intelligent young people (in their twenties and thirties, which seems young to me). Our talk was on the scriptures, and was introduced by Shane as follows:

> I'm aware that many people, in a community like ours, have moved on from an oversimplified, fundamentalist view of Scripture, but in that process it's been easier to drop it altogether. While it often takes a complete disengagement from something to be able to re-engage in a healthy way, I get the sense that a lot of us are somehow stuck in the twilight zone. We know how not to approach Scripture, but we haven't yet found a way to re-engage that feels safe, life giving, and authentic. I wonder whether there are two levels of disconnection here: technical and emotional; feeling ill-equipped and feeling traumatized.

Wow, I know of few churches that would be bold enough to introduce a discussion on the scriptures in such an honest and open way. I suddenly felt a bit nervous, but there is nothing like mulled wine to help you talk about the Bible. And so I rambled, and we all entered into conversation, and time marched by; and before I knew it, it was 9 p.m. and my taxi was at the front.

It was way past my bedtime, I was exhausted, and I had another bloody taxi ride. I shut my eyes, gritted my teeth, and eventually we made it to Glen Waverley. Jay steered me to the room, and for the third time that day, saw me nude, helping Lauren strip me down and wrangle me into bed.

As my eyes closed I reflected briefly on the day: sickness, piss, exhaustion, and a thoroughly enjoyable time.

August 3, 2013 (Friday)

Elly Clifton Journal

I've just received a phone call from the Campbelltown Arts Centre, telling me that the painting I had on exhibition has sold for $650, and that a second person had enquired as to whether I have any others in the same style. The piece in question is a large (100 cm x 70 cm) bromeliad garden. It's a plant that I've been fascinated by in recent months, and a journey into the Sydney botanical Gardens, with its stunning variety of densely packed bromeliads, inspired me to the design and the painting.

Six hundred and fifty dollars! I just can't believe it. I'm thrilled. I feel alive for the first time in ages, like a wounded bird suddenly discovering its wing is healed. Maybe that's an exaggeration. Perhaps the wing is healing, even though the bird is still caged? Clearly, analogies can't capture the ups and downs of life. It's enough to say that, for today at least, I'm happy.

More than the money, the sale is a validation of my work. Of course, the cash won't go astray. We try not to worry too much about money, and we seem to have enough to pay for our basic needs. But there's not much to spare, and I've been hoping to spoil Shane by updating his first generation iPad to the latest model. So following the good news, I logged on to the Apple Store and made the purchase. Now I'm giddy with excitement, and I hope it arrives quick-smart. I don't know how I'm going to contain myself, keeping the sale of my painting a secret while I wait for the delivery.

August 7, 2013 (Wednesday)

Shane Clifton Journal

Elly blows my mind.

I managed to get away from work early and met her at Gloria Jean's for coffee. When I arrived, she was grinning, her face as bright as sunshine, and she handed me a present. I'm pretty sure it was deliberately wrapped with sticky tape, making it hard for me to open, but I managed the task and uncovered a brand new iPad.

I will admit my first thought was, "can we afford this?"; but Elly, noting my hesitation, told me about the sale of her painting that funded the purchase.

What can I say that does justice to her love? With all the things she could have done with that money, she spent it all on me. She's turned her joy into generosity. What a blessed man I am.

September 18, 2013 (Wednesday)

Shane Clifton Blog Post: Trains, Sex, Buses, an Ambulance, the Emergency Department, and CT Scans

My day involved trains, sex, buses, an ambulance, the emergency department, and CT scans, so it was relatively exciting; and since I'm going to tell you upfront that I'm okay, there's no need for you to worry as you read on.

I had to be in Parramatta for a class at 9 a.m., which meant a far-too-early wake-up, and a morning preparation so rushed that I didn't get a proper shower, and so headed out the door with my hair looking a little like John Travolta in *Grease*. The train ride from Ingleburn to Parramatta has become boringly straightforward, except today. When changing trains, the ramp from the carriage to the platform wasn't held in place firmly enough by the attendant, so I ended up with my front castor wheels jammed between the train and the platform. No doubt, the five-minute delay needed to get me unstuck annoyed impatient commuters, but I am used to this sort of drama, and before long I'd changed trains and made it to Parramatta, and then to work.

My class was on sexual ethics. In Christian contexts, this is a topic fraught with controversy, and as we negotiated subjects that included dating, masturbation, and the ideals of transcendent sexual unity, I felt like shouting, "Stop over-thinking things. It's just an orgasm, and you should enjoy it while you can. I'd give anything to be able to experience that feeling again." But I restrained myself, and the class was fun—an open and engaging discussion on a topic dear to all of our hearts.

Following the morning class was an afternoon meeting at ParaQuad, where I had been invited to sit on the steering committee for a project set up to develop training programs for personal care at home. The ParaQuad offices are in Newington, and to get there I needed to catch a bus from the Parramatta terminus. When it pulled up, a crowd of people swamped inside, leaving me to wait for the bus driver to lower the ramp and usher me on. Bus corridors are narrow, and it takes a little bit of practice to negotiate the chair around the corner, past the driver's compartment, and into the designated wheelchair accommodation. This is near the front of the bus, with seats that fold up to make room for a chair, parking it facing the rear. Once in place, it wasn't long before we were under way and I was able to lose myself in dreams of adventure, listening to an audio recording of *The Count of Monte Cristo*:

> Life is a storm, my young friend. You will bask in the sunlight one moment, be shattered on the rocks the next. What makes you a man is what you do when that storm comes.

From Parramatta, the bus headed east toward the city along Victoria Road. You can tell when a driver is in a hurry by the extent to which aggressive acceleration and braking force you forward and then reverse-fling you into the backrest and headrest of the chair. But the journey today, while fast, seemed relatively normal, and I was relaxed and unconcerned. The crisis came without warning, as the bus looped left around a sweeping on-ramp from Victoria Road to the overpass on Silverwater Road.

Before I had any chance to react, my chair tipped and I fell to the side, smashed my head on the seating opposite, and then fell to the floor. It must have happened in a flash, but I can remember every instant of the fall. It was one of those moments when time seemed to slow, and I experienced the gut-wrenching sensation of a fall that I was utterly helpless to prevent. I didn't lose consciousness, and I ended up lying crumpled-up on my side, half-on and half-off the fallen wheelchair, with my face flat against the floor. I screamed in panic. The passengers, watching on in horror, shouted to the driver, and the bus pulled up.

A large and smartly dressed man (who later introduced himself as Michael) rushed over, made sure I was okay, and called emergency services.

They told him that I wasn't to be moved, but rather to wait for the arrival of the ambulance.

So I waited, with my face squashed against the dusty and unforgiving floor and my body twisted up like one of those oddly bent chalk drawings placed at the scene of the crime on TV procedurals. Memories of October 7, 2010 flashed into my mind, and I went from being panicked to feeling pathetically humiliated: a circus attraction earning the curiosity of the watching crowd. Before long, though, my mood switched to one of resignation. This sort of experience seems to be par for the course of SCI, and the way to get through it is to be patient and relax. What I can't change isn't worth worrying about, so I took the opportunity to shut my eyes and rest.

The ambulance seemed to take forever, although I suspect my sense of time was out of kilter. As I was lying there, I heard the bus driver talking to the passengers, defending himself:

"I didn't strap the seatbelt to his chair because most of them don't like it."

"I was only traveling at 30 km an hour, the normal speed—I wasn't driving too fast."

"I will probably be put on report and might be placed on suspension."

This self-interested justification irritated me, so I interrupted:

"Instead of spending this time worrying about yourself, why don't you get your priorities right, and show some concern about the quadriplegic lying on the floor of your bus?"

He gave a quick apology, and that was the last I heard from him. And still I waited. I'm pretty sure it was half an hour or more before another bus turned up to take the on-looking passengers the rest of their journey. I guess I should have felt a little sorry for the chaos I'd created, but I struggled to feel any real sympathy for them and their missed appointments. For that matter, it looked like I was going to miss my meeting. I figured that at least I had a good excuse.

The police arrived, and then firemen, and about twenty minutes after the fall, the ambulance roared in and the paramedics took charge. The team leader introduced herself as Claire, and while checking my vital signs she chatted and joked and made me feel at ease. It seemed likely that I was okay (well, I was still a quadriplegic—the fall hadn't cured me—but I didn't seem to be any *more* damaged), but Claire wasn't taking any chances. Since I was paralyzed, I needed to be treated as any other person subject to an SCI. The difficulty was that my weirdly contorted position, among the poles and seats of the bus, made a puzzle of the task of straightening me up. But a strategy was devised, beginning by placing my neck in a brace, followed by a series of cautious adjustments that eventually saw me lying flat on my back on a gurney. Thereafter, the task of getting me out of the bus and into the back of the ambulance was relatively simple.

Once settled, I was briefly interviewed by a police officer, and then asked whether there was anyone who should be apprised of the situation. Truth be told, I was reluctant for them to contact Elly. I knew that a call from the police would give her heart palpitations, and because I thought that I was probably fine, I contemplated keeping quiet, going to hospital for tests, and then trying to find my own way home. I quickly realized that not only was such a strategy stupid (really, did I imagine I could get myself home after an accident like this?), but that Elly would murder me if I didn't make sure she was notified. I instructed the officer to make the call, but to be as gentle and upbeat as possible.

At about 3 p.m., I took my first ride in an ambulance (my previous journey to hospital was in a helicopter), and I was ushered into accident and emergency at Concord Hospital. An hour or so later, I was transferred to radiology and given a CT scan of my head and neck. When I was returned to the ward, Elly was there waiting. This felt like old times—me staring at the ceiling with a neck brace, and Elly sitting alongside the bed. It must have been around 6 p.m. when I was given the all clear, and Elly took me home.

Later, I was talking to Kurt, and he declared that the whole thing was set up. He reckons that this mini-emergency had been planned to give me an exciting way to end the memoir based on my journals. "Finish it on a cliff-hanger," he said, "so that everyone will want to read the sequel."

October 7, 2013 (Monday)

Shane Clifton Journal

I've decided to take Kurt's advice. As is apparent in the space between entries, I've clearly been running out of steam, so this is going to be the final entry in this journal; the anniversary, three years on from the worst day of my life, seems an appropriate time to finish.

For obvious reasons, people like to read stories that resolve the tension that has sustained the narrative. In fiction, this might be the solving of a mystery, or the achievement of a goal. Resolution is equally important in autobiography, since the point of reading a true story is not merely to access facts about a life but, rather, to find some meaning in the progression of events. In the case of stories about disability, this normally involves an account of how hard work and perseverance achieve physical goals (the quadriplegic learns to walk, and if this is not possible, she achieves sporting glory at the Paralympics) or they tell of psychological success (the disabled person finds the courage necessary to flourish, and their capacity to live "happily ever after" challenges and inspires those of us with less obvious handicaps). In my case, I can see no way of accomplishing such resolution. I have achieved no great physical feat and have not arrived at the point where I am confident of living happily ever after. No doubt, I shall "live" and know moments of hope and joy, but I suspect that happiness will only ever be a tenuous accomplishment.

Of course, it might be better to give myself more time. People say that it takes many years to arrive at some degree of normalcy and contentment following a severe acquired injury. I concede the point but, nevertheless, I have come to believe that offering a neat and easy resolution (or any resolution at all) is disingenuous. And in any event, as I said right at the beginning, my purpose has been to invite you into my head, to see if I can help you to imagine what it has been like to experience the loss that comes with SCI and, thereafter, to think about life, loss, disability, happiness, faith and doubt, and above it all, hope. Whether or not I have succeeded, I've now (almost) run out of things to say.

I've been leaking again, most often at night, waking up in a wet bed. Apparently the phenol injection (which stops bladder spasm) dissipates, so the procedure needs to be redone every year or so. I'm now booked in for the operation in April, but the temporary solution is a uridom external catheter. If you're wondering what that is, the name gives away. It's essentially a condom, with a small amount of adhesive to keep it fixed in place, and an outlet at the end that connects to a bag. The only difficulty is that extended use irritates the skin and leaves me with delightful red sores. Obviously, it doesn't hurt (one of the compensations of SCI), but it's probably not good for me over the long run. I'm forced to weigh wetting myself against scabbing, so every second night I run the gauntlet, and then wake up in a puddle.

I've come to the conclusion, however, that it's no big deal. So I have broken-down plumbing. It doesn't seem to stop me sleeping, and it's easily enough cleaned up in the morning.

I'm reminded of the famous serenity prayer (my brother Daniel calls it "the back of the toilet door prayer"), apparently written by the theologian, Reinhold Niebuhr:

> God, give us grace to accept with serenity
> the things that cannot be changed,
> Courage to change the things
> which should be changed,
> and the Wisdom to distinguish
> the one from the other.

Up until now, this prayer has seemed to me to be bland, clichéd, and too passive—a capitulation to fate. I'm coming to realize, however, that the prayer has a deep insight. We often talk about life as a journey, and we imagine that we are at the wheel, steering by our choices. But I think that life is much more like a current, mostly out of our control and sweeping us along, and the challenge is to learn to go with the flow, not fighting it, but steering your way along it. As a surfer, one of the skills you learn is to use the rip to take you beyond the breakers. Every year at Australian beaches, people drown in rips because they get they get caught up in the flow, panic, fight against the current, tire, and then sink below the waves. To survive a rip, you have to go with it, and steer yourself out of danger. River rafting down rapids requires a similar strategy. The river will take you where it will, with plenty of bumps along the way, but if you're clever and lucky, you can gain enough steerage to avoid the worst of the rocks.

I can't fight SCI: my broken body is dragged along in what is often a filthy current of urine and feces, through bedsores and nerve pain. It's taking me in a direction I don't really want to go, away from things I would prefer to be doing. Yet I'm stuck in this current whether I like it or not, and I'm far too weak to swim against it. Even so, if I take the opportunities that arise along the way, I can find some fresh tributaries, and maybe even some moments of joy. If I hold on long enough, I might even earn some satisfaction at what I accomplish over the length of the ride. Then again, there is every chance I might still drown. After all, as someone once said, "Life isn't fair. It's just fairer than death" (*The Princess Bride*). In fact, death is the fairest thing of all. It's the end of *every* current; and because that's so, we'd best strap ourselves in, go with the flow, and make what we can of the ride while it lasts.

Made in the USA
Lexington, KY
12 December 2015